POLITICS, PRIDE AND PERVERSION

THE RISE AND FALL OF FRANK ARKELL

POLITICS, PRIDE AND PERVERSION

THE RISE AND FALL OF FRANK ARKELL

ERIK EKLUND

ANU PRESS

BIOGRAPHY SERIES

For nothing is hid, that shall not be made manifest;
nor anything secret, that shall not be known and
come to light.

— Luke 8:17

ANU PRESS

Published by ANU Press
The Australian National University
Canberra ACT 2600, Australia
Email: anupress@anu.edu.au

Available to download for free at press.anu.edu.au

ISBN (print): 9781760466794
ISBN (online): 9781760466800

WorldCat (print): 1481999533
WorldCat (online): 1481999524

DOI: 10.22459/PPP.2025

This title is published under a Creative Commons Attribution-NonCommercial-NoDerivatives 4.0 International (CC BY-NC-ND 4.0) licence.

The full licence terms are available at creativecommons.org/licenses/by-nc-nd/4.0/legalcode

Cover design and layout by ANU Press. Cover photograph: From the collections of the Wollongong City Libraries and the Illawarra Historical Society. P05293.

The Biography Series is an initiative of the National Centre of Biography at The Australian National University, ncb.anu.edu.au.

This book is published under the aegis of the Biography editorial board of ANU Press.

This edition © 2025 ANU Press
Second printing January 2026

WARNING: Readers are advised that this publication describes experiences of a highly sensitive nature including child abuse, graphic violence and murder, paedophilia and suicide.

Contents

List of plates		ix
Abbreviations		xi
A note about currency		xiii
Acknowledgements		xv
Introduction: 'Both a devil and a saint at the same time' — The life of Frank Arkell		1
1.	Family and kin: Growing up in Port Kembla and Steeltown	15
2.	School, family business and real estate	25
3.	'For the betterment of Wollongong': From new alderman to long-serving mayor, 1965–1981	35
4.	'Life in the city of Wollongong is never dull': Local and state politics, 1981–1988	55
5.	'A mindless vendetta against me': Declining popularity and increasing frustration, 1985–1991	69
6.	'Attempting to sell people a dream': Business dealings, networks and influence	85
7.	'Wonderful, wonderful Wollongong'? Arkell's vision for a post-industrial city	103
8.	'Commander Hook' and the Wollongong paedophile network	119
9.	Public and private: The evidence, the allegations, the charges	137
10.	A wide and diverse network of abuse	163
11.	The University of Wollongong and its paedophile past	179
12.	'People don't wave anymore': The diminishing years	195
13.	'Our brother Frank was suddenly and violently taken from us': The death of Frank Arkell	205

14. 'Wollongong is the "W" in NSW': Frank Arkell's political record	215
15. 'I would rather him face the courts': The aftermath and the legacy	229
Afterword	241
Arkell family tree	245
Frank Arkell: Timeline	247
Bibliography	251

List of plates

Plate 0.1 Lord Mayor Frank Arkell's official Wollongong City Council photograph, 30 July 1980   6

Plate 3.1 Frank Arkell escorts Prince Philip on his walk along Crown Street, Wollongong, 10 April 1970   38

Plate 3.2 Lord Mayor Frank Arkell at a 'Thank You' event in his honour hosted by the local Serbian community, just one of the countless events, festivals and celebrations he attended among Wollongong's faith and multicultural communities   42

Plate 3.3 The independent how-to-vote card for Ward 1 and for Lord Mayor for the September 1980 Wollongong City Council election   45

Plate 3.4 Frank Arkell plants trees along Northfields Avenue with Jan Ryan from the University of Wollongong Wives' Group, 3 September 1975   52

Plate 4.1 A publicity shot highlighting Wollongong City Council's sponsorship of 500cc world motorcycle champion Wayne Gardner, Belmore Basin, 14 March 1988   68

Plate 5.1 The North Beach International Hotel in North Wollongong, photographed from the beach, 17 November 1988   70

Plate 6.1 A copy of a cinema advertisement for the Arkell family's Cobbler's Hill Service Station shown in Wollongong cinemas in 1953   88

Plate 6.2 Frank Arkell (centre) stands out from the crowd at the opening and preview of the City of Greater Wollongong Art Competition in 1962   102

Plate 7.1 The lower end of Crown Street, Wollongong, looking east towards City Beach (officially, Wollongong Beach), 30 July 1981   111

Plate 7.2 The Wollongong City Council administration building, completed in 1988, photographed in 2008   113

Plate 7.3 Frank Arkell delivers a speech at the official opening of the Illawarra Performing Arts Centre, 30 January 1988, while Princess Diana looks on and Prince Charles takes notes   114

Plate 7.4 A public relations event celebrating the commercial partnership between Grace Bros, Kern Corporation and Wollongong City Council, 15 October 1984   116

Plate 8.1 Tony Bevan and 'senior flight crewman' Peter Foretic pictured at the Windang base in 1991   128

Plate 9.1 Lord Mayor Frank Arkell watches as NSW Premier Barrie Unsworth officially opens the Wollongong City Mall, 20 October 1986   158

Plate 10.1 Wollongong Bishop William Murray, left, with Luigi Barbarito, the Pope's personal representative in Australia, and Lord Mayor Frank Arkell, sometime between 1978 and 1984   166

Plate 11.1 The first University of Wollongong graduation ceremony, held in Wollongong Town Hall, 11 June 1976   181

Plate 11.2 Lord Mayor Frank Arkell unveils the plaque commemorating the official opening of the stage three extensions of the Wollongong University Union building, 2 April 1976   182

Plate 11.3 Edgar Beale and Frank Arkell at an Illawarra Historical Society event in 1983   185

Plate 13.1 Front page of the *Illawarra Mercury*'s 'Special Arkell Murder edition', 29 June 1998   208

Abbreviations

ASIC	Australian Securities and Investments Commission
BHP	Broken Hill Proprietary Company Limited
CBD	central business district
CPEU	Child Protection Enforcement Unit
DMR	Department of Main Roads
ER&S	Electrolytic Refining and Smelting Company of Australia Limited
ICAC	Independent Commission Against Corruption
MP	member of parliament
NSW	New South Wales
SCTLC	South Coast Trades and Labour Council

A note about currency

On 14 February 1966, Australian currency changed from pounds, shillings and pence to dollars and cents at a rate of £1 = $2.

Acknowledgements

The idea for this book sat in the back of my mind for many years. It came to light through conversations with Antoinette Holm. Her influence and inspiration can be seen on every page, and her enthusiasm and wise counsel helped me finish it.

Justine Greenwood was the ideal research assistant in the early stages. She enabled me to start this research despite the state lockdowns and border closures in 2020 and 2021, which meant I could not travel to Wollongong from my then home in Victoria. I am grateful to the many family members and friends who provided their own memories and stories, especially Peter Eklund, Anna-mai Taylor and Steve Taylor. Eva Eklund and Oliver Eklund both read and commented on drafts with enthusiasm and insight. Thanks to Andrew Ironside at the NSW Land Registry Services for helping me access the land title information. Thanks also to the librarians at the ABC Archive who uncovered large amounts of ABC Radio and ABC TV material on Frank Arkell dating back to the late 1960s. Jenny McConchie and the staff from the Local Studies unit at Wollongong Public Library offered much-appreciated help accessing the relevant records held in their collection, as did archives staff at the University of Wollongong. The university's online archive is a wonderful resource and I used it extensively to research this book (archivesonline.uow.edu.au). Thanks to Jennifer Sloggett from Museums of History New South Wales, who provided invaluable material that helped me firmly establish Frank's year of birth. I want to thank Peter Sheldon for his generous and collegial response to my questions about research that he completed almost 30 years ago. Thanks also to Frank Bongiorno and Jayne Persian for reading the entire manuscript and providing feedback and comments.

There was a further group of people who were contacted for information and advice and some of them were interviewed for this book. These people include: Andrew Anthony, Peter Bahlmann, Anne Baron, Gordon Bradbery,

Janine Cullen, Bevan Fermor, Harold Hanson, Nick Hartgerink, Ray Leary, Nick McLaren, Paul McInerney, Brett Martin, John Martin, Bill Parkinson, Andrew O'Hearn, Toni O'Loughlin, Mark Richmond and Antonios Tziolas. Without their generous input and lively engagement, this project would not have been possible. I hope I have done their memories justice. Thank you to my main contact at The Australian National University, Melanie Nolan, as well as members of the ANU Press Editorial Committee and the anonymous reviewers who provided thoughtful and invaluable feedback on the manuscript. Thanks to Jan Borrie for the exacting copyedit. Thanks also to my friend and colleague Keir Reeves for being there when it mattered.

I owe a special debt to Brett Martin, who shared with me his unpublished manuscript on the Wollongong paedophile network. It was through Brett that I gained access to the notorious 'Bevan Tapes'. Despite all these helping hands, I remain responsible for the final product. I have gathered and checked the facts as assiduously as I can and spoken to as many people as possible, but the final interpretation offered here is mine alone. In researching and writing this book, I have learned that just about everyone in Wollongong, and in many places beyond the borders of that city too, has an opinion on Frank Arkell, and many of them have an Arkell story. So, I look forward to the debate and discussion that I hope my book will provoke.

Every effort has been made to identify and contact the copyright holders of material reproduced in this book. We would be pleased to rectify any omissions in subsequent editions should they be drawn to our attention.

Introduction: 'Both a devil and a saint at the same time'— The life of Frank Arkell

Politics in regional cities rarely excites the imagination or makes the front pages of the capital city newspapers. But what if it was a city that experienced rapid economic growth, large-scale immigration and newfound cultural diversity? A city where opportunities to profit came through wheeling and dealing? A city where powerful, highly regarded men in positions of authority garnered respect and deference, but maintained hidden layers of vice, deception and greed? In this city, seemingly endless meetings, community events and festivals, wrapped up in the public face of respectability, cloaked a secret world of illicit liaisons. What if we described one politician with a modest utilitarian lifestyle but showed he concealed the kind of resources of which most locals could only dream? If we could do all these things, we would be describing the life of Frank Arkell, who was born in Port Kembla, New South Wales (NSW), in 1929 and became the most well-known and most controversial politician ever to hail from the city of Wollongong.

Wollongong is a regional city 80 kilometres south of Sydney. Its suburbs grace the narrow coastal strip between the Illawarra Escarpment and the Tasman Sea. After World War II, it grew rapidly through industrial and residential expansion. In the 1970s and 1980s, Frank Arkell became a fixture in the city. Frank hailed from a well-connected local Catholic family with business interests and a long tradition of involvement in civic affairs. After an apprenticeship in the family business and then in the business world in Sydney, he devoted his life to politics from his mid-thirties. Always well dressed in formal attire, with a distinctive rangy, tall physique, he could be seen everywhere. He was at every event, turning up at official openings, sporting events, festivals, school visits, even private parties, and dominated every media outlet. His political success appeared unstoppable as he progressed from newly elected alderman in 1965 to lord mayor in 1974, and to state member for Wollongong from 1984. It was Wollongong that became the centrepiece of Arkell's political philosophy, and its welfare the guiding light to his politics. Wollongong was his main issue so much so that he popularised the phrase 'Wonderful, wonderful Wollongong'.

But at the edge of public consciousness, within private circles, there was growing disquiet over Frank Arkell's secret life. There was talk of dealings with young men and even boys. There was talk of a network of men who traded in boys. There were allusions to an extensive empire of family businesses that many suggested made him independently wealthy. Then there is the manner of his death: a brutal murder that shocked the city and left Arkell's secret life, now solidified into police charges, unresolved by the courts. This man, who led such a remarkable public life full of energy, vigour and civic service, still divides people to this day. In this book, we will see how much of Frank Arkell's public life and secret depravity we can drag into the light. More than 25 years after his brutal murder, it is time for an assessment of this man and his contributions. This is the story of one man with an engaged public life hiding a dreadful private secret—all played out in a city that was growing and changing.

For the first time, this book brings together the evidence, the allegations, the stories and the rumours. But the focus is not just the child sexual abuse allegations levelled against Frank Arkell, as important as they are. It also covers Arkell's contributions, his family history and his remarkable energy and networking, trying to understand why he was so popular for so long. It is the very dissonance between Arkell's political success underpinned by committed civic energy and his private perversions that makes him such a compelling though difficult biographical candidate.

How Frank Arkell is remembered is influenced by what transpired in the last few years of his life and the nature of his death. In those final years, he was increasingly anxious and isolated. There had been a sharp decline in his public standing. After more than 25 years as a successful politician, things had begun to turn. 'Mr Wollongong', as he was popularly known, had served as the Lord Mayor of Wollongong (1974–91) and member of the NSW Parliament for Wollongong (1984–91). For decades, he worked tirelessly promoting the regional city. But in 1994, and again in 1996, he was named in the NSW Parliament and publicly linked to allegations of child sexual abuse. He failed to appear before the Royal Commission into the New South Wales Police Service. NSW Police subsequently charged him with 29 counts of child sexual abuse. Increasingly isolated, he was besieged by the media at his West Wollongong home and harassed by passers-by shouting 'paedo' or leaving graffiti on a nearby fence. It was a far cry from his halcyon days when he was widely lauded as our most loyal, committed and energetic local politician—a veritable one-man public relations machine in the service of all things Wollongong.

The last years of his life appeared to be moving towards a final act, a reckoning of sorts as police charges were confirmed and a trial date was set. But that was not to be. On the night of 26 June 1998, Arkell opened the door of his West Wollongong home to Mark van Krevel. The 19-year-old later told police: 'I felt that someone should kill him because of all the nasty things he had done to kids.' Mark van Krevel, who two months later changed his name to Mark Valera, had phoned Frank that morning saying he was a young gay man who wanted to talk.[1] In the months leading up to that visit from Valera, Arkell had continued to steadfastly maintain his innocence, stating that the mounting evidence of his alleged double life was simply not true. In November 1996, he told ABC TV News that he would sue his detractors: 'It's a terrible thing paedophilia, the worse thing in the world. Worse than leprosy, I'm sure.'[2] But that evening Valera was in no mood to talk. Arkell's final act was cut short. It was only a few minutes before Valera began attacking Arkell.

Over the course of Frank Arkell's life, and especially during his tenure as lord mayor and state member, Wollongong experienced rapid change. There was major industrial and residential growth and increasing cultural diversity with postwar immigration. This was followed by bouts of hardship and unemployment in the 1970s and 1980s as the region once dominated by mining and industry struggled to diversify its economy and move into a post-industrial phase. The place where Arkell was born and grew up transformed from a collection of rural townships, new industrial centres and the pre-existing commercial centre of Wollongong to become a larger, more unified area often known as the Illawarra region.[3] Utilising the

---

1   For ease of reference, throughout the book I will refer to Mark van Krevel, both before and after his name change, as 'Mark Valera'.
2   John Steward, *ABC TV News*, 4 November 1996, T315653, ABC Archives, Sydney.
3   The naming of this area is a complex issue about which I have written previously. 'Wollongong' is the commercial centre of the Illawarra region. The region extends from Nowra in the south to Helensburgh in the north, however, the boundaries of the City of Greater Wollongong, defined by the amalgamation of four council areas in 1947, have also come to be called 'Wollongong', despite town-based identities and interests. I use 'Illawarra' and 'Wollongong' interchangeably in the text and refer to Wollongong city or Wollongong CBD when referring to the commercial centre of Wollongong and the base for the City of Greater Wollongong Council.

resources and networks of the well-off farming families who adjusted to and prospered from industrialisation by moving into land subdivision, real estate and other small business ventures, Arkell made a successful move into local government as an alderman in 1965. Along the way, he gathered skills, experiences and contacts that would underpin his later political success, all while continuing to build extensive business interests in pastoral properties, a service station, a real estate agency and other family businesses. His single-minded determination saw him attend countless meetings, openings and media events as he championed plans for a new, greener, more cosmopolitan and cultured Wollongong. Whatever his faults, Arkell loved Wollongong, its people and its culture, and he was a leader with a vision of a post-industrial city. In exploring Arkell's story, we gain an insight into how the city changed over the course of his life. We also begin to understand the core elements of his political success since Arkell, whether by copying others or realising it for himself, was one of the first Wollongong politicians to come to terms with the emerging multicultural society.

But as Arkell let Mark Valera into his apartment at the rear of his home, the manner of his impending brutal death set the stage for how we see his life. Our life stories are often defined by how they end. Allegations of child sexual abuse followed by a brutal murder. It shapes everything. The nature of the ending frames all that has gone before it. As biographer Tom Frame found for Australian prime minister Harold Holt, who famously drowned in heavy surf off a Victorian beach, his was a 'life that should have overshadowed a death'.[4] Likewise, Arkell was murdered and how he is remembered has been shaped by that act of wanton cruelty and violence. He is remembered as the abuser, the paedophile, the man involved in Wollongong's secret network of abusers and the murder victim.

Many of the biographical profiles of Arkell that we do possess are in the form of sketches or overviews published not long after his death.[5] They came to light precisely through the fact of his murder—a kind of journalistic death notice that turned its gaze towards a subject at a moment of drama and tragedy. But what about Arkell as 'Mr Wollongong': a successful politician, an active figure in the community, businessman, devout Catholic and Christian Brothers Old Boy, a devoted son and a loyal servant to the Wollongong cause? And what does it mean that a man who was brutally

---

4 Tom Frame, *The Life and Death of Harold Holt* (Sydney: Allen & Unwin, 2005), 4.
5 Richard Guilliat, 'City of Secrets', [*Good Weekend*], *Sydney Morning Herald*, 22 August 1998: 22–27; Kate McClymont, 'The Demise of the Double Life', *Sydney Morning Herald*, 29 June 1998: 15–16.

murdered as a revenge attack for years of sexual abuse and predation carried the mantle 'Mr Wollongong' for more than 30 years? Does this say something about the city itself? Does the city embody a dualistic public–private split enabling public respectability and private abuse? The questions that propel this biography are twofold. What does the life of Frank Arkell tell us about Wollongong as the city grew and transformed over these decades? And what can we know about Arkell himself, a figure who straddled the industrial and the post-industrial phases of Wollongong's history? As a long serving and recent Lord Mayor of Wollongong, Gordon Bradbery, explains:

> The city was in a form of cognitive dissonance over Frank; he did such a lot for Wollongong. There was a great deal of respect and also, in a lot of people's minds, the reality of Frank's paedophilia, if I can put it like that, his past, or supposed paedophilia, and what was coming out … was too hard to take. Too hard to take onboard.

For the community of Wollongong to remember Frank Arkell was to enter this complexity 'and work out how he was both a devil and a saint at the same time. That put the community in a very interesting space.'[6]

***

In writing this biography of Francis Neville Arkell, born in Port Kembla in 1929 and murdered in West Wollongong in 1998, I am primarily motivated by a determination to bring the Frank Arkell story to a wider audience. I want to understand more about this complex and controversial figure, who still inspires equal measures of loyalty and affection, and hate and revulsion. There are also personal dimensions to this tale for this author. To explain this let me tell you three stories. They are in the nature of childhood memories, keenly felt but blurred at the edges, random images and snippets of recall that either come to me unbidden or have to be thought about and concentrated on to bring them into the light of the present.

In 1976 I played soccer for Balgownie Junior Soccer Club as the goalkeeper. We had some success, and I always enjoyed the gala days at which multiple teams came together to play shortened games round-robin style. I was driven south of Wollongong to the Oak Flats ground for one of these events by the coach, who had a large white van that during the week handled the bread deliveries for Balgownie and Fairy Meadow, two northern suburbs of Wollongong. I remember this day fairly well: during our warmup, I dived

---

6   Interview with Gordon Bradbery, 29 April 2023.

to save a ball from a teammate and landed on dog excrement. The coach's wife, a kindly woman with a strong Leeds accent, helped me clean it off my shorts. I always felt our team had some additional credibility because the coach and his family had English accents and, you know, England had won the World Cup in 1966 (even I knew that in 1976) and I watched Match of the Day every Sunday morning.

We won that gala day. I still have the winner's medal, but I don't recall experiencing the joy of winning. I do recall lining up and receiving the medallion. A huge table at the front of the presentation area had dozens of trophies and medals on it. My mother came to pick me up in our little grey Morris Mini. As we were walking away after the presentations, the Lord Mayor of Wollongong was leaving too. I seem to recall him about to get into a large white Ford sedan, maybe an LTD? Then my mother called out to him: 'Hello, Mr Arkell. How are you?'

'I am very well thanks, Heather. How's the family?'

Plate 0.1 Lord Mayor Frank Arkell's official Wollongong City Council photograph, 30 July 1980

Photo: From the collections of the Wollongong City Libraries and the Illawarra Historical Society.

INTRODUCTION

I was impressed that my mother knew the lord mayor. He was tall, well dressed and had a kindly round face. I was also amazed that he remembered my mother's name—just one of countless constituents and old contacts. Her name came easily to him. He was good at this. There was a certain familiarity between the lord mayor and my mother that my eight-year-old self could not fathom. Later I learned that Frank Arkell was from a large Port Kembla family and that his father had married an O'Donnell, who were well-known throughout the region. My mother knew just about everyone in Port Kembla. She told me before her death in 2017 that the real force behind Frank was 'Old Mrs Arkell'. She gave me the first of many clues that I would follow for this biography.

There is another memory. This one is not so nostalgic or positive. It was 1979 and I was in Year 7. My friends and I went down to Fairy Meadow Beach for a swim. We had a swim and one of them said, 'Let's go and find some poofters. They are up behind the dunes here. They are everywhere.' My friend was an ordinary Year 7 boy expressing the casual homophobia of that age. I dutifully followed him. We trudged through the dunes behind the beach in the stretch between the Fairy Meadow Beach clubhouse and where Fairy Creek flows into the lagoon at Stewart Park. We found one poor man behind the lip of the front dune who was sunbaking and reading a book. My mate threw some sand at him and we ran off, the heavy sand dragging at our young legs as we galloped away. 'There are poofs all through there. You might find Frank Arkell there too. He loves the Puckeys Estate.'

How was it possible that my mate knew about Frank in 1979? There was talk about Arkell simply because he was unmarried. In Wollongong in the 1970s an unmarried man who showed no apparent interest in women could be the subject of all kinds of speculation and prejudice. Was this what my mate was homing in on? Just that Arkell was a single man and therefore assumed to be gay? Or did he know, or had he heard, something more? This friend had gone to a Catholic primary school so this could have been the source of information. I recall other incidents that year when I heard that the lord mayor was gay. I went to an all-boys school in Wollongong, Keira Boys High School, and jokes and homophobic slurs about being gay were told every day, but among this cohort of boys there was always a joke about the lord mayor being a 'poofter' and that his favourite project was the rejuvenation of the Puckeys Estate behind Fairy Meadow Beach because everyone knew that was where the poofters hung out. The toilets at Fairy Meadow Beach and the area south of the clubhouse were indeed a gay beat. Again, it is impossible to know whether these bits of information gleaned from childhood memories were reflective of some real knowledge about Arkell and his preference for young boys or simply 1970s Wollongong homophobia.

Many in Wollongong would have had a similar experience. Like mine, their memories of Arkell will be of the public man officiating at functions or meetings and they too will have heard stories and rumours. But I am conscious of the perspective of those who knew the precise details, those who witnessed the things that became rumours or those who had family or close friends who suffered through them. For them, hearing the rumours must have been a bitter experience since they never gained the status of accepted fact but remained for too long just Wollongong folklore.

One final memory. In 1991 I was a casual tutor in the Faculty of Arts at the University of Wollongong. A friend who was a university student from another faculty told me that there was a paedophile ring of well-connected, powerful men operating in Wollongong. Like so many in Wollongong, I found it difficult to believe what was already an open secret to some. How could such a thing be possible? If this was true, how could powerful men in Wollongong, including Arkell, get away with decades of abuse?

With so many stories and half-remembered rumours, it is even more important to return to the evidence, to flesh out the Frank Arkell story with documentary evidence and carefully triangulated memories of those who knew him or had some significant insight into his public life as a successful politician or even his controversial private life. To the best of my ability, I present Arkell's life based on a critical reading of the evidence and an attempt to triangulate across sources and build confidence in the picture that emerges. Where there is uncertainty, even speculation, about an apparent fact or interpretation, I will indicate this in the text.

While both the legal system and historical analysis work with evidence, and its strengths and its limitations, there are different rules of evidence. The past is never perfectly recoverable. We search for its traces and echoes in written documents, photos and memories, but especially when we have a historical subject whose life was controversial, whose death was brutal and who seemed to live a double life, the best I can do is present the facts as they have been uncovered, offer the best interpretation possible and stimulate the mind of the reader with probabilities, possibilities and alternative readings. The work of the historian is not the same as the pronouncements of a judge or a jury. Arkell was never convicted of any crime, but not all verdicts on a life are made in a court. A historian can present the facts and their best interpretation, as I do here, and readers too will make their own judgements. This book will present all the evidence and make a judgement on what many knew as Wollongong's and Frank Arkell's open secret.

In this book, I use the term 'paedophile' in a very specific way. In Chris Brickell's discussion of sexuality and power, he suggests that the key axis of inequality where it exists in same-sex relationships is age. 'A typical dynamic,' Brickell argues, 'involves older men exercising coercive power over their younger counterparts.'[7] This is true of the paedophiles featured in this book. As the evidence will show, these were relationships between men and boys that were mostly about sexual contact. They occurred between two parties with vastly different resources and capabilities, so there was a major power imbalance. There was a significant age difference between the two parties and where there was another form of engagement this was often about securing or maintaining sexual contact through gifts, favours, money, duress, intimidation or sometimes blackmail on the part of the paedophile. I am aware that there is a vast literature on paedophilia. Many argue that 'paedophilia' should be a separate term from 'child sexual abuse', for example, since not all paedophiles act on their attraction to children. I make no claim that the characteristics of the Wollongong paedophiles are generalisable to other contexts and cases.

Biographers have long grappled with the question of whether to include material from a subject's private life.[8] There is also the related question about how much of this private world is accessible in any case. Tom Frame's biography of Harold Holt, which has been useful in understanding how the nature of a subject's death shapes our understanding of their life, argued that 'because some aspects of his private life found expression in his public duties they are legitimately the subject of comment and critique'.[9] Frame was interested in the private details of Holt's life only to the extent that they revealed something of the essence of his character. Historian and biographer Jenny Hocking goes further. In her efforts to reveal the details of the 'Palace Letters' regarding the dismissal of the Whitlam Labor government in 1975,

---

7   Chris Brickell, 'Sexuality and the Dimensions of Power', *Sexuality & Culture* 13 (2009): 57–74, doi.org/10.1007/s12119-008-9042-x.
8   Nicholas Brown, 'Public Lives, Private Lives: The Fundamental Dilemma in Political Biography', in *Australian Political Lives: Chronicling Political Careers and Administrative Histories*, eds Tracey Arklay, John Nethercote, and John Wanna (Canberra: ANU E Press, 2006), 35–42, doi.org/10.22459/APL.10.2006.05.
9   Frame, *The Life and Death of Harold Holt*, 4.

and in the face of arguments that this correspondence between the governor-general and the Queen's private secretary was 'personal in nature', Hocking has argued that 'all history should be public history'.[10] In an earlier piece on biography generally, she wrote: 'The very nature of political biography rejects the narrow construction of the subject as a decontextualised and isolated actor.'[11]

In the case of Frank Arkell, at the heart of our collective interest in him as a biographical subject is the relationship between public and private. Nicholas Brown maintains that this is a fundamental characteristic of all political biography.[12] In Arkell's case, the relationship between public and private is especially fraught. How can we reconcile the man whom many knew as an engaged, hardworking lord mayor and state member with the widespread rumours and later charges of child sexual abuse? If the rumours and substance of the charges can be verified, to what extent was this private world separate from his public self?[13] Many of the people I interviewed for this book grappled with this question as they offered their memories and perspectives. Some might argue that we should just write a history of Arkell's public positions and achievements and leave aside his private life. This book pursues a very different line of inquiry. It argues that Arkell built a public world that enabled him to facilitate his private depravity. It is not possible to separate the two. The public standing, widespread networks of colleagues, friends and supporters, financial resources and opportunities that public life brought him enabled his private illicit activities. Furthermore, many of his key contacts in the public world of politics and business shared his illicit predilections. Arkell's life shows us a case where a public and a private life simply cannot be untangled.

The first available reports of Frank Arkell being involved in sexual relationships with boys and young men date from the early 1970s. In Chapters 8, 9 and 10, I will discuss these reports and other evidence linking Arkell to a range of predatory sexual practices involving boys and young men. I have tried to maintain a careful focus on the evidence and

---

10   Jacquelyn Baker, 'Q&A with Jenny Hocking, Author of "The Palace Letters"', *Australian Policy and History*, 11 February 2021, aph.org.au/2021/02/qa-with-jenny-hocking-author-of-the-palace-letters/.
11   Jenny Hocking, 'It's a Ripping Good Yarn: Political Biography and the Creative Imagination', *Adelaide Law Review* 32, no. 1 (2011): 69–82, at 72.
12   Brown, 'Public Lives, Private Lives'.
13   In framing these questions, I have been influenced by Dan Davies's excellent biography of British DJ, media identity and philanthropist Jimmy Savile. Towards the end of Savile's life, but particularly after his death, compelling evidence emerged that he had engaged in long-term systematic child sexual abuse. See Dan Davies, *In Plain Sight: The Life and Times of Jimmy Savile* (London: Quercus, 2015).

not embellish or overinterpret what I have discovered in my research. This is not a work in the 'true crime' genre, so I have avoided the explicit detail that is characteristic of that genre and typical of some published material on Arkell's life, and in particular his brutal murder in 1998. However, when discussing Arkell's links with a network of senior Wollongong politicians, clergy and businessmen that operated to procure and groom boys and young men for sexual relationships, the material is both deeply troubling and at times unavoidably explicit. I have usually placed the word 'victim' in inverted commas to indicate that it is a word that does not capture the complexity of the lives of the boys and men dragged into the world of child sexual abuse. 'Victim' was often used by the police and courts as a specific descriptor of a person subject to an illegal act, but I am conscious of how this word fails to capture either the full breadth and nuance of a person's life or their agency within difficult and sometimes traumatic contexts. Many of those abused by the Wollongong paedophiles survived and have led remarkable lives despite their experiences.

This book argues that Arkell's story is closely linked with that of a contemporary who shared many of the same characteristics. Real estate agent and former Wollongong mayor Tony Bevan (1933–1991) led a kind of parallel life to Arkell's. Approximately the same age, both men were Catholic, both Christian Brothers Old Boys and both heavily involved in local government and real estate. Bevan was a central player in Arkell's alleged child abuse and his role will be explored and the evidence against him assessed. There is a large section of the report of the 1997 Royal Commission into the New South Wales Police Service (the 'Wood Royal Commission') that details Bevan's role as the linchpin of a Wollongong-based paedophile network.

Tony Bevan was in the habit of recording all his phone conversations—not just his business calls, but also those relating to his paedophile activities. He used a small tape recorder placed beside his phone in his office in the IMB Building in Crown Street, Wollongong. Bevan's efforts to document his activities and keep tabs on the participants in his network have bequeathed to us 150 hours of secret recordings of phone conversations between Bevan and the men who were involved in the network. It is through these recordings that we have a clear and certain idea of who the participants were. The tapes were copied and one set went to the Wood Royal Commission while the *Illawarra Mercury* acquired another set. The newspaper had them professionally transcribed and used them extensively in 1995 when journalist Brett Martin published his exposé on Tony Bevan. Son of Labor alderman John Martin, Brett started with the *Illawarra Mercury* in 1980 as a cadet and worked on the Bevan and Arkell stories in the 1990s. After Martin's 1995 exposé, Bevan's secret recordings became more widely known as the 'Bevan Tapes'. These tapes, copies of which were provided to me through the generosity of Brett Martin, have informed my understanding of Arkell and, in particular, his close and later increasingly fraught relationship with Tony Bevan.

Bevan was not the only well-to-do Wollongong businessman and/or politician involved in child sexual abuse. Others included Arkell's political and business associate Brian Tobin, old friend and fellow history enthusiast Edgar Beale, and factory owner and manager Tom Gaun, to name a few. All these men had links with Arkell in some way or another. Then there are the links with child abuse that emerged out of the Catholic Church in Wollongong, where Arkell was a devout adherent and key player. I will also consider his involvement with the many abusive clergy from Wollongong as another possible vector that connects him to a long-term and deeply entrenched culture of child sexual abuse.

At times I seek to summarise the perspective of certain key players in this part of Arkell's life without necessarily endorsing their views or their recollections. Readers likely to be affected by such material are advised to proceed with caution and seek professional help should they need it. The best way I know to honour the truth is to tell the story as clearly and as objectively as possible. If I find and report levels of uncertainty in some stories this in no way is meant to undermine the reality of abuse for its survivors. The truth will out and there is no need to embellish or exaggerate it. In its simple essence, it has a power to it.

But none of us is a one-dimensional being. We all have layers of experience, we all grow and change over time, just as Wollongong did over the 68 years of Arkell's life. The nature of the controversial and traumatic allegations about Arkell's child sexual abuse has, understandably, overshadowed other aspects of his life. Where did this man come from? Why was he so popular? What about his family life and education? What of his early political career and his business dealings? Just as Jenny Hocking discovered secrets in Gough Whitlam's family history, including the criminal convictions of Whitlam's grandfather, so too I have discovered secrets in the Arkell family's past.[14] Between Arkell's birth in 1929 and his murder in 1998, the city that he loved so much went through dramatic changes. Arkell's life reveals much about the transformation of Wollongong and its path towards becoming a modern post-industrial place. Paralleling the life of Frank Arkell was the growth and development of a city that he made the centrepiece of his political life, and I will follow the city's story too since it is so powerfully linked to Arkell's. So, let us begin with Frank Arkell and assess where he came from, who he was and what he achieved, before we return to that fateful Friday night in June 1998.

---

14 Jenny Hocking, *Gough Whitlam: A Moment in History. Volume 1* (Melbourne: Melbourne University Press, 2009).

1
Family and kin: Growing up in Port Kembla and Steeltown

Frank Arkell was born on 13 September 1929, only one month before precipitous losses on Wall Street in New York signalled the beginning of the Great Depression. He was the fourth and youngest son and arrived well after his three brothers. His was a family that had considerable resources and standing in the Illawarra region but would nonetheless face challenges from a shocking tragedy in 1941.

Frank's father, Sidney Arkell, was born on 21 October 1881 in the English town of Bibury in Gloucestershire.[1] Sidney was the second son of a large family of three boys and two girls. His elder brother was two years older than him while his youngest brother was born when Sidney turned 18. His mother and father were shopkeepers, and many of the siblings worked in the store in Bibury. In 1906, at the age of 26, Sidney decided to emigrate to the United States, boarding a ship in Liverpool bound for New York. Two years later, his elder brother, James Edward Arkell, joined him and, by April 1910, the US Federal Census shows the two brothers were employed as shepherds on a farm in Carey, Idaho.[2] The scant records available tell us little more about their life in the United States. It is hard to imagine a more isolated town in the US Midwest. Carey was a small farming community

---
1 Sidney Arkell's name is spelt 'Sidney' on his birth and death certificates and 'Sydney' on his marriage certificate and the electoral rolls. I have adopted 'Sidney' here but acknowledge that there were multiple spellings.
2 'Household Returns for Carey, Idaho', in *Thirteenth Census of the United States, 1910*, Microfilm Publication T624, Record Group 29 (Washington, DC: US National Archives and Records Administration, 1910), www.archives.gov/research/census/online-resources.

with a population of approximately 700 people, east of Yellowstone National Park and about 240 kilometres from the state capital of Boise. Sidney returned to Gloucestershire four years later for what the local newspaper called a six-month holiday.³ He was home long enough to be recorded in the 1911 UK census in which his occupation was listed as 'bicycle agent' in Bibury.

By the end of 1911, however, apparently neither the prospect of a return to the United States nor his continued presence at home appealed. On 10 November, a few weeks after his thirtieth birthday, Sidney departed London bound for Sydney on the *RMS Orama*, a new Orient Line vessel on its maiden voyage. The 12,000-ton (10,900-tonne) vessel was almost 174 metres long and carried 450 first and second-class passengers, as well as 800 third-class passengers, one of whom was Sidney Arkell. The press followed the *Orama*'s voyage with great interest as the new ship was such an impressive sight and the Orient Line had the government contract to carry the Australian mail. After calling at Fremantle, Adelaide and Melbourne, the *Orama* arrived in Sydney on 21 December 1911. More than 800 passengers disembarked at Sydney. Luggage was placed in a wharf-side shed in no apparent order, with some bags taking up to five hours to unload and clear customs. As one passenger complained to the *Daily Telegraph*: 'I have been here the best part of a day trying to sort out my luggage. I am tired, hot, dusty, thirsty and exceedingly annoyed.'⁴ Sidney negotiated this chaos, found his bags and completed the immigration paperwork. On the ship's passenger list, Sidney gave his occupation as 'foreman', perhaps more in hope than in accuracy.⁵ He was alone. None of his large English family accompanied him on his journey to Australia. In an oral history interview conducted in 1982, Frank Arkell was uncertain about the reasons for Sidney moving to Australia. He indicated that he thought his father arrived in 1918 or 1920: 'I think he was unsettled at home and he just moved off.' In this interview, Arkell also reveals that he knew of Sidney's move to the United States but was unsure of the dates.⁶

3   'The Cotswold Country', *Cheltenham Chronicle*, 27 August 1910: 4.
4   'An Ocean Greyhound', *Sydney Morning Herald*, 21 December 1911: 5; 'Sea Passengers' Luggage', *Daily Telegraph*, [Sydney], 23 December 1911.
5   'The UK 1911 Census', *UK Census Online* (Jersey: Genealogy Supplies Limited, 2024), ukcensus online.com/.
6   Winifred Mitchell and Geoffrey Sherington, 'Interview with Frank Arkell as part of research for the book "Growing Up in the Illawarra"', July 1982, D153/1/1, Archives Online, University of Wollongong, archivesonline.uow.edu.au/nodes/view/8780?keywords=Winifred+Mitchell+and+Geoffrey+Sherington &type=all&highlights=WyJ3aW5pZnJlZCIsIm1pdGNoZWxsIiwiZ2VvZmZyZXkiLCJzaGVyaW5nd G9uIl0%3D&lsk=6238d83bfcb11406c62b7ee12d25289c.

1. FAMILY AND KIN

A few days after Sidney's arrival, it was Christmas, but we have no information on how he spent it in his new country. It has not been possible to locate any information about Sidney during the time between his arrival in Sydney and his appearance in Wollongong in 1921. He is listed neither on the electoral rolls for Sydney or Wollongong over those nine years nor in any of the countless state and country directories that provide a snapshot of the trades and services available in each town and locality in the state.[7] Sidney finally fetched up at Kembla Grange working as a horse trainer. Kembla Grange is between Dapto and Unanderra, near the north-western edge of the bright, glittering expanse of Lake Illawarra, possessing its own small train station on the main South Coast Line. Solicitor, investor and NSW politician Sir Joseph Carruthers purchased land at Kembla Grange, designing and building a racecourse that emulated the dimensions of Sydney's Royal Randwick Racecourse. In 1912 a private branch line was built between the main South Coast Line and the racecourse to transport both horses and racegoers to the track.[8]

Sidney's solo journey to a new country was in stark contrast to Frank's mother, Marcella, who was a member of a well-known and large local family, the O'Donnells. The family had been resident in the Illawarra since 1853 when Michael O'Donnell was appointed manager and leaseholder of the Wentworth estate. Michael was an Irish bounty migrant from County Tipperary. He married Sarah Meade in County Cork, Ireland, in 1840 and together they migrated to New South Wales in 1841. After arriving in Sydney, the couple eventually transferred south to Wollongong. At 890 hectares, the Wentworth estate was one of the most significant landholdings in the area and Michael, initially in partnership with James Rigney and later on his own account, was resident manager until his death in 1861. One of Michael's sons, also named Michael, lived on the estate. For three generations, the O'Donnells were resident managers and many of their large clan lived on the estate, which, under their occupancy, was commonly known as the Five Islands Estate—an early colonial name for the area, after the five small islands that lie just off the coast between Port Kembla and Wollongong.

---

7   John Sands, *Sands Sydney, Suburban and Country Commercial Directory* (Sydney: John Sands Limited, 1912, 1915, 1917, 1920), City of Sydney Archives.
8   'Timeless Wollongong: Kembla Grange Marks 100 Years of Racing', *Illawarra Museum*, 8 September 2012, illawarramuseum.wordpress.com/category/kembla-grange-racecourse/; 'Kembla Grange', *Your Suburb*, [Online] (Wollongong: Wollongong City Libraries), wollongong.nsw.gov.au/library/explore-our-past/your-suburb/suburbs/kembla-grange.

In 1898 Marcella Veronica O'Donnell was born on the Five Islands Estate, the third child of seven to Ada and Michael O'Donnell Jr, who were residents on the estate. This area was part of Dharawal Country, cared for by the traditional owners and under the custodianship of the Dharawal people. As colonisation proceeded in the region, new names were coined or old names adopted and modified. The name 'Wollongong' was itself a rendering of a local Dharawal name, Woolungay, meaning either 'the five islands' or 'the sound of the sea'. 'Illawarra' is also clearly an Indigenous word or has Indigenous origins, but its exact meaning is obscure, at least to this non-Indigenous author.

In 1900 the state government resumed 162 hectares of the estate to begin work on harbour and breakwater construction at Port Kembla. The O'Donnells maintained their leasehold on most of this land but now leased it from the government rather than the Wentworth estate. Marcella completed her London College of Music preparatory exams in 1913 and, in 1915, achieved her junior grade in music theory through the Sydney College of Music, with both examinations held at St Mary's Convent in Wollongong.[9] We know little about her early life. She studied music and attended Catholic and Presbyterian fetes in Wollongong and Port Kembla. At the Presbyterian fete in 1916, she won a box of chocolates, which must have been a joy for the 17-year-old as the Great War loomed over the home front.

The O'Donnells were a large Catholic family with commercial, landholding and dairying interests throughout the region. They also excelled at municipal politics. Frank O'Donnell, Marcella's uncle and a noted breeder of Ayrshire cattle in the Illawarra (as were many of the O'Donnells), was a long-serving alderman on the Central Illawarra Council. The council had been formed in 1859, covering Figtree, Mount Kembla, Dapto, Albion Park, Lake Illawarra and what later became Port Kembla, with its chambers in Unanderra. Frank O'Donnell was an alderman throughout the 1880s, 1890s and early 1900s, and regularly served as mayor until his tragic death in 1906 from a horseriding accident. Frank had attended an Agricultural and Horticultural Association meeting in Wollongong and was riding home to Port Kembla at night when his horse tripped on a new wire fence erected near the Wollongong racetrack. The *Illawarra Mercury* reported the 'heavy gloom' that had descended on the district and noted the 'utmost sympathy'

---

9   *Illawarra Mercury*, 26 August 1913: 3; 13 July 1915: 2.

1. FAMILY AND KIN

that was expressed for the family. Frank O'Donnell's funeral was one of the largest seen in the district for many years, with more than 200 vehicles and riders covering 2.4 kilometres in a procession along Crown Street in Wollongong.[10] This O'Donnell, who had dominated municipal and civic life for many decades, was widely and genuinely mourned. It is possible that Frank Arkell was named after Frank O'Donnell and, if this was the case, success in local government was very much part of Frank Arkell's destiny.

Marcella's father, Michael O'Donnell, born on 17 June 1854 on the Five Islands Estate, also bred Ayrshire cattle and had extensive farming interests.[11] Michael Junior was one of eight children born to Mary and Michael Senior, and the family's name and reputation reached across the rural towns south of Wollongong. The sheer number and busy commercial and civic lives of the O'Donnells were in stark contrast to Sidney, who was without family in the region and, by the late 1920s, was earnestly working a trucking business as an owner–driver at the then new Port Kembla steelworks.

There is a family tradition of strong women behind the O'Donnells' success. When Michael Senior died at the age of 46 in 1861, Mary kept the estate running, taking over the management until her death in 1887.[12] Marcella's mother, Ada Isobel Smith, was a trained nurse and worked for eight years in a Sydney hospital before returning to the Illawarra in 1894, when she married Michael Junior.[13] When Ada O'Donnell died in 1937, aged 69, she was described as 'an energetic and industrious woman all her life'.[14] Alice Smith, Ada's sister, married Michael Junior's brother Richard. She was the postmistress at Unanderra from 1900, and was active in the local Red Cross and Parents and Citizens Association.[15]

If the O'Donnell women were not imposing enough, all the O'Donnell men had public profiles as businessmen, farmers and civic leaders. All five O'Donnell sons moved into farming and estate management in the region to the west and south of the Five Islands Estate, principally in Dapto, Kembla Grange, Figtree and Unanderra. The family had a lease with the Wentworth estate that expired in 1926, after which the land was resumed by

10 'Shocking Fatal Accident', *Illawarra Mercury*, 13 November 1906: 2.
11 'Obituary on Michael O'Donnell', *South Coast Times*, [Wollongong], 23 March 1945: 7.
12 Anon., 'O'Donnell Family History', [Online], www.wagsoft.com/FamilyHistory/ODonnell.pdf.
13 'Family Notices', *Illawarra Mercury*, 12 May 1894: 2. The marriage was held on 10 April 1894.
14 *South Coast Times*, [Wollongong], 26 November 1937: 19. See also *Illawarra Mercury*, 26 November 1937: 10.
15 S.C. Rose, 'Mrs Alice B.C. O'Donnell—An Appreciation', *Illawarra Mercury*, 14 July 1939: 1.

the trustees of the estate. It would soon be further subdivided, forming parts of the industrial area around the harbour and new dormitory suburbs just as sections of the estate had already formed the basis of the new town of Port Kembla in 1908. The vista of rolling farms and dairies from Port Kembla, Unanderra, Dapto and Albion Park, and around Lake Illawarra, was slowly but surely breaking up. Farmland was claimed by new industries, a major new deepwater harbour at Port Kembla and eventually residential subdivisions. The O'Donnells played a central part in that transition. Control over land, and its regulation and surveillance, heightened into the twentieth century. For the Dharawal people, campsites, both traditional and more recent, were increasingly controlled and often removed. The unfinished occupation of the nineteenth century was giving way to a more comprehensive dispossession as industrialisation and residential development became more widespread and land use more intensive.[16]

Marcella Veronica O'Donnell, aged 23, and Sidney Arkell, 39, were married on 10 June 1921 at St Paul's Catholic Church in Albion Park.[17] It is not clear how the couple met but Marcella's brother Richard lived at the Kembla Grange Estate, adjacent to the Kembla Grange racecourse, and the family was keen on horses and horseracing. Marcella's father, Michael O'Donnell Jr, owned racehorses and the O'Donnells entered horses in Kembla Grange race meetings. Sidney's religion had been listed as Church of England in the 1911 UK census, so to marry in a Catholic Church the couple would have required dispensation and Sidney some instruction in the Catholic faith. Only two months after the marriage, their first son, Richard Sidney Bruce Arkell, was born, on 8 August 1921 in 'Brooklyn', a private hospital in Kiama.[18] This was an unusual situation for the time. Marcella was seven months pregnant when she married Sidney, but it is not clear why the couple delayed their marriage until a time when Marcella would have been obviously showing. Father Joseph Donovan went ahead with the marriage at Albion Park despite Sidney's Anglicanism and Marcella's condition. The service was performed on a weekday (a Friday), which was not uncommon for Catholic marriages involving a spouse of a different faith.

---

16   I have written about this process and its implications for the Dharawal people in more detail in Erik Eklund, *Steel Town: The Making and Breaking of Port Kembla* (Melbourne: Melbourne University Press, 2002), 114–30. See also pp. 72–80 for information on the first subdivisions and commercial development of Port Kembla.
17   NSW Marriage Certificate, Sydney [sic] Arkell & Marcella O'Donnell, 10 June 1921, St Paul's Catholic Church, Albion Park, 9041/1921, State Records NSW, Sydney.
18   Birth Certificate for Richard Sidney Bruce Arkell, 38762/1921, State Records NSW, Sydney.

1. FAMILY AND KIN

After their marriage, Sidney and Marcella lived in O'Donnell Street, one of the more salubrious parts of the new industrial town of Port Kembla. As a family that was central to the history and management of the Five Islands Estate (commercially marketed as the 'Wentworth Estate'), the O'Donnells received a street named in their honour when the first subdivision for Port Kembla was surveyed in 1908.[19] Other children soon followed, including James Edward (Bill) in 1923 and Harold Francis Norman (Harry) in 1924.

The O'Donnell influence through Marcella, Marcella's father, Michael O'Donnell Jr, and the other O'Donnell uncles and cousins could explain Frank's interest in business and local government and his eventual move into municipal politics in the 1960s. The O'Donnells were also involved in land sales and subdivision development. Michael Alfred O'Donnell, son of Frank O'Donnell, was a principal of one of Wollongong's largest auction houses, O'Donnell & Stumbles, before his untimely death at the age of 42 in 1925.[20] Richard O'Donnell—according to family history, the most private of all the O'Donnell brothers—sold his farm to the Lithgow-based Hoskins brothers as their plans for a new iron and steelworks, first mooted in the early 1920s, came to fruition.[21] Michael Junior had acquired large tracts of land in the region and sold the bulk of it before his death in 1945. Sections that were left in his estate were passed on to his surviving relatives.[22]

On 13 September 1929, the final member of the family was born. The fourth and youngest son of Marcella and Sidney Arkell was christened Francis Neville but was always known as Frank. The name 'Francis' only ever graced the more formal entries on lists of Wollongong councillors, members of the NSW Parliament or voting papers. Sidney was aged 48 when Frank was born, so Frank had an unusually old father, while his mother was 31, which was also considered old to have a fourth child. The O'Donnell legacy would be an important shaper of Frank's life. Apart from the family resources, and the influence of the great uncle who was Central Illawarra's most favoured citizen and a long-serving alderman, Frank Arkell's supporters often introduced him in the 1970s and 1980s as a member of one of the region's earliest and most highly regarded 'pioneering families', obviously following the family line through his mother's side. The O'Donnells were

---

19 See Eklund, *Steel Town*, 77–79.
20 'Obituary for Mr M.A. O'Donnell', *South Coast Times*, [Wollongong], 13 March 1925: 8. See also Probate of Michael James O'Donnell, NRS-13660-26-6700-Series 4_304286, State Records NSW, Sydney.
21 Anon., 'O'Donnell Family History'.
22 See Probate of Michael O'Donnell, NRS-13660-26-6700-Series 4_304286, State Records NSW, Sydney.

Wollongong elite, heavily involved in the Catholic Church, farming, real estate and local government. Both Marcella and Frank carried that with them for the rest of their lives.

In 1930 the Arkells moved to the Steeltown Estate, sometimes rendered just as 'Steeltown', about 4 kilometres north-west of Port Kembla. James O'Donnell, a bachelor brother to Michael Junior, was a long-time Port Kembla resident and local agent for the Wentworth estate, who had acquired this land in 1894.[23] Uncle James left provision in his will to transfer this large holding to Marcella for the fixed sum of £500 when he died in 1918. Another uncle, Michael Alfred O'Donnell, from O'Donnell & Stumbles, was the executor of James's will but, as we have seen, Michael Alfred died in 1925. For reasons that are unclear, this provision in James's will was not formalised until 1959. Despite the legal complexities, about 4,000 square metres of Steeltown, where sales from the new subdivision began in 1928, was O'Donnell land and Marcella was on a legal promise that one day she would own it. When she finally acquired the title in 1959 it was for a fraction of the then market price.[24] By now Marcella was the only surviving daughter in the family as her younger sister Majorie had died in 1930 at the age of 27.

Steeltown Estate was situated between Wollongong and Port Kembla and adjacent to the new Port Kembla steelworks, which was owned and operated by Australian Iron & Steel Proprietary Limited. While from the 1830s Wollongong was the commercial hub of the region, the new industrial centre of Port Kembla developed in the 1890s as a coaling port and, from 1907, as a new home for industry. A copper smelter and refinery, the Electrolytic Refining and Smelting Corporation Proprietary Limited, had begun production in 1908, Metal Manufactures Limited started in 1918 and, in 1926, the Hoskins brothers, iron and steelmakers from Lithgow, announced their intention to relocate to Port Kembla. Steeltown was new so there were few houses and mostly vacant blocks surrounding the Arkells' new home.

The rapid industrial and urban development of Port Kembla and areas adjacent to it such as Steeltown benefited the well-placed gentlemen farmers of the district. Many lamented the loss of grazing land and the changes to the old rural society of the Central Illawarra. The more marginal farmers,

---

23   Deed of Sale, No. 6, Book 549, 17 July 1894, Land Titles Office, State Records NSW, Sydney.
24   Deed of Transfer, No. 276, Book 2483, 29 April 1959, Land Titles Office, State Records NSW, Sydney.

especially leaseholders on smaller dairying blocks, were not in a position to benefit and were more likely to be moved on as land was sold and subdivided. The gentlemen farmers like the O'Donnells, however, had large holdings across the region, extensive experience with buying and selling land and were well connected politically. Those who could, adapted to the rapid urban and industrial development by buying and selling land or even moving into real estate. As new land was opened for industrial and then residential purposes, the O'Donnells sold off key parcels of their holdings. Almost inevitably, at least for some members of the clan, they made the successful transition into real estate.[25]

The Arkell house in Birmingham Street, Steeltown, was only a short distance from the number-one blast furnace at Australian Iron & Steel. Steeltown grew with the steelworks and was just south of Five Islands Road. In 1939, with Frank just 10 years old, the suburb was renamed 'Cringila', once the Postmaster-General's Office changed the local 'Steeltown Post Office' to 'Cringila Post Office'.[26] The Arkells' home in Steeltown was in the middle of a large 4,000-square-metre block—the size of six typical suburban blocks. The family established themselves in Steeltown and Sidney's occupation was by now listed as 'labourer'. Sidney attended meetings of the Steeltown Progress Association and his eldest boys enrolled at Christian Brothers College in Wollongong. Christian Brothers was a new Catholic school, opened in 1926, which became a focus of Catholic life and education in the region. The Christian Brothers was a Catholic lay order founded by Edmund Rice in Ireland in 1802 and focused on educating the poor in Catholic communities. By the late nineteenth century, the order had opened schools in the Australian colonial capitals and expanded into regional centres such as Wollongong in the first three decades of the twentieth century.

This was the shape of life for the Arkell family by the early 1940s. The house, on its large block in Birmingham Street, was a sizeable three-bedroom timber home. Young Frank slept on the front verandah, which he stated in 1982 was 'for no other reason than I preferred to sleep on the verandah'. It was comfortable though not necessarily luxurious. The family acquired a large six-cylinder Essex motor vehicle in 1929. Arkell recalled the new vehicle had enough room to take the whole family to the beach on weekends. By the time he was a grown man, Frank developed a love of local

---

25   See Eklund, *Steel Town*, 95–97.
26   *Illawarra Mercury*, 21 April 1939: 13.

and family history, keeping files of material in his mother's home in West Wollongong, including the receipt for the purchase of the Essex. The years before the impending tragedy must have seemed idyllic.

In the early 1940s, the Arkells had a henhouse, fruit trees and a vegetable garden. Frank's three older brothers roamed the remnant farmland and yet-to-be-developed blocks. Richard, aged 20 in 1941, had a .22-calibre rifle and the older boys would go rabbiting in the area. Their home was surrounded by the accoutrements of rural living adjacent to the rising force of the modern industrial age—the new Hoskins iron and steelworks. The blast furnace, finished in 1928, towered 37 metres above the new suburb. The noise of the steelworks, the whoop of sirens, the rumble of trains and the roar of the furnace defined a new aural landscape beside remnant farmland and fenced paddocks. The steam from the coke works and the brown wispy smoke from the blast furnace were clearly visible from the surrounding areas, including the hilly vantage points on the Steeltown Estate. The Hoskins steelworks was altering the landscape as well as forging a new rhythm and structure to local society. The three shifts spread across 24 hours shaped tide-like surges of wage workers to and from the expanding industrial site. Port Kembla's rural fringes were being subdivided for industrial and residential purposes. The old Five Islands Estate was slowly shrinking. Bicycles, trucks, a few cars as well as men on foot traversed this changing landscape, especially now the steelworks had moved to wartime production as the war in Europe had been underway for two years.

The new furnaces and coke ovens ran day and night while the Arkells tended their large block and Sidney toiled away at the steelworks as a driving contractor. Apart from her landholdings and investments, Marcella generated additional income by supplying sandwiches for the truck drivers employed at the steelworks. But in late 1940, ill health forced Sidney to take a break from work. He spent time convalescing at home until 1941. On 23 March, a Sunday, 11-year-old Frank and his mother had departed for Canberra on a holiday when Frank's father, Sidney Arkell, aimed Richard's rifle at his right temple and fired.

2

School, family business and real estate

Richard's rifle fired at point-blank range. Sidney was dead. Earlier that morning, Frank and Marcella had departed for Canberra while the three older boys headed off to church; all were gone by 8.45 am. There are only a few hints at the reason for this drastic action by the married father of four. The coroner's inquest heard evidence that Sidney had been downcast about his work prospects. His 20-year-old son Richard, who found his father's body in the bedroom with blood pooling across the linoleum, told the inquest that 'ill health had forced his father to give up work as a truck driver some months before'. Marcella's evidence records that Sidney was no longer employed owing to poor health. She had reassured him that she would be able to take care of financial matters and reported that he had not told her of any financial worries.[1] When Marcella left for Canberra that morning, there was no inkling of what Sidney was planning nor any indication of a major problem. On 23 March 1941, what appeared from the outside as a comfortable, even idyllic life came crashing down. When Detective Devenport of Wollongong police inspected the scene at 11.15 am, the smell of gunpowder still lingered.[2]

Four weeks later at the coroner's inquest, Port Kembla doctor Archibald Malcolm Harper outlined the cause of Sidney's ailing health. Sidney had been seeing Harper for about 18 months for high blood pressure and a hernia. Despite this, nearly all the witnesses, including Marcella Arkell,

---

1   'Late Sidney Arkell', *South Coast Times*, [Wollongong], 18 April 1941: 10.
2   ibid.

Dr Harper and a police officer from Port Kembla, Sergeant King, were shocked by the event. 'His general conditions varied,' reported Dr Harper, 'but on no occasion did he give any hint he may take his own life.' However, the sheriff's officer at Wollongong Court, Thomas W. Reed, had spoken to Sidney in January of that year, serving him with papers for an unspecified legal matter requiring his appearance at the court in April. Reed gave evidence that Sidney had replied, on receiving the summons: 'I doubt if I shall be alive by April. I can hardly leave the house. I have turns and fall over.'[3] The unspecified legal matter scheduled for April remains a mystery and it is possible, though highly speculative, that it was another factor in Sidney's decision to end his life in March.

We shall see time and again in Frank Arkell's life that the suggestion of something untoward or unseemly was never far away. Not only was there the unspoken fact of Arkell's father's suicide and his unexplained court summons. There was something else. One of the few times that Sidney Arkell appeared in the written record was in 1934 as a jury member on a controversial case of alleged sexual assault of a minor in Nowra, a rural town 50 kilometres south of Wollongong. The jury was empanelled at the district court in Wollongong. The man charged with assaulting an 11-year-old girl was a truck driver and garage owner from Port Kembla and was well acquainted with Sidney Arkell. Sidney sat on a jury for the serious sexual assault trial of someone he knew. On hearing the verdict of 'not guilty', the accused, George Henry Phillips, turned to the jury and said: 'Gentlemen of the jury, I thank you.'[4]

Arkell rarely if ever spoke about his father. Sidney did not come up in speeches and no biographical sketch of Frank Arkell published so far has mentioned his father's suicide. In a 1982 oral history interview, Frank simply recounted that his father had died when he was very young: 'I didn't know him', he had said, but an 11-year-old would no doubt have had clear memories of his father. Frank never volunteered any further information about his father and certainly nothing about his suicide. By contrast, he spoke with considerable warmth about his maternal grandfather, Michael O'Donnell Jr. Sidney's suicide was not the kind of family story that was told and retold. Undoubtedly, the Catholic proscription against suicide as a mortal sin must have counted for a lot among this devout family. Sidney had

---

3   *Illawarra Mercury*, 28 March 1941: 1; 18 April 1941: 6. The inquest reported Sidney's age as 62 while his birth certificate indicates he would have turned 60 in March 1941.
4   *Nowra Leader*, 29 June 1934: 7.

gone against God's dominion over life and death in the most profound and irredeemable way. Even so, the well-connected O'Donnells still managed a Catholic funeral service, although Sidney is buried in the Church of England section at Wollongong Cemetery, so perhaps his conversion to the Catholic faith was incomplete or perhaps his suicide excluded him from a Catholic burial. It is also significant that his sons were at church on the morning of his death while Sidney stayed home.

Along with what appears to be an omission from the public record about Sidney's fate, there are several other inaccuracies or uncertainties about Frank's early life. There are multiple dates given for Frank Arkell's birth. Journalist Kate McClymont put Frank's year of birth as 1929 and a number of sources reported that he was 67 or 68 when he was murdered.[5] This was possibly based on evidence from Mark Valera's trial as the transcript of the judgement against Valera gives 68 as Arkell's age.[6] The court may have sourced its information from Australian Securities and Investments Commission (ASIC) records in which Frank is listed as being born on 13 September 1929 for various family companies.

The major alternative date for Frank Arkell's year of birth is 13 September 1935, which comes from Arkell's own parliamentary biographical entry. This information presumably came straight from Arkell and it roughly accords with one of the few times he provided his age in public life.[7] In 1969, in an *Illawarra Mercury* newspaper feature on candidates for the mayoral election, he was listed as being 36 years of age and that is at least close to a 1935 year of birth.[8] In New South Wales, birth certificates after 1923 are only available to family members so we must use other sources to confirm Frank's birth year. At Sidney's inquest in April 1941, Marcella referred to her son Frank being 11 years old, which is the clearest statement we have from a family source, and from his mother no less. Based on Marcella's testimony, court and ASIC records, Frank's year of birth was 1929 and not

---

5   McClymont, 'The Demise of the Double Life'; Greg Bearup, 'Death Surrounds Her', *Sydney Morning Herald*, 19 May 2001, www.smh.com.au/national/death-surrounds-her-20130524-2k6km.html; Pilita Clark, 'The Media and the Murder', *Sydney Morning Herald*, 4 July 1998: 33–34. The age of 68 comes from John Suter Linton, *Bound by Blood: The True Story behind the Wollongong Murders* (Sydney: Allen & Unwin, 2004), 34, who no doubt relied on the court transcripts.
6   *R v Valera* [2000] NSWSC 1220 [21 December 2000], www8.austlii.edu.au/cgi-bin/viewdoc/au/cases/nsw/NSWSC/2000/1220.html, para 12.
7   'Mr (Frank) Francis Neville ARKELL (1935–1998)', *Members*, [Online] (Sydney: Parliament of New South Wales), www.parliament.nsw.gov.au/members/Pages/member-details.aspx?pk=1930.
8   *Illawarra Mercury*, 10 December 1969: 1.

1935, as listed on the parliamentary website. Uncertainty about his age and the silence surrounding his father's suicide add up to a certain vagueness about Arkell's early history.

Frank attended Christian Brothers College in Wollongong. The Christian Brothers opened their school for boys at the top of Crown Lane in 1926.[9] The school's low fence and two-storey dark-brick buildings with distinctive arches greeted boys for decades until the move to a new site on Mount Keira Road in West Wollongong was completed in 1975. The Catholic curriculum at the time emphasised English, maths, science and religious studies. Church attendance was a regular feature of school life and the presence of Christian Brothers as teaching staff was a permanent reminder of the way that Catholicism and schooling were thoroughly infused.

The Tobins, the Bevans, the O'Donnells, the Arkells, the Dwyers and many more families had boys attend the school—all large Wollongong Catholic families connected by both church and school. Many of these boys would become Frank's political and business associates in later life and, in some cases, his rivals. At the annual end-of-year prize night in 1942, Frank received a prize for 'Christian Doctrine'. In his closing remarks that night, Father Cyril Callaghan 'urged the boys to be faithful to their religious duties. Those leaving school would meet opposition to their Catholic faith', he said, continuing that 'if they failed to uphold their principles, their Catholic education would have been useless'.[10] In 1941 Tony Bevan appeared in one sketch at the Christian Brothers annual concert in a mock debate for which the topic was 'Should School Be Abolished?' Bevan and others were dressed in suits and fake beards and reportedly 'caused much amusement'.[11] In 1944 Frank received his first-year certificate, while his younger contemporary Brian Tobin received his fourth-class certificate. At the 1946 annual concert, Frank appeared in a sketch in which two burglars attempted to steal from a waxworks.[12] At the end of 1946, at the age of 17, Frank received his leaving certificate. Tony Bevan and Brian Tobin would remain a part of Arkell's life into adulthood. Bevan became mayor of Wollongong and Tobin was a close political ally, and both will appear again in the Arkell story.

---

9   Stuart Piggin, *Faith of Steel: A History of the Christian Churches in the Illawarra, Australia* (Wollongong: University of Wollongong, 1984), 191; *Illawarra Mercury*, 17 December 1951: 2.
10   *Illawarra Mercury*, 18 December 1942: 8.
11   *Illawarra Mercury*, 19 December 1941: 12.
12   *Illawarra Mercury*, 5 December 1944: 9; 'B. Tobin 4th Year Certificate', *South Coast Times*, [Wollongong], 7 April 1944: 11; *South Coast Times*, [Wollongong], 23 August 1946: 10.

Frank's Catholic schooling was the wellspring for a life of religious devotion and church attendance. The prize for 'Christian Doctrine' was not an outlier. Frank and Marcella were a common sight at St Therese Catholic Church in West Wollongong. Arkell's attendance at church became less regular after his mother's death in 1979. One member of the congregation remembered 'occasionally' seeing him at the back of the church.[13] Arkell described himself as a 'devout Christian' and others have made the point that he took a keen interest in Catholic spirituality and religious beliefs in general.[14]

Frank went to school with boys who would form the cornerstone of his business, political and friendship network for decades. The Catholic Church and his high school, Christian Brothers College (renamed Edmund Rice College in 1962), provided formative experiences for him and shaped his adult life in Wollongong. That the high school was later revealed to be at the heart of a network of serial abusers and paedophiles is a fact that cannot go unremarked. We do know that Frank went to school with the likes of Tony Bevan, Peter Lewis Comensoli and Brian Tobin—all later alleged to be child sexual abusers and, in Comensoli's case, charged and convicted. Extensive historical research by the Royal Commission into Institutional Responses to Child Sexual Abuse found that the Christian Brothers were some of the worst offenders and that Wollongong had the fifth highest rate of offending among Catholic clergy in the country. These rates of child sexual abuse were not exclusive to Wollongong, or even Australia, but were also seen in other countries where the order was active, including Ireland, the United Kingdom, Canada and the United States.[15] Between 1950 and June 2015, 11.7 per cent of the Catholic clergy in the Wollongong diocese were sexual offenders. The royal commission's report found that 22 per cent of all clergy from the Christian Brothers were sexual offenders, second only to the Brothers of St John of God at 40.4 per cent.[16] Frank Arkell was a faithful and committed Catholic and there was something deeply problematic at the heart of most Catholic parishes, schools and institutions throughout this period.

---

13   Interview with Peter Bahlmann, 8 July 2023.
14   Gordon Waitt, 'A Place for Buddha in Wollongong, New South Wales? Territorial Rules in the Place-Making of Sacred Spaces', *Australian Geographer* 34, no. 2 (2003): 223–38, doi.org/10.1080/00049180301733.
15   Desmond Cahill and Peter Wilkinson, *Child Sexual Abuse in the Catholic Church: An Interpretive Review of the Literature and Public Inquiry Reports* (Melbourne: Centre for Global Research, School of Global, Urban and Social Studies, RMIT University, August 2017), religionsforpeaceaustralia.org.au/download/child-sex-abuse-and-the-catholic-church.pdf.
16   *Royal Commission into Institutional Responses to Child Sexual Abuse. Final Report*, 17 vols (Sydney: Commonwealth of Australia, 2017), www.childabuseroyalcommission.gov.au/.

Sidney's death prompted major changes, as one would expect. The remaining family, Marcella and the four boys, moved from Birmingham Street. Their home was physically moved to the edge of the large block and sold. The block was further subdivided and sold off, too.[17] This was a perfectly understandable response after Richard had discovered his father's body in a pool of blood in the bedroom. One of Frank's older brothers, Harry, travelled to Sydney and enlisted in the Royal Australian Air Force (RAAF) in December 1942—a good option after the traumatic events at home the previous year. That Frank was only 11 years old at the time of his father's death further underlines the age difference between him and his older brothers.[18] Marcella took her boys to her father's house in Kembla Grange, a fine old estate home that the O'Donnells had purchased in the 1890s. As always, it was the O'Donnell family who nurtured them, its large network of kin, property and farming interests providing a solid base that would enable Marcella eventually to rebuild, though she had her own reserves of strength and character on which to draw too.

Frank's grandfather, Michael O'Donnell Jr, the patriarch of the Kembla Grange home, was the boys' favourite. In 1982 Frank remembered his grandfather as a kindly gentleman who could get on with anyone. Frank's recollections of his family—the clipped reply about his father versus the warm, generous comments about his grandfather—are a fascinating contrast. Arkell was always a very careful, reserved interviewee. He kept his responses simple. He never elaborated or offered extended comments. His political skill resided in keeping his message clear and easily digestible. Two extended Arkell interviews from 1974 and 1982 are readily available. A young *WIN TV* reporter, Paul Bongiorno, conducted the 1974 interview. The 1982 interview was for the oral history project conducted by academics Geoffrey Sherington and Winifred Mitchell. His tone in both was reserved to the point of wary suspicion. But when it came to talking about his grandfather, as he did in 1982, there was a warmth in his voice that was only rarely heard.

After a few years at their grandfather's home in Kembla Grange, the family moved again, this time to Wollongong. Their initial move, sometime around 1945, was to a house at 11 Reserve Street, West Wollongong, and

---

17 'Cringila', *Your Suburb*, [Online], Wollongong City Libraries, wollongong.nsw.gov.au/library/explore-our-past/your-suburb/suburbs/cringila.
18 Harry Francis Normal Arkell, Service Number 73391, 1942–1948, A9301, 73391, National Archives of Australia, Canberra.

2. SCHOOL, FAMILY BUSINESS AND REAL ESTATE

later to 1 Reserve Street, where Frank set up a home as a young man and lived with his mother for many decades.[19] It was this three-bedroom timber house with an apartment out the back that would be home for Frank as his political fortunes rose through local and then state politics.

My mother, Heather Eklund nee Halcrow, was born in 1927 and grew up in Port Kembla. Throughout her life, she had a gift for storytelling underpinned by an excellent memory. She knew many of the Port Kembla families including the O'Donnells and the Arkells. Her own background was in the Presbyterian Church, but in the 1930s and 1940s, Port Kembla was still small enough, with a population of 4,000 to 5,000, for there to be interaction and knowledge shared across class, social and religious groupings. She could talk as easily about the local doctors and senior company staff in Port Kembla and their families as she could about the 'Darcy Roaders', a group of working-class, often Catholic residents who had a reputation for toughness. My mother admired Frank for his achievements and his sheer energy, though, like many in Wollongong, she was dismayed by the revelations that came in the last few years of his life. Her main point about Frank Arkell—and she would always remind me—was that 'Mrs Arkell was the real strength behind him'.

There are tantalising glimpses of the strength and capacity of Marcella Arkell. Her words of comfort and support to her ill husband, repeated at the coroner's inquest, give some indication of this. When Sidney was unable to continue working as a driver, she showed a determination to succeed and a willingness to help the family survive financially if necessary. In an age when women were often relegated to a secondary position in financial matters, if accorded any standing at all, Marcella, like the other O'Donnell women, became active in business, commercial life and the voluntary sector. Indeed, by the 1940s and 1950s, she was herself running a successful garage in Figtree and a real estate business, thus setting up the opportunities for Frank to take over when he was old enough. By 1954, Marcella Arkell was also involved in the Wollongong Crippled Children's Society and, by the 1970s, she was a major patron of the Wollongong Art Gallery, which expanded dramatically during the years when Frank was lord mayor.[20] Her interest in art was also underpinned by her own artistic practice.

---

19 The obituary for Michael O'Donnell Jr (Marcella's father), indicates that Marcella and her three sons were living in West Wollongong by 1945. *South Coast Times*, [Wollongong], 23 March 1945: 7.
20 *Illawarra Mercury*, 6 April 1954: 5.

POLITICS, PRIDE AND PERVERSION

In 1952 the commissioner for road construction resumed a large parcel of land in West Wollongong approximately 5.3 hectares in size and jointly owned by the surviving O'Donnell family, including Marcella, for the purpose of road construction. The O'Donnells were influential landowners in this part of West Wollongong and this helps explain the family's move from Steeltown to West Wollongong via Michael Senior's estate at Kembla Grange.[21] The resumed land became the construction site for the major new Wollongong bypass in 1963, which allowed ever-increasing numbers of vehicles to avoid the central business district of Wollongong and pass to the west of the growing city. New concrete bridges were built over the bypass, including the bridge at Reserve Street just near the Arkell residence. The Wollongong bypass was a clear sign of the city's rapid postwar population growth, much of it through the arrival of migrants from Central and Southern Europe.

After leaving school, Frank worked in the Arkells' garage on the Princes Highway in Figtree. There is a photograph of the garage taken in 1953 for an advertisement to be played during intermission at the local cinemas showing Frank standing out the front of the building (Plate 6.1). At 24 years of age, he was tall and lean, yet to grow into himself. After several years working at the Figtree garage, Frank moved to Sydney and secured employment initially with the Sydney Stock Exchange and later with the ANZ Bank. The years in Sydney are another curious silence in the Frank Arkell story. Like his father's suicide, this was a part of his life of which he never spoke. Perhaps to acknowledge he had lived in Sydney would have broken the spell of his uncompromising and resolute commitment to Wollongong, which later became the hallmark of his politics.

While Frank was in Sydney, Tony Bevan took over his father's business, in 1960, and the following year went into local government as an alderman for Ward 3, which covered the Wollongong central business district (CBD). Bevan was not aligned with either the Labor or the Liberal parties and was seen as a pro-business independent candidate. Bevan would go on to secure a three-year but rather unremarkable stint as Mayor of Wollongong, from 1965 to 1968. There had been others who pursued independent representation using this political strategy. Alderman Rube Hargrave was the only woman on Wollongong Council between 1959 and 1971,

---

21 'Transport (Division of Functions) Act, 1932–1952—Main Roads Act, 1924–1954—Proclamation', *Government Gazette of the State of New South Wales* (Sydney: NSW Parliamentary Counsel's Office, 1901–2001).

representing Ward 1, which covered the coastal villages and towns in the north of the region around Woonona, Thirroul and Bulli.[22] Alderman Hargrave maintained an extensive community and civic presence and served as deputy mayor in 1970. She also ran as an independent in 1965 for the state seat of Bulli, which Labor's Rex Jackson had held since 1955. Hargrave received 2,388 votes or 10 per cent of the vote.[23] In 1968 she ran in the state seat of Corrimal, to the south of the seat of Bulli, where she was less well known. She secured 671 votes or 3.6 per cent.[24] Likewise, Bevan followed his three-year term as mayor with an attempt to run as an independent for the state seat of Wollongong in 1968.[25] 'It is true to say of course,' claimed Bevan in announcing his candidacy, 'that Wollongong has not received equitable treatment from either of the political parties that have controlled New South Wales Governments in the past.'[26] In this case, Bevan secured 16.4 per cent of the vote or 3,345 votes with his preferences helping Liberal candidate Jack Hough win the seat.[27] In the mid to late 1960s, both Hargrave and Bevan were pursuing a form of non-Labor politics that they presented to the electorate as independent and which had some success at least at the municipal level.

Bevan and Hargrave seemingly provided a template for Frank Arkell but there was also Frank's own family history traced through his mother's side. The O'Donnells had been adept at exercising their influence on the old Central Illawarra Council with great uncle Frank O'Donnell, a reassuring and widely respected presence. At more than 1.8 metres tall, Frank O'Donnell was a towering figure and a similarly tall Frank Arkell clearly took after his great uncle in this regard. We cannot be sure but the O'Donnells had experience of family representation on the council and this may have influenced Frank's plan to seek office as an alderman on Wollongong Council. His mother and his older brothers were well established in various business

---

22 Kerrie Anne Christian, 'Alderman Rube Hargrave—Ward 1, Wollongong City Council', *Linga Longa: Stories of Women and Thirroul*, 27 March 2009, lingalongathirroul.wordpress.com/2009/03/27/alderman-rube-hargrave-ward-1-wollongong-city-council/. In her short piece, Christian acknowledges the excellent research by community historian Mick Roberts.
23 Parliament of New South Wales, State Election Results for the Seat of Bulli, 1965, www.parliament.nsw.gov.au/electionresults18562007/1965/Bulli.htm.
24 Parliament of New South Wales, State Election Results for the Seat of Corrimal, 1968, www.parliament.nsw.gov.au/electionresults18562007/1968/Corrimal.htm.
25 See Terry Moore, 'Tony Bevan to Run for Parliament', *WIN4 News*, 31 January 1968, Archives Online, University of Wollongong, archivesonline.uow.edu.au/nodes/view/14768.
26 ibid.
27 Parliament of New South Wales, State Election Results for the Seat of Wollongong, 1968, www.parliament.nsw.gov.au/electionresults18562007/1968/Wollongong.htm.

ventures that included landownership, subdivision development, residential and commercial real estate, as well as earthmoving and large equipment contracting. A family voice on the council could be an especially desirable asset. Frank returned to Wollongong from Sydney in 1964. Marcella and Frank were now joint proprietors of Arrow Real Estate Proprietary Limited and the family businesses included an impressive portfolio of property in Wollongong, the Central West of New South Wales and in Canberra.[28] In December 1965 Arkell successfully stood as a candidate for alderman for Ward 5, which included Figtree, Unanderra and Dapto. At the age of 36, his career in local government began but his business activities continued as well. Frank Arkell was back and, as far as he told the story, he had never left 'wonderful, wonderful Wollongong' at all.

---

28   *Canberra Times*, 25 March 1964: 64.

3
'For the betterment of Wollongong': From new alderman to long-serving mayor, 1965–1981

Having returned to Wollongong and worked to establish and further the family businesses on a firmer footing, Frank Arkell's plans turned to local government. After 1945, the small rural towns, dirt roads and open farmland where many of the O'Donnells had run their farms only a few decades before were fast turning into new suburbs and a major industrial zone as Wollongong and Port Kembla expanded. The rural land between Port Kembla, Figtree, Lake Illawarra and Unanderra was now dotted with suburbs and hostels to cater for the growing labour force at the BHP steelworks. There were opportunities for projects in land subdivision, commercial and industrial development and residential real estate, but rapid growth also presented major challenges for the newly formed City of Greater Wollongong.

The City of Greater Wollongong was formed in 1947 when four smaller local government areas amalgamated: the Bulli and Central Illawarra shires and the municipalities of Wollongong and North Illawarra. In 1965, when Frank Arkell first sought election to the council, Wollongong was a prosperous industrial region with a strong coal mining sector, a rapidly expanding industrial heartland in Port Kembla and a well-established commercial and retail hub in Wollongong itself. In the postwar years, regional society had been transformed through large-scale migration of mostly European workers and their families. In 1966 the Commonwealth census recorded a population of 149,506 living in the City of Greater Wollongong. There were more males than females in the area—78,020 to 71,486, respectively—a result of the demand in the male labour market for industrial jobs in the BHP steelworks and its related industries in and around Port Kembla.[1]

This was a multicultural region with many European migrants settling in the area. Dramatic changes in the makeup of the population occurred after World War II. By 1965, 13 per cent of the region's population had been born in the United Kingdom or Ireland while almost 30 per cent had been born in Europe. Of the Europe-born, the major contributors were Italy (4 per cent) and Yugoslavia (3 per cent) as it was then called, a nation-state that, at that time, included Serbs, Croats and Macedonians, among others. A significant number of Macedonians had settled in and around Port Kembla, while 2 per cent of the Illawarra's residents were born in Germany and 1.5 per cent each in the Netherlands and Greece, with smaller numbers from Spain, Malta, Poland and Austria. Arkell himself was fond of saying 'there are 76 migrant groups in Wollongong, all making up part of our wonderful community'. This was a message he delivered time and time again and was one element of his electoral popularity in a region that was rapidly changing.

The amalgamation that created the City of Greater Wollongong had been strongly contested by the Central Illawarra Shire and the Bulli Shire, and divisions and rivalries continued well into the tenure of the new council in the late 1940s, 1950s and into the 1960s. There were five wards, each of which elected three aldermen.[2] Arkell was nominated for Ward 5, which included Unanderra, Figtree, Dapto and Albion Park, and he was elected in December 1965. This ward was very much home turf for the O'Donnells and the Arkells, and the base for their businesses and extensive landholdings. Arkell secured third spot in Ward 5—a very creditable result—coming in just behind sitting aldermen Harry Graham and I.V. Ryan. Of the 10,720 votes cast in Ward 5, Labor's Ryan secured 3,113 for the top position. The long-serving Graham, who had been the first mayor of the newly amalgamated Council of Greater Wollongong in 1947, was second on 2,964, while Arkell polled 2,633 votes. In a surprise result in the

---

1   Australian Bureau of Statistics, 'Part 1: New South Wales', in *2106.0 Census of Population and Housing, 1966. Volume 4: Population and Dwellings in Local Government Areas* (Canberra: Commonwealth of Australia, 1966), 30–32, www.ausstats.abs.gov.au/ausstats/free.nsf/0/D311C20059D36DDFCA2578 80008306D7/$File/1966%20Census%20-%20Volume%204%20Population%20and%20Dwellings %20in%20LGA%20-%20Part%201%20NSW.pdf.
2   Peter Sheldon, 'Local Government since 1947', in *A History of Wollongong*, eds Jim Hagan and Andrew Wells (Wollongong: University of Wollongong Press, 1997), 115–28.

mayoral contest, Tony Bevan from Ward 3 comprehensively defeated the expected frontrunners: the Labor candidate, J.J. Kelly, and former Labor mayor Albert Squires. Labor's vote had been evenly split after Alderman Squires left the party and ran as an independent. Squires polled 12,832 votes while his replacement on the Labor ticket, Alderman J.J. Kelly, polled 13,614 votes. Labor disunity delivered the mayoral position to Bevan. Not for the first time, the independents on Wollongong Council—a broad collection of candidates not aligned to a major political party and usually from the conservative or pro-business side of politics—benefited from Labor's mistakes and missteps in the region. At 33, Tony Bevan became the youngest mayor elected to Wollongong Council. This is a record that has never been publicly acknowledged or promoted given Bevan's name later became synonymous with the Wollongong-based paedophile network.[3]

Extensive economic and social changes coupled with urbanisation and industrial development created a complex and challenging environment for any local government authority. While this and later chapters present material that is critical of the City of Greater Wollongong, it is well to remember that this under-resourced level of government had to play a key role in ensuring orderly growth and the preservation of urban amenities during this period of rapid change. By 1966, Wollongong Council covered an area of almost 445 square kilometres, with 41,135 dwellings of which 38,640 were private dwellings. The lack of funding from the state government was a recurring theme in Wollongong politics and an issue that the independents on the council would exploit very effectively.

After a short stint as deputy mayor in 1969, Arkell won the position of lord mayor in September 1974. At the time, the position—a title the City of Wollongong secured by royal assent in 1970—was voted on by all 15 aldermen. Arkell's victory showed his standing among the group and meant the non-aligned independents had gained a majority on the council. In 1971 the previous lord mayor, Labor's John Parker, had indicated that he was willing to stand again in 1974 but clearly he failed to secure the numbers on the new council.[4]

---

3   'Landslide to Alderman Bevan in Mayoral Poll', *Illawarra Mercury*, 6 December 1965: 1, 3. The Ward 5 results are on p. 3.
4   'Lord Mayor of Wollongong Interview', *WIN TV*, 1971, WIN4 Collection, D75/sr/1971/SR65/pt2, Archives Online, University of Wollongong, archivesonline.uow.edu.au/nodes/view/4075. Amendments to the *Local Government Act* in 1992 formally changed the title of elected council representatives from 'alderman' to 'councillor' so 'alderman' is used throughout this book since the change occurred after Arkell had left the council. Once Rube Hargrave left the council in 1971, it was not until 1983 that the arrival of Pat Franks and Norma Wilson heralded the next wave of women aldermen.

Plate 3.1 Frank Arkell escorts Prince Philip on his walk along Crown Street, Wollongong, 10 April 1970

Note: Despite being only an alderman, Arkell secured a prominent position in the official party welcoming the royal entourage of Queen Elizabeth II, Prince Philip and Princess Anne when they visited the city.

Photo: Wollongong City Libraries, copied from negative filed at MSS 1563/3 FM2/346/2, No. P30975.

3. 'FOR THE BETTERMENT OF WOLLONGONG'

In a *WIN News* interview conducted by Paul Bongiorno, Arkell nominated pollution and the environment as key issues and emphasised the challenge of improving the image of Wollongong. Arkell was asked whether his election as lord mayor was 'the fulfilment of a life's ambition in any way'. He replied:

> Not really, but it is very exciting. It is quite a challenge. I hope to work with the team and as a team and, if we can project a better image of council to the people and take council to the people, I think we will achieve what we are after. Pollution is a big issue and the environment. And this is generally a big worry to the people of Wollongong. In other words, we want to make Wollongong a much better place to live in.[5]

His style was characteristically focused with an almost flat, monotonal delivery. The sentiments themselves were potentially quite rousing but Arkell's media performances always came across as workman-like rather than polished. His great strength was his consistency. His ability to stay on message even in the face of apparently quite tough questions was almost legendary. In the same interview, Bongiorno asked the new lord mayor whether he was concerned about the commercial interests of aldermen affecting council decisions. The journalist asked:

> Local government is often prone to the sort of criticism that many people become aldermen so they can advance their own interest. Do you think you have to be particularly sensitive about this area given you know land development, zoning and things like this?

Arkell simply ignored the substance and possible implication of the question and made a generic statement about the quality of the aldermen being elected:

> Yes, I do honestly feel that Wollongong is the second city of New South Wales and it's developing very fast and I am very pleased with the calibre of the aldermen being elected. We have some very fine aldermen ... With the regional planning coming in, this will be planning on a broader scope, leaving detailed planning to Wollongong Council, where they will have to expand the town planning section of the council whereby people will have more say in terms of what they want in their community.

---

5   Paul Bongiorno, ' Interview with Lord Mayor Frank Arkell', *WIN4 TV*, 29 September 1974, WIN4 Collection, D75/srs/1974/09/29/pt3, Archives Online, University of Wollongong, archivesonline.uow.edu.au/nodes/view/4338.

Among the issues noted by Arkell for attention in his first term were the council's deficit, moves to computerise the council's works register, the need for differentiation of rates between residential, industrial and farming communities, and the opportunities presented by an increasing amount of funding from the Commonwealth Government.

When asked whether he believed the independents would caucus together and 'become more like a party', Arkell answered: 'No I don't. I feel we can work within Council, we can get together and unite and go forward for the betterment of Wollongong.'[6] This was a common refrain from Arkell. He almost always emphasised unity and working together for the greater good of Wollongong. His public statements focused on opportunities and talked about a bright future. The underlying message was always: trust me, things will get better.

Despite Arkell's assessment in 1974 that the independents would not become like a party, they soon emerged as a party-like grouping and were eventually tagged 'the Arkell Independents'. Bevan Fermor from the Labor Party recalled that when he first stood for election in Ward 5 (Arkell's ward) in 1977, he found in Arkell 'quite a formidable opponent' and 'the Arkell team were very well organised'. Fermor spent 10 years on the council and noted that Arkell's personal vote in Ward 5 was always so strong that his independent team secured first and second places, with Arkell first and his running mate second, while the Labor Party secured the third remaining position for the ward.[7] It was not until the 1977 council election that Labor representatives were able to form a slim majority over the Arkell and non-aligned independents.

One of the keys to Arkell's electoral success was his positive disposition towards recent migrant families. Arkell was a regular speaker at migrant associations and had good links with communities beyond the British and Irish diaspora, especially the Italian and Polish communities, with whom he shared the Catholic faith of many families. This carried over into his later successful political career as a state member. Arkell's embrace of ethnic diversity contrasted to the Anglo dominance of some union leaders and Labor candidates at local and state levels. At the branch level, Labor was a rich amalgam of local cultures, but the party kept endorsing candidates who had Anglo-Australian, British or Irish heritage. At an address to the West Wollongong Rotary Club, of which he was an active member, Arkell

6   ibid.
7   Interview with Bevan Fermor, 22 March 2023.

observed: 'Immediately after the War people from all over the world came to our city as refugees. Today there is [*sic*] over 76 national groups in the City of Wollongong.' Again, with Arkell, we see the typical repetition of favourite facts. Many people in Wollongong will have heard those same sentiments and statistics in many of Arkell's speeches, as reported here in a *Rotary News* summary of Frank's speech:

> The City has an Anglo-Celtic base added to which has been a small French component and a large Italian element. The Italians started coming back in the 1880's from Piedmont to build the railways. Today the Italians are the largest national group with the Yugoslavians being the largest of the recently arrived national groups. We welcomed all these people into our city. There were no riots there was no jealousy 'Great Workers—Great People'.
>
> It was in such a way [that] Frank explained how he saw the uniqueness of Wollongong. A unique city today because it has [a] wide ethnic base with its citizens working constructively side by side to build great industries.[8]

Nick Hartgerink, a journalist with the *Illawarra Mercury* and later its editor, who first met Arkell in 1977, recalled:

> [Frank] was a very effective politician. He used to have a technique of walking into a function, saying hello to everybody and walking out the back door. He would have only been there for 10 or 15 minutes, but everybody would have said I saw Frank Arkell at this function or that function. He was particularly good at going to events organised by migrant communities. So, if, for example, the Polish Club had a national day event he would be there. He might only be there for 10 or 15 minutes, but everybody would remember that the lord mayor had been there.[9]

Arkell's embrace of multiculturalism was crucial in the 1970s when Wollongong society was changing so rapidly and ethnic and cultural tensions between established residents and new migrants were often manifest. As Hartgerink noted: 'For a lot of migrant communities that was a really big deal. It gave them an imprimatur that they mattered and it gave Frank a very loyal voter base. No question, he was a smart politician.'[10]

---

8   Rotary Club of West Wollongong, 'President's News, 1975 to 1983', [Notes from meeting dated 13 August 1975], *Rotary News*, www.rotarynews.info/2/club/4445/3239 (site discontinued).
9   Interview with Nick Hartgerink, 24 November 2022.
10 ibid.

Plate 3.2 Lord Mayor Frank Arkell at a 'Thank You' event in his honour hosted by the local Serbian community, just one of the countless events, festivals and celebrations he attended among Wollongong's faith and multicultural communities

Note: The caption reads: 'Wollongong Serbian community members Helen Delich (left), Radmilla Pupovac and Dushanka Tatalovic (right) in their national dress to welcome Senator Misha Lajovic, Father Jovo, Wollongong Lord Mayor Ald Frank Arkell and Serbian Society president Michael Delich at the "Thank You" dinner for Ald Arkell, 20 July 19??.'

Photo: *Illawarra Mercury* Image Collection and Wollongong City Libraries, Image no. P24751.

Another story of Hartgerink's highlights Arkell's proactive engagement with the press and his intuitive understanding of the importance of their coverage and their view of him. Shortly after the new journalist had attended his first council meeting in 1977, Hartgerink had a dinner date at the Italian Centre with his girlfriend, who would later become his wife. As he recalls:

> We were sitting down to our meal and a carafe of wine was delivered to the table. And I said, 'I didn't order this wine.' And the waiter said, 'Oh, the lord mayor sent you this wine.' And Frank Arkell had sent me over a carafe of wine, which I found quite embarrassing. My wife thought it was impressive. Or my girlfriend at the time, my new girlfriend. She thought it was quite impressive that the lord mayor thought enough to send me a carafe of wine. I, on the other hand, was not comfortable at all. And I don't think we drank a sip of it. When the waiter told me who had given it to me and he pointed

to Frank, who was standing at the bar or at the other end of the restaurant, I can't remember the details, and he just nodded to me. Well, I thought: interesting.[11]

Even in 1990, towards the end of his political career, Frank was still meeting and greeting new journalists. Newly appointed *Illawarra Mercury* journalist Paul McInerney arrived in Wollongong in August 1990 and attended his first official civic function. He was introduced to Arkell, whose first words to him were: 'Welcome to wonderful Wollongong. Don't believe everything you've heard about me.' This was a welcoming line McInerney would never forget and again showed Arkell's capacity to work with journalists but also his attempts to frame their reading of a new situation and anything they might hear about him. Arkell's reference is enigmatic. It shows him alluding to rumours and issues about his reputation but attempting to promote an element of doubt. It was a bold move but showed him fighting back on the reputational front. As John Martin, a Labor alderman on Wollongong Council from 1977 to 1987, recalls:

> [Arkell] cultivated the media and through the media the population as a whole. In the main he was good at avoiding controversy and at presenting himself in a good light. This was his full-time preoccupation as Lord Mayor and he was good at it.[12]

Despite his reservations, McInerney was still alive to the consummate politician in action: 'Every time I saw him, he moved with a bounce. He walked into a room and he became the centre of attention. Before he walked in, he squared his shoulders back and put a smile on his face.'[13]

Arkell's height, at 193 centimetres, gave him a natural advantage. As he aged, he filled out and his frame thickened. The gaunt, skinny youth photographed out the front of Arkells' garage in 1953 was long gone. By the time he was lord mayor, he possessed a commanding physical presence— the stature of political and financial authority.

Arkell's energetic networking, continually attending meetings, events and celebrations, as well as the media coverage that he so effectively courted, meant that his popularity continued to rise throughout the 1970s and early 1980s. The energy he devoted to the task at hand was remarkable. He was simply relentless. He once told a journalist from the *Wollongong Advertiser*:

---

11 ibid.
12 John Martin, Personal communication, 23 April 2023.
13 Notes from an interview with Paul McInerney, 21 November 2022.

'I'm scared to death of not being busy.'[14] Peter Bahlmann, an Edmund Rice College student and later a Wollongong-based solicitor, recalled that Arkell appeared at a school function in the late 1970s—no doubt just one of many he attended across the region. As Balhman recalled, Arkell talked about being on the council and all the activities he undertook. A student asked him where he found the energy for his work. Paul remembered his answer: 'He said, "I have powernaps. I just go and lie on the couch for 15 minutes and then I just get up."'[15]

This activity paid dividends. We can gain a snapshot of Arkell's electoral popularity across the five wards of the City of Greater Wollongong by looking at the results of the first popular ballot held for the lord mayorship in 1980. The NSW Labor government had amended the *Local Government Act 1976* for the City of Greater Wollongong Council, with the sole purpose, many argued, of trying to unseat Arkell.[16] The reasoning here was that Arkell could never win a popular vote across the whole electorate as his support base was limited to Ward 5.

Arkell proved the Labor schemers wrong. At the 1980 election, Arkell topped the poll with 38,453 votes, with the second-placed candidate, Labor's John Parker, receiving 31,037 votes. Two high-profile independents, the highly respected alderman Ernie Ford, and Bernie Groben from the Ratepayers' Association, secured 3,862 and 3,287 votes, respectively. But there was no need for preference distribution: Arkell had won almost 52 per cent of the primary vote. This was an impressive result as Parker was no political newcomer. As a former lord mayor and Labor stalwart on the council, he had been a serious contender backed by the Labor Party's branch network.[17] In Ward 5, Arkell won 12,212 votes to 6,656 for Labor's Bevan Fermor, while Arkell's running mate, John Schipp, secured 1,131 votes. Arkell's result in the ward represented 57 per cent of the total votes cast and was enough to secure the Arkell Independents a quota of two aldermen for the ward.[18]

---

14   Lachlan Harris, 'Mr Wollongong Plans a Long Run as Mayor', *Wollongong Advertiser*, 29 January 1986.
15   Interview with Peter Bahlmann, 8 July 2023.
16   The Act stated that in Wollongong and Newcastle 'the mayor or president of an area to which this section applies shall be elected by the electors of that area'. This was introduced by the then new Wran Labor government, which came to office in May 1976 and passed this amendment in December of that year. *Local Government (Elections) Amendment Act 1976* No. 70 (NSW), schedule 2, section 25a, www8.austlii.edu.au/cgi-bin/viewdb/au/legis/nsw/num_act/lgaa1976n70382/.
17   'Local Government Election Details: Wollongong', *Illawarra Mercury*, 22 September 1980: 10.
18   ibid.

3. 'FOR THE BETTERMENT OF WOLLONGONG'

Back in 1968, at the end of his first term, Arkell had only just outpolled the Labor candidate in Ward 5 by slightly more than 100 votes. By 1980, his personal vote was more than double that of his main Labor rival.[19]

While Hartgerink, McInerney, Fermor and Martin could see the effectiveness of Arkell's approach and even admired his energy and commitment, they expressed reservations about the substance of his ideas and plans. John Martin remembered Arkell as a gregarious and affable man who tried to make him feel welcome on the council when Martin was a new alderman in 1977. Martin would sometimes accompany Arkell on his round of social visits and events after council meetings. But he also found Arkell lacked substance. 'I came to form the opinion,' Martin recalled, 'that he was essentially a political lightweight who sought popularity and avoided confrontation as a political tactic.' In all the time Martin spent with Arkell outside council meetings, Arkell never discussed his plans or his vision for Wollongong nor did he ever talk about his religious or spiritual convictions. Martin, like many, found a frustrating lack of heart and soul in Arkell.[20] It was difficult, almost impossible it seems, to pierce that usually affable exterior.

Plate 3.3 The independent how-to-vote card for Ward 1 and for Lord Mayor for the September 1980 Wollongong City Council election
Note: Pictured (left to right): Frank Arkell, Brian Tobin (who held the number-one spot for the independents) and Phil Cram (who held the number-two spot).
Photo: University of Wollongong Archives, Collection C1/19/04, Item IDC1/19/04.

---

19   'Labor's Team May Control City Council', *Illawarra Mercury*, 9 December 1968: 1.
20   John Martin, Personal communication, 23 April 2023.

During this period things were changing for Arkell in his home life. Apart from the few years he spent in Sydney in the late 1950s and early 1960s, he had lived all his adult life with his mother in Reserve Street, West Wollongong—initially at number 11 and, from about 1960, at 1 Reserve Street. Marcella occupied the house at the front of the block and Arkell lived in an apartment at the rear. A photo album Arkell donated to the Local Studies Collection at the Wollongong City Library includes photos of Frank and Marcella attending dances and commemorative events at AGA Club Germania and the Polish Club that date from the early to mid-1970s.

Even in these photos, Marcella looks old and frail. In the last few years of her life, she developed dementia. Living across the road from the Arkells, the D'Souza children would often find Mrs Arkell wandering the streets looking lost, and their mother would ask them to take her home. At times Mrs Arkell became worried about the lights on in the D'Souza house. She would come over and ask whether they were okay. At the time, Michael D'Souza's mother explained to him that Mrs Arkell:

> often thinks back to when she was a little girl. And when she was a little girl, there was a fire in the barn or something in her early life, there was a fire, and so Mum was explaining to us, she sometimes remembers that and she's worried ... [that] the lights might cause a fire.[21]

There was indeed a tragic fire in the O'Donnell family history. In 1895, just a few years before Marcella was born, the O'Donnell home on the Five Islands Estate caught fire. Despite the best efforts of Marcella's father, two of her uncles (James and John) and two employees died, and the house and all its contents were completely destroyed by the fire, the origin of which, according to the *Illawarra Mercury*, was 'shrouded in mystery'.[22] In her frail and weakened state, Marcella may have been channelling family memories of the 1895 fire.

It was during this time, from about 1976, that Marcella disappears from Frank's photos. Perhaps she was no longer able to attend functions with him? Marcella died on 3 April 1979. She was buried in the Catholic section of Wollongong Cemetery, separated from Sidney, who rests in the Anglican section, but we do not have any indication of how this affected Frank.[23]

---

21 Interview with Michael D'Souza, 21 November 2022.
22 'A Disastrous Fire', *Illawarra Mercury*, 7 December 1895: 2.
23 'Obituary for Marcella Arkell', *Sydney Morning Herald*, 4 April 1979.

From that date, after his long days and nights as lord mayor, he came home to an empty house. As best as I can discern, the private, secretive Arkell never shared with anyone how he coped with his mother's death. He stayed on at 1 Reserve Street, keeping the house more or less the same as when his mother was alive. He continued to live in the rear apartment but would occasionally entertain in the big house, where he also stored his papers, records and local history collection.

After Marcella's death, the public Arkell continued with barely a misstep and there were no references to his late mother, and no personal anecdotes or recollections ever graced his speeches. *Illawarra Mercury* journalist Paul McInerney found Arkell's speeches underwhelming: 'He never said anything very critical. Everything was positive, wonderful Wollongong. The speeches weren't much really. Typical politician-type thing.' As fellow journalist Nick Hartgerink acknowledged, it was difficult for a politician to be candid with a local journalist but even off-the-record chats about politics, spirituality and other big ideas were absent. 'He would say what he had to say and talk about wonderful Wollongong,' recalls Hartgerink, 'but beyond that you couldn't really talk about anything significant, or [of] a personal nature, or what your hobbies were or this or that.'[24]

Another clear reason for Arkell's enduring success in local government was the quality of the team of independents who coalesced around him. He surrounded himself with very effective, competent people. Naturally, the independents benefited from being associated with the high-profile Arkell, but some of the popularity and standing of his independent running mates rubbed off on Arkell, too. Ted Tobin, a senior manager at John Lysaght (Australia) Proprietary Limited and a highly respected sports administrator, served on the Wollongong Council from 1971 to 1984. Tobin (no relation to another Arkell ally, Brian Tobin) received an Order of Australia medal for services to local government and, like Arkell, a Knighthood to the Order of Merit of the Italian Republic for his work among the Italian community in Wollongong.[25] Ted was a close political ally of Arkell's and a long-serving independent alderman. Representing Ward 3, which covered the Wollongong CBD, Tobin was on the council at the height of Arkell's popularity. After leaving the council in 1984, he remained closely aligned

---

24 Interview with Paul McInerney, 21 November 2022; Interview with Nick Hartgerink, 24 November 2022.
25 Michelle Hoctor, 'Ted Tobin: A True Gentleman of the Illawarra', *Illawarra Mercury*, 9 February 2010, [Updated 5 November 2012], www.illawarramercury.com.au/story/626361/ted-tobin-a-true-gentleman-of-the-illawarra/.

with Arkell and continued to support him politically.[26] Peter Hilton, a senior BHP employee, was heavily involved in sports administration, not-for-profit boards and charities throughout the region. Hilton's role on the Commonwealth Government's Good Neighbour Council gave him a good profile among the region's migrant communities. Hilton would later act as campaign manager for Arkell in his lord mayoral and state election campaigns.[27] Local solicitor Harold Hanson, a Wollongong Council alderman from 1968 to 1977, was one of the architects of the independents' manifesto issued in 1974 that articulated many of the policy positions Arkell would advocate in the late 1970s and throughout the 1980s.[28]

The Arkell Independents showed that Arkell was a figure with a wide support base of well-connected professional middle-class men and women who supported and, indeed, arguably first articulated the vision for a newer, better Wollongong that Arkell subsequently made his own. With strong support from urban professionals, senior staff at the BHP steelworks and other industries as well as senior University of Wollongong staff, Arkell had captured the natural constituency of the Liberal Party, which had always struggled in this region with its strong Labor traditions and union presence. The Labor Party was aware of Arkell's success and his ability to command the natural constituency of the Liberals, so much so that they attempted to undermine Arkell's claim to be an independent by suggesting he was the Liberal Party's man in Wollongong. 'It must remain clear,' claimed no less a figure than premier Neville Wran in NSW Parliament in 1983, 'that the Liberal Party's man in Wollongong, Frank Arkell, has been put up for an election, is still a supporter of the Liberal Party, and has their support.'[29]

Across all sectors of society, from the Wollongong Rotary Club to the Illawarra Historical Society, from the Polish Club to AGA Club Germania, Arkell had strong standing and high levels of respect. Bevan Fermor's memories of council election day in Ward 5 were that the Arkell team was very well organised and volunteers included a mix of friends, business associates, members of various ethnic groups as well as small business and professional people—in other words, a diverse cross-section of Wollongong

---

26 ibid.
27 Brett Cox, 'The Hawks Fan Who Lived to Help Others', *Illawarra Mercury*, 26 October 2009, [Updated 5 November 2012], www.illawarramercury.com.au/story/623533/the-hawks-fan-who-lived-to-help-others/.
28 Notes of an interview with Harold Hanson, 3 April 2023.
29 Neville Wran, in NSW, *Parliamentary Debates*, Legislative Assembly, 22 September 1983, 1113, api.parliament.nsw.gov.au/api/hansard/search/daily/searchablepdf/HANSARD-290296563-1047.

society. Rotary awarded Arkell the Paul Harris Fellowship in 1985 'in recognition of his services to the City of Wollongong' and later conferred on him honorary life membership.[30] Arkell was a member of the Lions Club and a recipient of the Melvin Jones Fellowship. Local author and historical society member Joseph Davis penned a short but heartfelt obituary of Arkell, praising 'our past patron', who 'worked tirelessly for the local community'. 'It was common knowledge,' wrote Davis, 'that everywhere Frank Arkell travelled, he always touted the beauties and benefits that belong to this beautiful area and his informative input to our meetings will be sorely missed.'[31] In April 1991, for example, Arkell was part of a group of Wollongong-based lobbyists and politicians who were able to secure heritage listing for the 1881 shipwreck the *Queen of Nations* off the Illawarra coast near Towradgi Point, after reports that items were being removed from the wreck by divers.[32]

Arkell's interest in the Illawarra Historical Society was a longstanding one. He was among some of his closest friends and most committed supporters there, especially in the 1960s and 1970s. The founder of the society, Bill McDonald, was an old friend, and Arkell was made its patron in 1985. Well-known to Arkell, Wollongong solicitor Edgar Beale was one of the society's most influential members and probably its most gifted historian.[33] Arkell's long-term lawyer and close associate, Peter Daly, was also active there. Arkell had been an active member since at least 1960 and, on his elevation to the lord mayorship in 1974, the society proudly congratulated him. Bill McDonald wrote in the society's *Bulletin* for November 1974:

> Ald. Arkell, a member of an old Illawarra family has long shown a keen interest in local history and in the work of the Society. We hope that his new responsibilities will still leave him time to put in an occasional appearance at our meetings.[34]

---

30   Comments by Albert Cachia, in 'The Presidential Years, 1994 to 1999', *Rotary News*, www.rotarynews.info/2/club/4445/3241 (site discontinued).
31   Joseph Davis, 'Obituary: Frank Arkell, the Public Face', *Bulletin*, [Illawarra Historical Society], September 1998: 72.
32   Michael Organ, 'The "Discovery" of the Wreck of the Queen of Nations', *Bulletin*, [Illawarra Historical Society], March 1992: 14.
33   See, for example, Edgar Beale, *Illawarra Sketchbook*, Illustrations by Gillian Trigg (Adelaide: Rigby, 1977); Edgar Beale, *Sturt, the Chipped Idol: A Study of Charles Sturt, Explorer* (Sydney: Sydney University Press, 1979).
34   Bill McDonald, 'Personal', *Bulletin*, [Illawarra Historical Society], November 1974: 2, archivesonline.uow.edu.au/nodes/view/13784#idx107590.

In his 1982 oral history interview, Arkell revealed that he had family records that included the purchase details for the family car, the Essex, which had been acquired in 1929. He later became a patron of Vintage Illawarra, and his home in Reserve Street was known to have large collections of files and cabinets containing historical material. He donated a portion of his collection to the Local Studies collection at the Wollongong City Library and he was also a keen bottle collector.

As much as he was interested in Wollongong's past, he made the city's future his political focus. In three key areas, Arkell showed an interest in a future for Wollongong that was more than mining and industry. He showed his Labor rivals that leading on issues beyond the old industrial and mining economy could be electorally successful. In the first area of interest, Arkell was, above everything else, a patriot for Wollongong. He celebrated the city and its achievements and wanted to improve it through investment in large retail, hospitality and tourism development in particular, but also through better cultural facilities. 'We have pride in our City,' he told a Rotary Club meeting in 1975, 'but we do not say it often enough. You have to wear it on your lapel.' His career on the council and later as the state member for Wollongong revealed a single-minded focus on the city and—one of his favourite phrases—'its betterment'. His approach remained remarkably consistent across more than two decades. Putting Wollongong first meant rising above party politics and personal conflicts. In 1974, on his election to the mayorship, he said: 'If we can place the city above politics, above personalities, and work for the good of Wollongong, I think we can get together, unite and go forward for the betterment of Wollongong.' Election after election this clear, relatively simple message gained the support of the majority of voters in Ward 5 and across the City of Greater Wollongong.

In the second area of interest, Arkell provided extensive support to the University of Wollongong at a time when it had just achieved autonomy and was slowly but surely becoming a major employer in the region. Arkell attended the autonomy celebration held in 1975 and was a regular visitor at graduations, prize-giving events, building openings and tree plantings. He was chair of the Friends Membership Committee from 1981 to 1984. By 1985 the university enrolled 5,400 students at the undergraduate level and its first-preference counts from NSW school-leavers had more than doubled in two years.[35] In a city where the BHP steelworks and the coalmines

---

35 *University of Wollongong Gazette* 3, no. 1 (1985): 1.

dominated the labour market, and where education and training had been utilitarian, Arkell's support for the university broke the mould of the typical postwar regional leader. Arkell embraced education and the service sector whereas many of his predecessors were former miners, labourers, union officials or businessmen who had other priorities. A subsequent chapter will fill out the details of his relationship with the university and its predecessor organisations. In 1985 he was calling for a doubling of the university's enrolment to 10,000 students. By that time, the university's success was becoming more evident, increasing numbers of international students were coming to Wollongong and more domestic students from the southern suburbs of Sydney were finding Wollongong a congenial and affordable alternative to the Sydney-based universities.

In the third area of interest, Arkell exhibited a 'hands on' kind of environmentalism. He was rarely critical of the polluting industries that underpinned the regional economy but looked for community projects to clean up creeks, lakes and beaches. He was a strong supporter of parks and gardens and rehabilitating green spaces, which came from his lifelong interest in gardening. The Keira Green Corridor Project, for example, involved coordinating private landowners, government departments and the University of Wollongong in clearing the exotic weed bitou bush and planting trees. Improvements were made to the Mount Keira Summit Park, and Northfields Avenue at the front entrance to the university was narrowed near the Wollongong Botanic Garden. Another area of activity was Puckeys Estate, the slice of land sandwiched between the front dune of Fairy Meadow Beach and Squires Way. Arkell helped bring in the service clubs to assist in the task of clearing this area and removing invasive weeds including bitou bush. The Rotary Club, with which Arkell had close and enduring ties, was heavily involved.[36] The project to rehabilitate Puckeys Estate made local high school boys laugh. We thought it was funny that Arkell championed a project at a site that was adjacent to the gay beat south of the Fairy Meadow Beach clubhouse and carpark.

---

36 *University of Wollongong Campus News*, 2 December 1983: 2.

Plate 3.4 Frank Arkell plants trees along Northfields Avenue with Jan Ryan from the University of Wollongong Wives' Group, 3 September 1975
Note: Arkell attended numerous openings, graduations and events at the university.
Photo: University of Wollongong Archives, Collection U25/n2a/26/15.

3. 'FOR THE BETTERMENT OF WOLLONGONG'

The outlines of Arkell's key messages would be clear by the late 1970s. First trialled during the recession of 1974, his views and plans were honed and refined in time for the second major economic challenge to confront Wollongong: the major job losses at the BHP steelworks that would begin in 1982. Arkell was a shrewd publicist and promoter of the city. He gave his seemingly endless amounts of energy and optimism to Wollongong's development and especially its diversification away from the traditional heavy industry and coal mining base. As much as he and his family were grounded in the old Anglo-Celtic families of the Illawarra, he embraced cultural diversity and multiculturalism. His concern was as much about the image of the city as it was about the reality of diversifying its economic base.

But in 1983 Arkell would face a major political hurdle. On 15 September 1982, the state Labor member for Wollongong, Eric Ramsay, had made serious accusations in parliament about corruption and waste at Wollongong City Council. Specifically, Ramsay alleged that Lord Mayor Arkell had used his influence and position on the council to further his business interests. The Department of Local Government commissioned an inquiry to be headed by Peter Smiles, its chief inspector of local government accounts. Arkell had garnered a range of enemies in business and in politics. Tony Bevan, who had fallen out with Arkell over the stymied sale of the historical property known as 'Gleniffer Brae', which cost Bevan dearly, was now a powerful enemy. With the help of Bevan and his contacts on the council, the Labor Party began gathering evidence of alleged corruption at Wollongong City Council. On the eve of the 1983 council election—with timing that could only inflict maximum political damage on Arkell—the NSW Labor Party released the final report authored by Chief Inspector Smiles.

4

'Life in the city of Wollongong is never dull': Local and state politics, 1981–1988

By 1981 Frank Arkell was a dominant figure in Wollongong politics. The Labor Party's attempts to discredit him through the council corruption inquiry in 1982 and 1983 show the full extent of the threat he posed and how seriously his political enemies regarded him. Seven years as the Lord Mayor of Wollongong had given Arkell considerable political standing and widespread recognition. Through his endless rounds of engagements, meetings, events and media appearances, he had built a formidable network and support base. It was time for a new challenge.

Arkell turned his attention to state politics and the seat of Wollongong. This marked a new phase in Arkell's career, but it clearly built on earlier efforts. While many outlines of his political career cover his unsuccessful 1981 effort to win the seat of Wollongong and his successful 1984 campaign for the same seat, his attempts to move into state politics in fact began in the early 1970s. Arkell first stood as an independent candidate for the state seat of Illawarra in 1971 against a new Labor candidate George Petersen. This early test of Arkell's electoral support, before he had served as lord mayor, returned him 12.9 per cent of the primary vote, with Petersen taking the seat with 59.74 per cent.[1] The seat included areas that would become Arkell's stronghold in the future, including Figtree, Unanderra and Dapto—the towns where the Arkell family was well known and that formed the base of his Ward 5 constituency.

---

1   Parliament of New South Wales, State Election Results for the Seat of Illawarra, 1971, www.parliament.nsw.gov.au/electionresults18562007/1971/Illawarra.htm.

It is also significant that in 1968 Tony Bevan ran as an independent candidate for the state seat of Wollongong. Bevan was coming off the end of a three-year term as mayor and, as we noted, secured a credible 16.4 per cent of the primary vote. Bevan's preferences, however, flowed overwhelmingly to the Liberal candidate Jack Hough and ensured Hough's election over Labor's Eric Ramsay.[2] Bevan had articulated a policy of securing a better deal for Wollongong based on an independent holding the seat. So, where Bevan went, Arkell eventually followed with much the same political message.

In 1978 there were press reports that Arkell was considering running for the NSW Upper House, the Legislative Council.[3] These early attempts to move into state politics indicate that it was always part of Arkell's thinking to run at the state level, even before he became mayor in 1974. Once he achieved that high-profile position, however, he was able to dramatically increase his media presence, so the move from municipal to state political representation became even more possible. Arkell eventually achieved what Bevan had sketched out but failed to realise.

Rapid urban development and social change continued in the region. In the 1970s, there were underground coalmines beneath the escarpment to the north of Wollongong and to the south past Mount Kembla, including the Nebo, Huntley and Avondale mines. Over the Illawarra Escarpment towards Appin and the Burragorang Valley, new coalmines had opened in the previous decade. Around the industrial hub of Port Kembla, there had been significant expansion of the harbour facilities and associated industries. This expansion spilled out towards the suburbs of Berkeley, Unanderra, Primbee and beyond. Large-scale immigration had helped populate the region and fill many of the new postwar suburbs. Cringila, where the Arkells had lived in the 1930s and 1940s, was now an increasingly multicultural growth suburb fringed by company and Commonwealth–provided housing for single men or entire migrant families. Many of these recent migrants found jobs at the steelworks and its associated industries.

---

2   Parliament of New South Wales, State Election Results for the Seat of Wollongong, 1968, www.parliament.nsw.gov.au/electionresults18562007/1968/Wollongong.htm.
3   *Illawarra Mercury*, 11 September 1978.

The 1981 campaign for the state seat of Wollongong

Arkell contested the 1981 state election and came very close to defeating sitting Labor member Eric Ramsay. 'Wollongong' had been defined as a state seat only in 1968. Ramsay had held it since 1971 when he defeated the sitting Liberal member, Jack Hough. Ramsay slowly built Wollongong into a safe Labor seat with the height of his dominance revealed at the 1976 election when he won against the Liberal candidate, Ron Brooks, with a 7.8 per cent swing, capturing 73.8 per cent of the two-party preferred vote to the Liberal challenger's 26.2 per cent.[4] This made Wollongong one of the safest Labor seats in the state and a crucial seat in the then-narrow majority held by the new state Labor government under premier Neville Wran.

In 1981 there was only a small field of candidates for the seat of Wollongong. The Liberals, with Ron Brooks running again, ran a low-profile campaign and polled only 9.8 per cent of first-preference votes. Ramsay polled 46.47 per cent of first preferences to Arkell's 41.34 per cent. There were only 142 votes for independent candidate Ellen Love, most of which were distributed to the Liberal candidate. There were 974 votes for the Democrat candidate, Meg Sampson, most of which were distributed to the Liberal candidate with the remainder split evenly between Arkell and Ramsay. The Liberal candidate's preference distribution was where Arkell may have expected to overtake his Labor rival. Indeed, 77 per cent of Brooks's preferences flowed to Arkell but the low primary vote for Brooks, and the fact that 593 voters had preferenced Brooks first and Ramsay second, meant that Ramsay had enough votes for a majority. The final two-party preferred margin was 50.09 per cent to Ramsay and 49.91 per cent to Arkell. Ramsay won by a mere 51 votes.[5] The *Illawarra Mercury* argued that the controversial Port Kembla coal loader was a decisive factor holding down the Labor vote.[6] The new jobs on the loader were welcome but the region was paying a high price in the clouds of coal dust that blanketed Wollongong every time a southerly change came through and coal trucks continued to be a hazard on the roads.

---

4   Parliament of New South Wales, State Election Results for the Seat of Wollongong, 1976, www.parliament.nsw.gov.au/electionresults18562007/1976/Wollongong.htm.
5   Parliament of New South Wales, State Election Results for the Seat of Wollongong, 1981, www.parliament.nsw.gov.au/electionresults18562007/1981/Wollongong.htm.
6   *Illawarra Mercury*, 20 September 1981.

Despite the narrow loss, the electoral result was a remarkable achievement by Arkell. NSW Labor under Premier Wran did very well at this election, winning with an enhanced majority, so Arkell had come close despite the statewide swing to Labor. Labor now held 68 seats to 28 for the Coalition of the Liberal and National Country parties. Only two independents were returned at this election. Arkell, like any hopeful independent, would need a statewide swing against the party of the sitting member as well as a strong local campaign.

The council 'sit-in'

Labor was clearly worried, so much so that on the eve of the 1983 council elections the state Labor government released Chief Inspector Smiles's report on possible corruption in the Wollongong Council.[7] This was an attempted knockout blow on Arkell orchestrated by NSW Labor in league with Tony Bevan. We now know of Bevan's crucial role because he habitually recorded all his telephone conversations and these show that he was using his Wollongong Council contacts to secure inside information for the government to assist with their inquiries into the state of the council. Bevan worked with Labor Cabinet minister Rex Jackson and talked to him about speaking to 'Eric': 'I've sent out bloody smoke signals, and they reckoned you're in … somewhere. Listen, this dynamite on Her Majesty [Arkell], Eric's got it. It's a three or four-page document together with supporting evidence.'[8]

What would later come to light was that Bevan was feeding information into Eric Ramsay's office to discredit Arkell. He was even discussing with Ramsay his parliamentary tactics. As he says to Jackson:

> I said to Eric, well … He said, 'Well speak to Reg, and see if he can, for Christ sake, lean on him, because there might be a bit of pressure being the last week, a lot of bloody members want to get on the stump. If I can't get on the adjournment motion,' he says, 'because it's going to take me five minutes to go through this.'[9]

---

7   Peter H. Smiles, *Report of an Inspection of Wollongong City Council under Section 212 of the Local Government Act (1919)* (Sydney: NSW Government Printer, 1983).
8   Transcripts of the Bevan Tapes, No. 11.
9   ibid.

The detailed findings of the report are discussed more fully in Chapter 5 but the crucial point here is that the government held onto the report and released it at what appears to have been the most damaging time for Arkell: the week before the Wollongong Council elections. The government had defined the key election issue as Arkell's potential corruption. What Arkell did next was one of the shrewdest and most audacious manoeuvres in his political career.

In the face of Labor's continued criticism of both Arkell and the Wollongong City Council inside and outside state parliament, Arkell deftly turned the attention of the media and the public away from the corruption allegations and firmly onto Labor's threat to dissolve the council and cancel the September 1983 mayoral elections. Arkell staged a 'sit-in' in the lord mayor's chambers that showed off all his media skills and experience. With Arkell photographed sitting in the mayor's office talking on the phone to constituents and in person to independent aldermen who came into the office to join him, the story was now about the state government undermining democratic choice in Wollongong. 'It is for the people of Wollongong to make a judgement through the ballot box and to elect a council of their own,' countered Arkell, 'not dictated by anyone else.'[10] Having spent his political career singing the virtues of the city and its right to make its own decisions and influence its own fate, this was a gift to Arkell.

In parliament, the state Labor member for Wollongong, Eric Ramsay, had called for the council to be sacked and the elections suspended. Surely Ramsay had overplayed his hand? Labor had made the patrician and occasionally autocratic Arkell look like a radical democrat. The true defender of Wollongong appeared to be Arkell—holed up in his office, acting like he was under siege from hostile forces. Ultimately, Labor's threat to sack the council remained just that and the minister for local government Alan Gordon received the Smiles report but did nothing further. There was no follow-up from the police and there were no criminal charges to be considered. Labor's attempt to remove Arkell from office had failed.

---

10   Frank Arkell, cited in 'Wollongong Inquiry Welcomed', *Canberra Times*, 23 September 1983: 3.

POLITICS, PRIDE AND PERVERSION

The 1984 campaign for the state seat of Wollongong

The fortunes of NSW Labor had declined by the time of the 1984 election. There was a recession in the early 1980s with significant job losses. Regions such as Newcastle and Wollongong were hit hard by reductions in the manufacturing and coal mining workforce. Unemployment and the consequent economic distress and social misery were vital issues, especially in the regional industrial centres. Premier Wran nonetheless won his fourth term as leader, making him one of the most successful Labor politicians of his generation. Labor had a sizeable majority and could afford a 7 per cent statewide swing against it, but a palpable anti-government sentiment was just the condition that would allow a well-run independent campaign to ride the wave against the party of the sitting member. What's more, there were significant issues at a local level that were hurting the state government. The perennial question of local roads, railway and port infrastructure, including the Port Kembla coal loader, remained unresolved. The road transport of coal from the mines in the northern suburbs of Wollongong, and from those around Appin and the Burragorang Valley, was proving to be a major headache for Labor. The long-suffering residents of Wollongong, especially those who regularly commuted on these roads or who lived nearby and dealt with the patina of coal dust on their windows and the clothes on their washing lines, were becoming more vocal.

Arkell's long-term battle with NSW Labor and Labor Party members of parliament continued in earnest at the 1984 election, but this time the outcome was different. Arkell was elected state member for Wollongong, joining three other independents in the new parliament. This was the culmination of more than 10 years of effort since his first attempt to contest the state seat of Illawarra. The other independents elected or re-elected in 1984 were John Hatton (member for the South Coast), Ted Mack (North Shore) and Robert Bruce (Lismore). Arkell finished just ahead of the Labor candidate, Rex Connor Jr, on first preferences, reversing the outcome in 1981, when Ramsay had just pipped Arkell on first preferences. Arkell polled 44.7 per cent while Connor polled a creditable 43.5 per cent. Despite the statewide 7 per cent swing against Labor, in Wollongong, the Labor vote was down only 3 per cent. But Labor's creditable local performance would not be enough. With the Liberals running a 'dead' campaign and only a handful of other independents picking up a very small percentage of votes, Arkell garnered enough preferences to defeat Connor 54.2 per cent to 45.8 per cent two-candidate preferred.[11]

While Arkell battled with the Labor Party, his relationship with local unions and their representative bodies was also fraught. The Municipal Union, which represented most of the workforce at Wollongong Council, was a strong critic of Arkell's style. Even after just three years of Arkell as lord mayor, the union publicly stated its opposition for the upcoming 1977 council elections. After Frank's death, *Illawarra Mercury* journalists wrote of his reputation within the council, describing him as being difficult to work with, bad-tempered and not averse to haranguing staff. One story recounted a common saying in Wollongong that Arkell's campaigns always had to assume that every single council employee would be voting against him. A former alderman colleague and fellow independent, Harold Hanson, described Arkell as headstrong and sometimes difficult to work with.[12] The voting public had rarely if ever seen this side of him, but these traits became more prominent after his election to state parliament.

The other key battle in Wollongong was between Arkell and the South Coast Trades and Labour Council (SCTLC), the peak regional body covering all affiliated unions in the Illawarra. In the 1970s and 1980s, the Labour Council was a powerful industrial and political force with extensive membership coverage across Illawarra's heavy industry, transport and coal mining workforce. Historian Frances Laneyrie noted that the SCTLC and Arkell were engaged in a battle over who could best represent the city of Wollongong. Was it the avuncular lord mayor, who, by the 1980s, was an increasingly well-known figure, or the broadly representative industrial muscle of the peak union body? Laneyrie charts these divisions playing out over feminism and women's rights, especially arrangements for the Wollongong events and activities for the 1975 International Women's Year (IWY). Through the intervention of the lord mayor, the two Wollongong events—participation in International Women's Day in March and a 'happening week' in June—were organised by separate committees, roughly equating to a split between SCTLC-supported activities and council-supported activities:

---

11 Parliament of New South Wales, State Election Results for the Seat of Wollongong, 1984, www.parliament.nsw.gov.au/electionresults18562007/1984/Wollongong.htm.
12 Notes of an interview with Harold Hanson, 3 April 2023.

> The different directions of the two women's committees for the IWY celebrations reflected the tensions in ongoing patterns between the SCLC [Labour Council] and the Wollongong City Lord Mayor Frank Arkell (1974–1986) [sic] about who represented the collective 'voice' of Wollongong.[13]

This tension between the SCTLC and Arkell would play out again when the Labour Council secured a proactive and media-savvy secretary in the form of Paul Matters, who served from 1988 to 1999.

Arkell's message: Themes in the 1984 campaign and beyond

There were several key themes in Arkell's political messaging to which he returned time and again. He appeared to have an uncanny ability to stay focused on a handful of main points. Arkell plugged into a sense that Wollongong's needs were being overlooked and neglected. The major parties took Wollongong for granted and strong independent representation would change all that. 'I think we've been sadly neglected,' he told *ABC TV News* in April 1984 after his election. Arkell's main prescription to address this neglect was private and public investment secured by singing the praises of the city and its virtues. Arkell believed he could reduce consumer spending outside the region and diversify and improve Wollongong's economy almost through force of will alone. It was a belief from which he never deviated. 'Life in the city of Wollongong,' as Arkell said in his first speech to parliament in September 1984, 'is never dull.'

Election as state member of parliament (MP) for Wollongong also raised the issue of how Arkell would juggle his position as lord mayor and Wollongong's state representative in the Legislative Assembly. Arkell himself, when asked by an ABC journalist, was certain that the:

> two jobs are complementary … It will give Wollongong an opportunity to have a platform in Sydney to promote Wollongong, to work on the job opportunities we so badly need to attract industries and commerce to broaden the economic base.[14]

---

13 Frances Laneyrie, 'Between Class and Gender: Female Activists in the Illawarra 1975–1980' (PhD diss., Auckland Institute of Technology, 2010), openrepository.aut.ac.nz/items/da3c59fa-da19-4c82-b8e1-0371d7bc550c, 159, see also p. 140.

14 Interview with Frank Arkell, the new member for Wollongong, in 'The Winner', *ABC TV News*, 4 June 1984, T4397, ABC Archives, Sydney.

There was little that was concrete in his platform. He talked about making Wollongong 'a growth centre' and bringing it 'to the notice of the State government as a growth centre, something like Campbelltown, something like Albury-Wodonga'. This interview, conducted shortly after his election victory, was typical of Arkell. The main messages included statements that were broad generic positions, but he seemed somewhat more nervous than usual and spoke at a remarkably fast pace. 'I'll be working hard to create job opportunities in Wollongong', was his closing statement, having spoken at almost 160 words per minute.

The state government would ultimately pass the *Local Government Amendment (Members of Parliament) Act* in 2012 preventing the holding of 'dual roles' such as that of mayor and state parliamentarian as a revision of the *Local Government Act 1993*. There was support for the change especially where the specific roles and responsibilities overlapped or were potentially in conflict. Arkell's assertion that the two roles were complementary was at best an oversimplification. Might there be times when a city mayor and a state member could be representing different interests and exercising different responsibilities? Having different individuals in these roles also operated as a check and a balance. Importantly, however, the state government's action in preventing 'dual roles' by legislation did attract the ire of the Local Government and Shires Association, which responded that it was 'up to the community, not the Minister to decide if they wish their mayor or councillor also to be a Member of the Parliament of NSW'.[15]

Arkell established his electoral office on the top floor of the T&G Building in Crown Street, overlooking the corner of Crown and Flinders streets and with spectacular views south towards the Port Kembla industrial complex and the coal loader. He employed highly capable staff, creating an innovative research role within his office and once again showed his capacity to surround himself with effective and competent people. Making good on his long-time support for the University of Wollongong, Arkell employed one of its graduates, Martin O'Shannessy, as the new research officer. This additional role in his office was paid for from Arkell's own parliamentary salary.[16] This was another sign that Arkell's wealth could bankroll his career in state politics as it did his career in local government. With his family and

---

15   Paul Hemsley, 'No More Government Dual Roles', *Government News*, [Sydney], 5 April 2012, www.governmentnews.com.au/no-more-government-dual-roles/.
16   Paddy Ginnane, 'Frank Arkell', [*Weekend Magazine*], *Illawarra Mercury*, 17 August 1985.

individual wealth and income behind him, he was in no way reliant on the modest pay that came from local government or even the somewhat more substantial salary of a state parliamentary representative.

Within the first 12 months, his electoral office, and the research officer in particular, had compiled a high-quality 'progress report' detailing all his work and achievements. In his first term, Arkell was involved in various petitions, questions without notice and constituency matters that reflected some of his interests and priorities. He asked about police numbers and foot patrols for the Wollongong CBD and was concerned about the poor state of the Wollongong Police Station. A new station for the city was announced in March 1986.[17] He made representations about Warrawong High School, which had a very small library, and spoke out publicly in March–April 1986 when the school lost three demountable buildings used for English-language classes. Arkell argued that per capita health spending in the region was very low and advocated for the expansion of Wollongong Hospital and the retention of casualty services at Port Kembla Hospital. The bulk of his questions in the Legislative Assembly during his first term covered health (42), transport (22), education (13), public works (12) and youth and community services (8).[18]

Reflecting his concern for the environment and pollution, he sponsored a petition supporting:

> the removal of sewage pollution from our beaches, the rehabilitation of impoverished soils, the careful use of our resources and for the maintenance of the health of our citizens, measures be taken to put an end to the waste of our recyclable resources so that our used water is treated, purified and recycled for maximum use.

Arkell also showed his hand on social affairs, supporting petitions that sought to overturn the homosexual law reform championed by the Wran government and specifically by the premier himself. He also opposed law reform that gave de facto couples equivalent rights in law to married couples. In the assembly, as a general rule, he often voted with the government on procedural matters but on matters of policy and legislation, he usually voted with the Opposition.

---

17 Peter Clarke, 'Police Station Planning Begins', *Illawarra Mercury*, 1 March 1986: 7.
18 'Office of the Member for Wollongong, Research Centre, First Progress Report covering the period January 1985 to April 1986, WPL & Arkell media release, 27 March 1986', Wollongong City Library.

The 1988 campaign

At the time of the 1988 election, NSW Labor's difficult electoral fortunes continued. The glory days under Premier Wran were now a distant memory. Wran retired in 1986 after initially stepping aside in 1983–1984 while the Street Royal Commission heard allegations of corruption.[19] Wran's replacement as premier, Barrie Unsworth, was infamously endorsed by a former federal Labor leader and foreign minister in the Hawke Labor government, Bill Hayden: 'If you're the sort of person who enjoys the simple things in life, like tearing the wings off butterflies, then Barrie Unsworth's your man.'

Given this statewide political picture and the continued challenges for the now ailing Labor government, Arkell's chances of retaining the seat of Wollongong for a second term were good. But NSW Labor regrouped and selected a proven winner as a candidate. Laurie Kelly had been a member for Corrimal, based in the northern suburbs of Wollongong, from 1968 to 1988. Since 1976 Kelly had been speaker of the assembly under successive Labor governments, but a 1988 redistribution had abolished the seat of Corrimal, so Kelly stepped in to challenge Arkell in Wollongong.

This seemed to be a positive move from Labor but the regrouping process itself became highly problematic and deeply embarrassing for the party. Moving Kelly from the disbanded Corrimal to contest Wollongong—a move engineered by officials from the party's head office in Sussex Street in Sydney—had caused ructions within the local branch network and severely disappointed the 1984 candidate, Rex Connor Jr, who had planned to run again in 1988. Rex was the son of former minister for minerals and energy in the Whitlam Labor government, Rex Connor Sr. Rex Junior exercised strong personal control over the branch network, especially the large Warrawong branch of which he was president. Kelly and Connor Junior clashed, with Connor calling Premier Unsworth a 'political buffoon of the first order' and Kelly 'a coward' and a 'political wimp', among other things.[20] For publicly criticising a Labor premier and a Labor MP, Rex Connor Jr was suspended from the party and subsequently expelled. While not every local party member was a strong supporter of Connor, rank-and-file members

---

19   Rodney Tiffen, 'Was Neville Wran Corrupt?', *Inside Story*, [Melbourne], 31 August 2021, insidestory. org.au/was-neville-wran-corrupt/.
20   'Unsworth a "Buffoon", Says Connor', *Sydney Morning Herald*, 15 January 1988: 4. See also Tracey Aubin, 'Mr Speaker Is Called Out of Order', *Sydney Morning Herald*, 14 January 1988: 3.

never welcomed Labor Party head office intervention overturning local preselection processes. It is fair to say that the local Labor branches were in disarray leading up to the 1988 state election and at least some party members had their loyalties tested when it came to publicly supporting Laurie Kelly in Wollongong. Approximately 65 members left the Labor Party and joined the newly formed 'Rex Connor Senior Labor Party'. Rex Connor Jr planned to contest future elections under the banner of his new party, named in homage to his father. Public disunity in the Labor ranks was another sign that Arkell's prospects for the 1988 election were very good. Kelly had even announced his resignation from parliament before being dragooned into running in Wollongong.[21] He now had to backtrack and convince voters that he was a genuine candidate.

The Liberal–National Coalition under premier-elect Nick Greiner won the 1988 election with a statewide swing of 3.62 per cent, with the Liberals picking up 17 additional seats and their Coalition partners securing a swing of 2.9 per cent and five additional seats. In the face of this swing against Labor, Kelly performed well but not well enough. Arkell secured a solid margin in the primary votes, polling 45.51 per cent to Kelly's 38.83 per cent. After preferences, Arkell won 55.48 per cent to Kelly's 44.52 per cent on a two-candidate preferred basis.[22]

In a relatively straightforward four-candidate race, Arkell and Kelly received most of the first preferences, leaving Graham Roberts from the Illawarra Workers' Party (IWP) and John Masters from the Liberals to be excluded first and second, respectively. The IWP received only 2,028 votes or 6.99 per cent. Somewhat unexpectedly, only 57 per cent of these preferences flowed to Kelly, which was not enough to get him over 50 per cent or even put him ahead before the preferences of the Liberal candidate were distributed. The exclusion of the Liberal candidate with more than 80 per cent of preferences flowing to Arkell meant Arkell secured the win.[23]

Arkell's re-election was a sign of the drift away of normally solid Labor voters as the NSW party lost its way in the 1980s. Flirting with large-scale privatisation and tough austerity budgets, the party had alienated Labor voters in the Wollongong region, which it had typically held since 1921, and in Newcastle, as the success of independent candidate George

---

21   Robert Haupt, 'With Rex, There's a Fight in the Heir', *Sydney Morning Herald*, 2 March 1988: 1.
22   Parliament of New South Wales, State Election Results for the Seat of Wollongong, 1988, www.parliament.nsw.gov.au/electionresults18562007/1988/Wollongong.htm.
23   ibid.

Keegan had shown. So much of Arkell's political career was shadowed by the performance of the NSW Labor Party and, in particular, the state of the party in the Wollongong area. After the major job losses at the BHP steelworks in the early 1980s, the government closure of the state-owned Tallawarra Power Station in 1986 with the loss of a further 600 jobs was a major blow to the regional economy. Arkell spoke out strongly against the closure and against electricity privatisation. David Campbell, Arkell's successor as lord mayor and later the Labor member for Keira, described Arkell in the NSW Parliament as 'the nemesis of the Australian Labor Party in local politics in the Illawarra region'.[24] This was true but what Campbell did not acknowledge was that heavy-handed control by the head office in Sussex Street, and an unrelenting campaign against many Labor left-wingers, including former member for Illawarra George Petersen and federal member for Cunningham Stewart West, alienated large sections of the party membership. Petersen had resigned his membership in 1987 rather than vote for proposed workers' compensation legislation that he saw as profoundly draconian, while West, a former Cabinet minister in the Hawke government, was undermined by the dominant right faction in the party. Following a redistribution of the seat's boundaries, West lost in a preselection battle in 1993 to Stephen Martin.[25] Arkell was Labor's nemesis in the Illawarra but the factional players in Sussex Street were just as effective in undermining the standing and morale of the party in the region where Labor had been dominant for so long.

Arkell was at his political zenith. He had defeated Labor for a second time in the contest for the state seat of Wollongong. This was a remarkable achievement. There were moments when everything appeared to be working in his favour and he appeared to be genuinely enjoying himself. In October 1987, a local boy from Balgownie, Wayne Gardner, won the world 500cc motorcycle championship. For Arkell, this was also a victory for the city since the council was one of Gardner's official sponsors, and Gardner loudly proclaimed his allegiance to his hometown. 'He's given us a higher profile worldwide,' Arkell said, 'and we are grateful for that.'[26] A huge civic reception for Gardner was held in Wollongong on his triumphant return,

---

24   David Campbell, MLA for Keira, in NSW, *Parliamentary Debates*, Legislative Assembly, 8 August 2000, 'Condolences', www.parliament.nsw.gov.au/Hansard/Pages/HansardResult.aspx#/docid/HANSARD -1323879322-86942/link/6.
25   'Condolence Motion for George Petersen', in NSW, *Parliamentary Debates*, Legislative Council, 4 April 2000, www.parliament.nsw.gov.au/Hansard/Pages/HansardResult.aspx#/docid/HANSARD-18 20781676-20237, 61–71.
26   'Gardner Was on the Verge of Quitting', *Sydney Morning Herald*, 19 October 1987: 59.

with Arkell as the master of ceremonies. Arkell presented Gardner with the keys to the City of Wollongong. Gardner sat in an open-top vehicle and was driven through the Crown Street Mall with cheering crowds looking on. The weather had threatened but the rain held off and the city was blessed with a sun-drenched parade. Commenting on the miraculous weather change, Arkell told journalists, with a huge smile on his face, 'I just made a phone call … a local call, of course.'[27] Here was Arkell suggesting he had a direct line to God (who lived locally, of course) and that he could influence Wollongong's weather. In the bonhomie of the occasion, the media lapped it up. Things were looking good for Arkell but beyond the smiles, the civic receptions and even the triumphant 1988 election result, storm clouds were gathering. Not everything had gone his way in the past four years.

Plate 4.1 A publicity shot highlighting Wollongong City Council's sponsorship of 500cc world motorcycle champion Wayne Gardner, Belmore Basin, 14 March 1988

Note: Gardner is to the left of Arkell and, to the right, is Wollongong rider Ron Sumskis.
Photo: *Illawarra Mercury* Image Collection and Wollongong City Library, Image no. P23074.

---

27   ibid. See also 'Welcome Home Brings a Tear to the Champ's Eye', *Sun-Herald*, [Sydney], 18 October 1987: 3.

5

'A mindless vendetta against me': Declining popularity and increasing frustration, 1985–1991

Frank Arkell's popularity was based on his boundless energy, his strong connections with migrant communities and civic associations, and his unfailing ability to stay positive and on message. His positivity was a bright spot in the otherwise troubling economic landscape of the 1970s and 1980s. As one long-form piece in the *Sydney Morning Herald* commented, 'when hope seemed dead, Arkell's energy and enthusiasm rekindled some pride'.[1] But there were events and issues that showed him in a less positive light and these help explain the steady decline in Arkell's primary vote, which, as we will see, eventually led to electoral disaster at both state and council elections. So, we must briefly rewind the clock to 1985 and review the issues over which Frank Arkell's usually astute political judgement failed or his luck deserted him.

Before covering these issues, it is important to point out that Wollongong was also changing in the 1980s and 1990s. Population growth was modest, rising from 165,086 in 1981 to 173,764 in 1991. The strong demand for labour that had attracted new migrant workers and their families in the 1950s and 1960s had given way to stubbornly high rates of unemployment. What's more, migration patterns changed and larger numbers of Vietnamese migrants arrived in the region in 1979, later joined by migrants from Turkey, Iran, Iraq

---

1   Michael Cordell, Geraldine O'Brien, and John O'Neil, 'Labor's Lost Heartland', [*Spectrum*], *Sydney Morning Herald*, 26 March 1988: 61.

and Lebanon. Some of the changes, such as the growth of the tourism sector and the rise of the services industry as a proportion of the workforce, were welcomed and indeed encouraged by Arkell. He had a habit of adding the total public and private sector investment in Wollongong over multiple years and presenting that figure as a great achievement of his time as both lord mayor and state member. He loved to talk about 'money pouring' into the city. The new 10-storey North Beach International Hotel (Plate 5.1), opened on a site across the road from Wollongong's North Beach in 1983, was indicative of the kind of large-scale projects that followed. When the owners painted the imposing new building pink it was a clear statement of the brash, showy development projects that were to become the hallmark of the 1980s and 1990s. The economic development of Wollongong represents a classic shift from a postwar coal mining and manufacturing hub that often endured sharp downturns and job losses towards a city with a large service sector, including health, education and government services. By 1986, personal services and recreation employed more workers in the Wollongong statistical district (4.9 per cent) than mining (4.6 per cent) although the manufacturing sector remained large and the region was vulnerable to further job losses, which continued to be an issue well after Arkell's death.[2]

Plate 5.1 The North Beach International Hotel in North Wollongong, photographed from the beach, 17 November 1988
Photo: *Illawarra Mercury* Image Collection and Wollongong City Library, Image no. P26184.

---

2   Patrick Mullins, 'Cities for Pleasure: The Emergence of Tourism Urbanization in Australia', *Built Environment* 18, no. 3 (1992): 187–98, at 191.

Legionnaire's outbreak in the CBD

In 1985 and then again more seriously in 1987, Wollongong experienced an outbreak of what was later found to be legionnaire's disease. The mystery illness was a great concern to many but the location of the outbreak, ultimately determined to be in the Wollongong CBD, raised much bigger issues, including concerns about the council's plans for the Crown Street Mall and a growing sense of frustration with what seemed to be a steady decline in the commercial health of the Wollongong shopping district. The legionnaire's outbreak was a clear symbol of a wider malaise that was taking hold in the city and the council's and the lord mayor's responses were less than reassuring.

Legionnaire's disease is a bacterial infection primarily acquired through inhalation of air from contaminated airconditioning units, cooling towers or hot water systems. The legionella bacteria thrive in warm water. There had been cases in 1985 linked to a Wollongong club but in 1987 a more substantial outbreak occurred in the city. It was originally traced to the airconditioning unit in the Crown Gateway Mall, but subsequent analysis indicated the exact origin was an airconditioner on the roof of a chemist shop adjacent to the mall. It is thought that the unit, which had been turned off for the previous months and not serviced recently, ejected an airstream laden with bacteria that then infected the Crown Gateway cooling unit.

There were 120 suspected cases of which 60 were positively identified. Wollongong Hospital was able to secure data on 59 of those 60, all of whom had visited the Crown Street Mall in Wollongong in March or April 1987. The major symptoms included a fever, a productive cough, breathing difficulties and joint and/or muscle pain. Fifty-seven of the 59 cases were hospitalised, with 14 of those going into intensive care. Eleven patients whose records were tracked for this study died during the outbreak.[3] Thirteen deaths were recorded. At the height of the outbreak in March, April and May 1987, residents were wary of visiting the CBD, which was already suffering from competition from large retail developments in Shellharbour, Figtree and Warrawong as well as regular visits by Wollongong residents to Sydney to shop at places like Roselands shopping centre and Miranda Fair in Sutherland Shire.

---

3   Beverly Anne Ring, 'Legionnaires' Disease: The Wollongong Experience', *Australian Journal of Physiotherapy* 35, no. 3 (1989): 167–76, doi.org/10.1016/S0004-9514(14)60506-7.

In response, Arkell arranged a breakfast in the Crown Gateway shopping centre with local business owners. His plan was to demonstrate that the CBD was safe but, in this case, his unalloyed positivity came across largely as denial of the problem. 'All clear', Arkell proclaimed, even while the nature and origin of the disease were still under investigation.[4] Arkell was claiming that the city had to prove to the world that it was disease-free. The city's image was always his priority, even when his people needed him. This was a time to look inward and attend to the promotional and city image issues at some later date. Later that year, after another mystery illness had affected a resident, Arkell called for state government assistance to help Wollongong improve its image—as though the disease outbreak and its potential return were only ever a public relations problem and not a real tragedy for the 13 people who died and their families and friends.[5] For a city that had experienced its fair share of disasters and tragedies, Arkell was not the leader to turn to for comforting words.

The fact that Wollongong Council co-managed the Crown Gateway centre with the Kern Corporation placed the council at the heart of the problem. Notwithstanding the large development that had been completed on the old council library site in Crown Street (which was initially occupied by Grace Bros and other tenants), the Wollongong CBD was struggling. Blocking Crown Street to traffic and turning the area between Keira and Kembla streets into a pedestrianised mall in 1986 had polarised the community. Small business owners felt that the council was working primarily for the bigger tenants rather than for them. Even today if there is one issue that will fire up some of the 65,000 members of the Facebook group 'Lost Wollongong', it is the state of Crown Street, the mall and various council plans over the past four decades to address the future of the CBD.[6]

It was bad luck that a serious infectious disease broke out in the Wollongong CBD in 1987, but Arkell's response was clumsy and lacking in warmth and empathy. This lack of empathy was something close observers noticed at several crucial moments in his life. In 1986, the D'Souza family living across

---

4   'Wollongong Shopping Centre All Clear', *Canberra Times*, 21 May 1987: 8. For the business breakfast, see *Canberra Times*, 20 May 1987: 8.
5   John O'Neil, 'Epidemic's Source Still Not Certain', *Sydney Morning Herald*, 19 May 1987: 4.
6   See, for example, the post by Chris Rogan, 22 October 2022, on the Facebook group 'Lost Wollongong', which features a photo of a busy Crown Street in 1964: 'Back before it all went down the toilet … 😊 We'll build a Mall, they said … to invigorate the town they said. We'll bring the people back into the main street … they said … What could go wrong … ?? They said … 🙄.' www.facebook.com/photo/?fbid=8979991775360355&set=gm.2360586534098414&idorvanity=185002564990166.

the road from Arkell suffered a tragedy. Mrs D'Souza died in a car accident. Family and friends gathered at the house and Arkell came over 'to give his condolences', but, as Michael D'Souza remembers it:

> You could even see then he wasn't really capable of giving sincere, emotional 'I feel for you, I'm sorry for what's happened to you'. It was more a case of slap you on the back, it will be okay. I remember he said [to my Dad] as he went out, 'Have a scotch, make it a double.' I remember my elder brother standing out there as he walked out and looking at him, and not saying it to him, but saying, 'Wow, what a prick.'[7]

The Coledale mudslide

In April 1988 the Wollongong region was drenched with more than 600 millimetres of rain. On 30 April, on a hilly street at Coledale just below the Illawarra railway line, a major landslide killed two members of the Hagan family, Jenny and her son, James. Huge volumes of water had built up behind a blocked railway drainage system and overwhelmed an earthen embankment at the top of the street. This produced a devastating flash flood and mudslide. Wollongong Council was the subject of criticism as many residents believed the council knew the risks but had not informed local landowners. Arkell's response to the tragic loss of lives was to say that it was not the council's fault, although he did express his sadness.[8] This was a ham-fisted initial response to a terrible incident. The people of Wollongong wanted to hear reassuring words of sympathy while statements about responsibility could have been made later.

Once again, Arkell's lack of empathy showed. He came across as heartless. The following month angry residents attended a council meeting that was 'interrupted by continual heckling from the packed public gallery, with calls for aldermen and city officers to resign'. One resident said she had been assaulted by council staff when she tried to take photos near the site of the mudslide and Arkell replied by saying that 'council staff would not do that'.[9] Arkell's demeanour was angry and unsympathetic. Terry Hagan, who lost his wife and son in the mudslide, said he had met Frank Arkell 18 months before the tragedy to express his concern: 'I had been alerted that something

---

7   Interview with Michael D'Souza, 21 November 2022.
8   'Body Retrieved Near Marulan', *Canberra Times*, 2 May 1989: 3.
9   'Flood Aftermath 1: Call for Inquiry into Mudslide Deaths', *Sydney Morning Herald*, 3 May 1988: 1.

might go wrong. They [the council] just fobbed us off, saying that a report had said everything was safe.'[10] A trial of four senior State Rail Authority employees for manslaughter and criminal negligence found them not guilty, much to Hagan's profound disappointment. A group called the Escarpment Coalition was subsequently formed to highlight dangerous development along the Illawarra Escarpment. The coalition surveyed all local government candidates for the 1991 council elections and was particularly disappointed that Arkell had been silent on the issue.[11]

Major projects and big plans

Arkell loved a major development project with ambition and scale. The North Beach International, for example, was an excellent development in Arkell's view because it gave Wollongong a hotel of international standard and allowed it to compete on the international conference circuit.[12] He sought external and, in some cases, international investors to bring large amounts of capital to the region. There were numerous major proposals with which Arkell was associated from 1984 until his loss of office at local and state levels in 1991. There are too many to cover them all—which is itself a reflection of both Arkell's priorities and his never-ending energy—but we can sample some of the most important to gauge how Arkell's thinking was changing after the 1982–1983 recession.

Arkell was a man in a hurry. In his rush to remake Wollongong, he moved fast and often in secret. He was very plain about his methods, telling ABC TV *Four Corners* journalist Mark Colvin that he invited developers to lunch at Parliament House, thus creating an obligation that they visit Wollongong.[13] With this method, he often failed to take the community with him and the response to these grand schemes was often critical. Arkell's argument was that the region was losing millions of dollars in 'escape spending'—his phrase to describe the flow of residents who travelled away from the region to shop in southern or western Sydney. In January 1986, Arkell suggested that the region was losing $100 million to 'escape spending' and that the $62 million of investments planned for Wollongong, Dapto, Woonona

---

10 Lindsay Simpson, 'Verdict a Blow to Father', *Sydney Morning Herald*, 4 April 1990: 2.
11 Paul Bailey and Danielle Cook, 'Candidates Agree on the Monorail: It Has to Go—Local Government Elections', *Sydney Morning Herald*, 14 September 1991: 6.
12 Lachlan Harris, 'The Great Jobs Boom', *Illawarra Mercury*, 29 January 1986: 1.
13 Mark Colvin, 'Independents' Day', *Four Corners*, [*ABC TV*], 7 March 1988, T87476, ABC Archives, Sydney.

and Warrawong would help recoup this loss and create hundreds of new retail jobs. His approach to regional development was very much top-down. Deals could be done, phone calls could be made and meetings arranged.

In this vision, Arkell as well as a select group of experts in the council, the state government or in lobby groups such as the regional tourism board all knew best. The people of Wollongong would inevitably benefit. This became a major flaw in his otherwise energetic and committed work within the community. He largely failed to articulate his vision and bring his constituents along with him. This was where Mr Wollongong needed to find the substance to fill out his dreams for the city. He needed to go beyond the simple and so-far successful strategy of being overwhelmingly positive and start a genuine conversation about the future—not only its possible benefits but also its challenges.

At times the community responded with dismay to what were often vague ideas and thought bubbles. His single-minded determination could come across as insensitive. One curious case concerned a proposed resort for Japanese seniors in the Wollongong region with the Japanese city of Kawasaki as the key investor. Australia had concluded a trade treaty with Japan in 1957. Extensive Japanese investment had occurred in mining and minerals processing from the 1960s and in tourism and real estate, especially on the Gold and Sunshine coasts in Queensland, from the early 1980s. Japanese tourists in tour groups who often stayed at Japanese-owned resorts or hotels became a sensitive issue. Wollongong Council established a sister city relationship with Kawasaki in 1988. In August 1990, a delegation from Wollongong including Arkell and senior council staff visited Kawasaki. The Dapto RSL responded critically, with sub-branch secretary Doug Rymer arguing that Arkell's courting of Japanese investors and Japanese tourists was an affront to the many Australians who served and died in the Pacific War.[14] Arkell was unmoved and in response conceded that the 'war was a terrible thing but Australia now is very much a part of the Pacific and Asia and we have to learn to live with our neighbours'.[15]

The South Coast Trades and Labour Council placed a ban on any project to build a resort for elderly Japanese tourists, calling the idea 'exceptionally offensive and racist'.[16] For the Labour Council, any facility for foreigners

---

14   Geoff Failes, 'Ex-Diggers Object to Japanese Resort Plan', *Sun-Herald*, [Sydney], 18 September 1988: 41.
15   ibid.
16   Natasha Bita, 'Club Gong?—Forget It, Unions Tell Japanese', *Sydney Morning Herald*, 2 August 1990: 1.

was an affront while elderly Australians were not adequately provided for. Rod Oxley, Wollongong Council CEO, suggested that the SCTLC was being precipitant since there was no formal proposal to build a resort, just an agreement to encourage elderly Japanese tourists to visit Wollongong.[17] But evidence from Kawasaki's then mayor, Kiyoshi Takahashi, indicated that Arkell had formally agreed to the proposal for the city of Kawasaki to build 'facilities in Wollongong for senior citizens of Kawasaki City. It was intended that the Japanese would arrive in groups of 30 to 50 to stay for six or eight weeks.'[18] Kawasaki City planned to rent accommodation to begin with but eventually finance and build a resort, and later hand ownership over to Wollongong Council. Purnendra Jain, an academic researcher who interviewed Mayor Takahashi shortly afterwards, noted that 'Kawasaki's mayor had expressed his disappointment over the misunderstanding that followed in the wake of this proposal'.[19] This was typical of Arkell's approach to such ambitious projects. He appeared to be pushing forward with ever more haste, getting well ahead of consultation and discussion. As soon as these schemes were revealed to Wollongong residents, there was the inevitable critical response. He had an almost reckless indifference to the political consequences. Arkell was losing focus and discipline, especially by 1990. In his haste, he ended up achieving very little except generating good headlines for the Wollongong and Sydney newspapers.

Arkell and the independents in state parliament

Successful independent candidates did not emerge at once and often the reasons for their success were highly localised, but by the time Arkell reached state parliament there were four independents in the NSW Legislative Assembly including Arkell: John Hatton (South Coast), Ted Mack (North Sydney) and Bruce Duncan (Lismore). There were also two independents in the Legislative Council: the Reverend Fred Nile and a former Liberal, Jim Cameron. This was part of a broader pattern as independents began to challenge the dominance of the major parties. At the Commonwealth level, the major parties (Labor, Liberal and the Nationals) consistently won

---

17   ibid.
18   Purnendra Jain, 'Japan's Urban Governments, Their International Activities and Australia–Japan Relations: An Exploratory Essay', *Policy, Organisation and Society* (Summer, 1991), [Special Japan Issue]: 33–44.
19   ibid., 39.

approximately 92 per cent of first-preference votes from 1950 to 1980, but this declined to 84 per cent by 1990. In state parliaments across Australia, first-preference votes for independent candidates 'increased from 3.15 per cent in the 1960s to 5.8 per cent in the 2000s'.[20]

Jim Cameron was forced to resign due to ill health and was replaced with Marie Bignold. After the election of Elaine Nile to the Legislative Council in 1988, this grouping became a party registered as the Call to Australia— Fred Nile Group. Research by political scientists Mark Rodrigues and Dr Scott Brenton found that many of the successful independents in the NSW Parliament were former mayors, with Labor most often the losing party to what they described as candidates who 'had strong local profiles and no party affiliation'.[21]

Perhaps the most obvious parallel with Arkell is John Hatton, the independent member for the South Coast, who was elected in 1973 and served until he retired in 1995. While there are initial similarities, there are also crucial differences. Hatton was an astute and well-connected community campaigner like Arkell but Hatton's tenure in parliament was as much about accountability and anticorruption activities as it was about regional development. Hatton, for example, is perhaps best known for his casting vote to set up the state's anticorruption authority, the Independent Commission Against Corruption (ICAC). Arkell and Hatton were both avowed social conservatives, but Hatton was able to keep his seat for much longer and maintain the kind of long-term personal popularity that Arkell sought but never quite attained. Arkell also never showed a sustained interest in government transparency or anticorruption measures.

The group of independents towards whom Arkell gravitated was the evangelical-inspired religious conservatives led by the Reverend Fred Nile. By 1984, there were two members of the Fred Nile Group in the Legislative Council. Arkell and Nile's group coalesced around resistance to the socially progressive reform agenda, which the Wran government was leading from 1984. Arkell shared some characteristics with the popular independent

---

20 Mark Rodrigues and Scott Benton, *The Age of Independence? Independents in Australian Parliaments*, Parliamentary Library Research Paper, no. 4, 2010–2011 (Canberra: Parliament of Australia, 21 September 2010), parlinfo.aph.gov.au/parlInfo/download/library/prspub/228202/upload_binary/228202.pdf;fileType=application/pdf#search=%22Mark%20Rodrigues%20and%20Scott%20BENSON,%20The%20Age%20of%20Independence?%20Independents%20in%20Australian%20Parliaments,%20Research%20Paper%22.
21 ibid.

from Newcastle George Keegan, who won his seat from Labor in 1988. Newcastle is a large regional city north of Sydney with an important industrial and mining history, so it has crucial synergies with Wollongong. Newcastle also had a tradition of popular mayors who made the transition to state parliament. The irrepressible Frank Purdue, with stints as Mayor of Newcastle in the 1950s and 1960s, was also a state member for the seat of Waratah from 1959 to 1962 and from 1964 to 1965. George Keegan, like Arkell, had a background as a successful real estate agent and had an active civic life as a member or patron of a myriad Newcastle clubs and societies, including the Chamber of Commerce and the Cruising Yacht Club. Both Keegan and Arkell were successful in their respective seats through the wave of anti-Labor sentiment that characterised the 1988 election.[22]

Despite a strong local profile, Keegan was unable to win his seat for a second time in 1991, losing to Labor candidate Bryce Gaudry. Gaudry was an old-school Labor candidate and local member who did a prodigious amount of constituency work. I had moved from Wollongong to Newcastle in 1994 to take up a position at the University of Newcastle. Living in suburban Newcastle in the mid-1990s, we received house calls from Gaudry and his spouse, Barbara (who was herself a Newcastle city councillor), when they took the time to talk about local matters. Constituency work like this gave Gaudry a detailed picture of local issues and sentiment. It was this type of Labor member who could compete and compete successfully with the active, networked and popular independent candidates. Gaudry could have been the model for the type of candidate that Labor preselected for the 1991 state election for the seat of Wollongong. Labor's Gerry Sullivan would be hard to beat and, by now, as we have seen, Arkell was taking political damage across multiple issues.

The 1991 state campaign

If the 1988 election had delivered a major swing against the Labor government and against many Labor candidates, the 1991 state election did the opposite. The Liberal–National Coalition government under premier Nick Greiner was a controversial one with an ambitious reform agenda

---

22 Martin Dinneen, 'Tributes Paid to George Keegan', *Newcastle Herald*, 26 November 2008, [Updated 1 November 2012], www.newcastleherald.com.au/story/490466/tributes-paid-to-george-keegan/; 'Mr Ernest George KEEGAN (1928–2008)', *Members*, [Online] (Sydney: Parliament of New South Wales), www.parliament.nsw.gov.au/members/Pages/member-details.aspx?pk=1876.

that was unpopular by the eve of the May election. NSW Labor had found a credible opposition leader and excellent media performer in Bob Carr. In Wollongong, Labor preselected a capable candidate with strong links to the community, local schoolteacher Gerry Sullivan.

Labor did well across the state at the election, pushing the Coalition government under Greiner into minority status, forced to govern with the help of four independents, but Arkell was not one of them. Sullivan had won the seat back for Labor. Labor performed much better than expected, with a 7 per cent swing towards it in Wollongong, and other regional independents, such as George Keegan in Newcastle, also losing to Labor. The 1991 state election gave the Coalition 59 seats in the 109-seat parliament.

Arkell's primary vote declined to 29.66 per cent—a dramatic and decisive blow to any hopes of retaining the seat. Sullivan performed so well that he won on first preferences, recording 50.25 per cent of the primary vote and ultimately 58.6 per cent of the two-candidate preferred vote compared with Arkell's 41.4 per cent. 'Mud sticks,' Arkell told Danielle Cook from the *Sydney Morning Herald*: 'I've been blamed for not creating jobs in the Wollongong area.'[23] This was Arkell's take on the election loss, but Sullivan's campaign was focused and disciplined, pulled together by his long-time friend and campaign director, Warwick McMillan. Arkell suffered a 10 per cent decline in his primary vote compared with Sullivan's increase of 11.4 per cent. Arkell lost and lost comprehensively.[24]

According to Paul Crittenden, Labor member for Wyong, NSW party officials gave Sullivan little chance of success. Speaking to a condolence motion after Sullivan's untimely death in 2000, Crittenden noted that 'Gerry and his team believed that Arkell was the triumph of style over substance'. They ran a strong, issues-based campaign: 'Gerry held the view, both privately and publicly, that a person's sexual preference should not be a weapon in the armoury of a political campaign.' The analysis from Sullivan's Labor team in 1991 that Arkell lacked substance also resonates with former Labor alderman John Martin's view that Arkell was a 'political lightweight'. Labor had feared Arkell in the 1970s and 1980s and had even tried to engineer a corruption finding against him, but by the time of the 1991 state election, they were convinced he had fatal weaknesses. The voters

---

23   Danielle Cook, 'Gong Upset Stunned the Winner—The Cliffhanger', [*Spectrum*], *Sydney Morning Herald*, 27 May 1991: 7.
24   Parliament of New South Wales, State Election Results for the Seat of Wollongong, 1991, www.parliament.nsw.gov.au/electionresults18562007/1991/Wollongong.htm.

of Wollongong responded strongly to the Sullivan campaign and much credit should go to Sullivan and McMillan, but it was also true that Arkell's simple message had lost its appeal by 1991.

There was to be another test that year: the council elections were scheduled for September. Arkell was adamant he would run again despite close political allies trying to convince him that he should not. 'The only blue I ever had with him,' recalled former Arkell Independents team member Ted Tobin, 'was when we tried to talk him out of standing again as Lord Mayor in 1991 … We had a classic run in when we told him he would lose.'[25] Determined to push ahead, Arkell set up his 1991 mayoral campaign asking voters to let him complete the work that he had championed for decades. His pamphlets and posters proclaimed: 'I work hard for Wollongong because I love this city. Let me finish my work.'[26]

The voters were not convinced although Arkell's mayoral vote held up much better than his state election results. In a close contest, Arkell polled 47,779 votes or 43.6 per cent of the formal votes cast, but his Labor rival, David Campbell, polled 49,996 votes or 45.6 per cent. Labor had finally recaptured the lord mayoralty at Wollongong City Council. Campbell was another long-serving mayor and held office until 1999 when he too made the transition to state politics as the Labor member for the seat of Keira. He was the first Labor mayor since John Parker lost to Arkell in 1974. Arkell's incredible dominance of Wollongong Council was finally over. It was the end of the Arkell era and even Campbell could hardly believe he had defeated Mr Wollongong.

What explains this double blow to Arkell's political fortunes? If Arkell had channelled the zeitgeist in the 1970s and 1980s with a simple message about valuing the city and improving its image and its environment, by the late 1980s and early 1990s, he had failed to adapt and update his political messaging to address more contemporary concerns. By 1991 there were a range of issues on which he was seen as a political liability. High-profile battles with the secretary of the SCTLC Paul Matters, controversy in Wollongong over the council's new administrative building, the legionnaire's disease outbreak in the Crown Gateway Mall, the poor handling of the 1988

---

25   Ted Tobin cited in Geoff Failes, 'The Arkell Murder: Death Shocks and Saddens Colleagues', *Illawarra Mercury*, 29 June 1998: 7.
26   Danielle Cook, 'Labor Ends Arkell's Reign—Local Council Election', *Sydney Morning Herald*, 16 September 1991: 6.

Coledale mudslide and disquiet over large hotel and resort developments—all blunted the edges of the 'wonderful, wonderful Wollongong' message. The halcyon days for Mr Wollongong were well and truly over.

More than this, the tenor of Arkell's ideas and proposals began to shift by the late 1980s. He retained a base in community groups and assiduously attended meeting after meeting, but increasingly he was linked with major corporate deals, whether it was negotiating with a Japanese city to bring a resort to Wollongong or working with major retail and supermarket developers to expand in the Wollongong CBD and in Warrawong. Time and again, Arkell appeared to side with developers, allegedly engaged in secret meetings and publicly criticised union leaders for blocking new development proposals.

Perhaps Arkell's relationship with Frank Lowy best epitomised this shift towards a more corporate and elite style of development politics. Lowy was one of the best-known shopping centre and property developers in Australia as chairman of the Westfield Development Corporation. Westfield built multiple shopping centre precincts in Australia from 1977, including Westfield Figtree not far from the Arkells' Cobbler's Hill Service Station. Westfield was eventually successfully listed on the Australian Stock Exchange. As a Hungarian migrant who built a property empire, Lowy was an uncompromising and highly successful businessman.

It is difficult to trace when Arkell first met Lowy and the precise nature of their relationship. An *Australian Financial Review* story on Arkell's business dealings in 1987 was the first major public revelation of the relationship although council insiders were aware of the links before that date. It could have been Arkell's election to state parliament in 1984 that led to his introduction to Lowy. In 1988 Arkell told *Four Corners*' Mark Colvin in a very disarming, upfront manner how he used his parliamentary position to attract investment to Wollongong. In fact, the story specifically mentions Westfield. As Arkell said to Colvin:

> When I get the Westfield people into Parliament House they are very happy to accept an invitation to come to lunch. I take them, you know, well, and then they are under an obligation. I then invite them to Wollongong. They then come to Wollongong. I show them the investment opportunities. As a result of that something like $1.7 billion has been and is being spent in the city at the moment.[27]

---

27   Colvin, 'Independents' Day'.

But, as noted above, Arkell was a man in a hurry. New investments with significant planning implications were not a matter of transparent planning and open discussion. These proposals may have been the best options for Wollongong (though many doubted it), but the first ratepayers heard of them was a story in the *Illawarra Mercury*. Even fellow aldermen were not brought into Arkell's confidence. Mr Wollongong in this light was less a man of the people and more a member of the 'white-shoe brigade'—that much-reviled coterie of businessmen and politicians who were wheeling and dealing on the Gold Coast and in Brisbane in the 1980s. That form of development and its insidious corrupt links with politics had been painfully exposed by the Fitzgerald Inquiry into police corruption in Queensland. Given that the Wollongong Council conducted a number of high-profile 'fact-finding missions' to Queensland to visit shopping centres and malls, including one attended by all 15 aldermen as well as numerous senior council staff, there was a tangible connection between Wollongong Council and the increasing concern about corruption and high-rise development in Queensland. The Fitzgerald Inquiry was in session for almost two years of investigation and evidence gathering, finally reporting to parliament in July 1989. Wollongong Council was sending delegations to Queensland at the very time when that state's politics was imploding.[28]

This sense of rushing towards some distant goal also compromised Arkell's community work. Well known and respected for attending multiple meetings in an evening every night of the week, he was, by the late 1980s, gaining a reputation for turning up and then disappearing very quickly. As former alderman John Martin commented, there was a feeling that Arkell would come in the front door and disappear out the back. There were supporters at the Italian Club and the Hellenic Club who found Arkell had left almost as soon as he showed up. This change in his behaviour was another factor that helps explain the decline in Arkell's primary vote. The workload of being the lord mayor and the state member was huge and surely more than one man could bear. Many commented on an increasingly ill-tempered Arkell, prone to becoming frustrated and angry very quickly. The seeds of these traits were there in the late 1970s, but they manifested much more clearly in the mid-1980s.

---

28   'The Fitzgerald Inquiry', *Our History*, [Online] (Brisbane: Crime and Corruption Commission Queensland, 2019), www.ccc.qld.gov.au/about-us/our-history/fitzgerald-inquiry.

5. 'A MINDLESS VENDETTA AGAINST ME'

Arkell's relationship with the *Illawarra Mercury* also deteriorated in the late 1980s. Arkell was incensed when the paper published a Morgan Gallup opinion poll indicating that Arkell was less popular than SCTLC secretary and key Arkell critic Paul Matters, and that almost 48 per cent of people disapproved of his work. He issued an angry press release condemning the paper. Arkell stated, 'The poll represents nothing more than another slanderous attempt by the *Mercury* to discredit me', and further claimed that the paper was continuing to 'wage a mindless vendetta against me'.[29] The steady deterioration of the relationship between the region's main newspaper and its most prominent politician eventually culminated in Arkell issuing a writ for defamation against the paper in early 1998. For more than two decades, Arkell had steadfastly focused his public comments on positivity, optimism and opportunity. He had rarely if ever publicly criticised opponents and never publicly commented on press coverage. Now he had broken his own rules but, more than that, his language was unrestrained and intemperate.

Arkell's press release was a sign of a personality trait that for the most part had been hidden from the public but was becoming increasingly apparent. Nick Hartgerink recalled:

> He could be quite catty and critical … I certainly saw instances of that when he could become very short-tempered and catty with people. So, I guess that sort of filtered through and more and more people had experience of that, or their friends did or their family did … [and] the glow got a bit tarnished, I think.

Hartgerink agreed that this change coincided with Arkell's election to state parliament, where 'he might have had a bit much on his plate'.[30] Rod Oxley, who was Wollongong Council's treasurer in the early 1980s and CEO from 1988, praised Arkell 'for being an inspiration to many people', but recalled that he became more difficult to work with from the mid-1980s: 'He started to become obsessive and less tolerant of people. He became frustrated and took this out on staff.'[31] Another long-serving senior council staff member, Michael Gross, recalled after Arkell's death that Frank:

---

29 'Arkell Slams Mercury Morgan Group Poll', Press Release from the Office of the Member for Wollongong, 23 June 1989, WLP.
30 Interview with Nick Hartgerink, 24 November 2022.
31 Rod Oxley cited in Failes, 'The Arkell Murder'.

was a man full of extremes—full of support and encouragement for those he regarded as positive in helping shape his vision, hostile to those who were negative or whom he regarded as a barrier to the realisation of his work.

According to Gross, Arkell was known inside the council as 'Cranky Franky' for his short fuse and ill temper.[32]

But here we leave aside the dominant public thread of Frank Arkell's political life. Hidden beneath the successes and failures and the regular rounds of media coverage and public engagements was Frank Arkell the businessman. The foundation of Frank's public life, which enabled him to devote his entire life to politics, was the income generated by inherited wealth and a network of interlocking family businesses.

---

32 Michael Gross cited in Geoff Failes, 'Friends Praise Arkell: "We Hope the Good … Will Be Remembered"', *Illawarra Mercury*, 7 July 1998: 5.

6

'Attempting to sell people a dream': Business dealings, networks and influence

Frank Arkell's long political career dominated the public domain. Stories about Arkell tagged him as the former mayor and former state member but rarely covered his life before politics or his continuing business interests while he was still active in politics. For the first time, the extensive network of Arkell family businesses is outlined, which has otherwise been kept hidden. The Arkells possessed a network of interlocking businesses in landownership and subdivision, a service station, pastoral activities, commercial and residential real estate, and heavy machinery, construction and earthmoving hire. They also had smaller sidelines in insurance and a sandwich shop. Frank's political career carried on without any reference to the nature and extent of his ongoing work in business. Except for election material that presented Arkell as a 'businessman', no details or even the most basic information were placed on the public record. Only those who knew the family or had some inside knowledge knew of their business activities.

What follows is a more detailed discussion of the ways in which Frank Arkell's business interests intersected with his political life. At the core of this was the collision of two parts of his life that ideally should have been separate. This led to various claims that Arkell utilised his political influence on the council to help further his business interests. These claims, especially those coming from his political enemies, will be carefully assessed against the available evidence. It is important to stress that Arkell was never charged with, much less convicted of, corruption or fraud. However, there is evidence that he did benefit financially from his political standing and access to key decision-makers at Wollongong City Council.

Frank's start in the world of business—especially land development, subdivision and real estate—was the continuation of a long-established pattern in the O'Donnell family. Indeed, as we shall see, Arkell was a direct beneficiary of the assets and connections that came from the broad interests of the O'Donnells, including those that came to him from his mother, Marcella. Land sales, rezoning and subdivision provided ideal wealth-making opportunities as regional population and industrial growth proceeded apace. After the war, the patchwork of farms and cleared land slowly receded as rural land was subdivided, houses were built and farms were taken up for housing, new highways and industrial and commercial precincts. By the 1970s, farms on the edges of growing towns were a curiosity. Running a few head of cattle or some horses, these farms were a holdout against the rising tide of growth. At the back of Figtree, a Mr Gibson held onto his farm along Cordeaux Road until the late 1960s. It was finally sold for a new subdivision and the site of Figtree Private Hospital, among other things. The McPhail farm along West Dapto Road was another survivor from a period when farmers dominated the Central Illawarra, and when the McPhails were dairy farmers, not real estate agents. The Duncan family ran a dairy farm at Lake Heights well into the 1970s. Seemingly in an instant, one could observe the sprawling suburbia along Flagstaff Road and then be among rural scenery of paddocks, cows and old fences on the Duncans' farm. This was a hilly country so not easily developed, unlike the relatively flat expanse of nearby Berkeley.

From the top of Lake Heights, the growth of the suburb of Berkeley from the mid-1950s would have been an impressive sight: a spreading vista of weatherboard homes and new schools as the Department of Housing planned a whole new suburb and built houses—all framed by the arc of the distant escarpment.[1] My mother's sister, my uncle and cousins lived in Berkeley and we were regular visitors in the 1970s and early 1980s. Another aunt and uncle lived in Albion Park Rail. The road we took south to visit them, with the escarpment on our right, was fringed by farmland but also subdivisions and new homes, a ribbon of which was arranged around Port Kembla, the BHP steelworks and the commercial hub of Wollongong.

---

1 Kathleen H. Barwick, *History of Berkeley, New South Wales* (Wollongong: Illawarra Historical Society, 1978), ro.uow.edu.au/ihspubs/21, 12–16.

6. 'ATTEMPTING TO SELL PEOPLE A DREAM'

Coming on top of the suicide of Frank's father in 1941, there were important changes for the wider O'Donnell family in the 1940s. The Kembla Grange Estate where Marcella had taken the boys in 1941 was in possession of Uncle Richard (Dick) O'Donnell. Frank's grandfather and Marcella's father, Michael O'Donnell Jr, and his first wife, Ada Isobel, built a new home at Figtree in the 1930s. After the death of Ada in 1937, Michael Junior remarried and moved to Sydney, with the Kembla Grange Estate being Dick's sole provenance.[2] In March 1945, Michael Junior died, aged 90, in a private hospital in Ryde, a suburb of Sydney.[3] Dick stayed on the property for only another five years after his first wife, Daphne, died in 1941, selling his herd, all the estate furniture and the home itself in 1946.[4] By the age of just 15, Frank had lost both maternal grandparents. Losing both grandparents and his father at such a young age inevitably meant that Frank's mother would become the rock on which he based his life.

Probate and land title records indicate that the O'Donnell estate was a sizeable one, albeit with the numerous O'Donnell children inheriting parcels of land in the Port Kembla, West Wollongong, Figtree and Kembla Grange areas. In May 1941, two months after Sidney Arkell had died, Marcella purchased land and houses in Reserve Street, Wollongong. The Arkells lived at 11 Reserve Street from 1945 to about 1960 and then Frank and Marcella moved to 1 Reserve Street. Marcella owned at least one other block of land in Reserve Street, at number 3, next door. Marcella, along with her five brothers, had inherited an equal share of her father's estate in 1945, which was worth more than £16,000 and included shares, cash on hand, land in the Central Illawarra Municipality, as well as a house and property in the Sydney suburb of Kogarah, where he had lived with his second wife, Alma O'Donnell.[5] As we have seen, Marcella was also due to inherit land at Cringila through the estate of her Uncle James, who died in 1918. This finally came into her possession in 1959. Her portfolio of property interests was beginning to develop.

---

2   *Illawarra Mercury*, 26 November 1937: 10.
3   *Sydney Morning Herald*, 20 March 1945: 10; *Illawarra Mercury*, 23 March 1945: 5.
4   *Illawarra Mercury*, 13 December 1946: 9.
5   Probate of Michael O'Donnell, NRS-13660-10-261-Series 4_130195, State Records NSW, Sydney.

Plate 6.1 A copy of a cinema advertisement for the Arkell family's Cobbler's Hill Service Station shown in Wollongong cinemas in 1953
Note: This retouched advertisement shows a tall, thin Frank Arkell in his early twenties standing in front of the business.
Photo: Bill Parkinson's Interval Slide Collection via 'Lost Wollongong' Facebook group.

A short drive from the new family home in West Wollongong was Cobbler's Hill Service Station in Figtree. The family opened this business about 1950 at 51–53 Princes Highway, near where the much newer 'Arkell Drive' meets the highway (Plate 6.1). In 1954 Marcella applied to Wollongong City Council for a permit to extend the commercial building. The extensions were valued at £3,000 and the application was approved. A reference to this in the *Illawarra Mercury* reveals Marcella's central role in the family business—in this case, as the key applicant for the building extension.[6] A much-altered commercial building is extant on the site. As I found more evidence of Marcella's property records and her business activities, I was beginning to see the meaning of my mother's enigmatic comment that the real force behind Frank Arkell was 'old Mrs Arkell'. Marcella was setting

---

6   The council noted that M.V. Arkell received permission to build additions worth £3,000 to the garage on the Princes Highway, Figtree. See *South Coast Times*, [Wollongong], 21 June 1954: 11.

up a family enterprise and her sons were slowly taking on a greater role. In 1954 Frank was only 25, but his brother Richard was 33, James (Bill) was 31 and Harold (Harry) was 30 years old. Even so, Marcella was the driving force in the application to extend the business. Business records from 1960 held by the Australian Securities and Investments Commission (ASIC) indicate that Cobbler's Hill Service Station was a family-owned business with Marcella and her four sons as joint owners. This was an ambitious family enterprise with local advertising purchased for display during the interval at local cinemas (Plate 6.1).

Next door to the service station was a lockup yard where a second family business operated: Arkell Brothers Proprietary Limited, a plant hire company later renamed Wollongong Plant Hire Proprietary Limited. Arkell Brothers was operating by at least 1950, with an advertisement in the *South Coast Times* from May of that year showing it offering for sale three loaders, two second-hand and one brand new.[7] This was the only family business that did not include Marcella as a director. The four brothers—Richard, Bill, Harry and Frank—were listed as directors in ASIC records from 1960. It is clear that the site on the Princes Highway at Figtree was an important base for the Arkell family enterprises. The service station and lockup were on a prime site that could attract traffic travelling north from Dapto and Unanderra or south from Wollongong and Figtree. This was also familiar territory. It was not too far from their grandfather's old estate house at Kembla Grange, in the town to which Michael Junior and Ada had moved after living at Kembla Grange.

There is little detailed information available on Frank Arkell's activities between leaving school and entering local government in December 1965. The cinema advertisement from 1953 shows Frank, tall and lean, standing in front of Arkells' garage, so we know he worked in the family business for a time after leaving school. The NSW Parliament website, which includes a short biographical statement for each MP, indicates that Arkell worked for the Sydney Stock Exchange and then for a Sydney branch of the ANZ Bank. It also lists his interests as squash and tennis. In one interview in 1968, he told an *Illawarra Mercury* journalist that he had studied economics at the University of Sydney.[8] Again, in 1974 on an election pamphlet, he stated that he had 'completed his studies in Sydney in accountancy

---

7   *South Coast Times*, [Wollongong], 11 May 1950: 14.
8   'You Pick the New Mayor', *Illawarra Mercury*, 10 December 1968: 1.

and economics', which was a slightly more generic claim.⁹ I searched the University of Sydney calendar from 1953 to 1970 trying to find his name listed as a graduate but to no avail. I also asked the university archivist to check student records to see whether Arkell had perhaps completed one or two years of a degree without graduation but again there was no record of his enrolment.¹⁰ The NSW Real Estate Institute does have a record of him possessing a real estate agent's licence and this required some professional training to secure. Perhaps the reference in the 1977 pamphlet refers to this training but the 1968 claim to have studied at the University of Sydney is certainly not correct. Electoral roll records of the time show Frank still registered to vote in Wollongong at the Reserve Street address so it could be that he found lodgings while in Sydney and returned to Wollongong for weekends.

The *NSW Government Gazette* shows that Arkell became a justice of the peace (JP) in 1956. This was an important service to the community but also a useful facility for those in the business world. Frank's eldest brother, Richard, followed and became a JP in 1956.¹¹ As we saw from the discussion of the probate records and the family businesses, Richard died in 1963, aged only 41, of renal failure in a hospital in Hampstead Heath, London. Thereafter, it was usually the three brothers, Harry, Bill and Frank, along with Marcella until her death in 1979, who shared the directorship of their various companies and business enterprises.

Labor criticisms of Arkell

Unease about the relationship between Arkell's business and political interests was expressed even in the very early stages of his political career. His Labor opponents would be vocal critics throughout his time in politics and, in 1973, George Petersen, the state Labor member for Illawarra, called Arkell a 'wealthy land developer' and expressed concern about his role as a Wollongong alderman. Petersen made specific mention of the Masters Road deviation, asserting that Arkell financially benefited from the rezoning of land and the construction of an access road. Petersen also

---

9   'City of Wollongong, How to Vote Independent for Ward 5, 23 September, 1977', Collection C1/10/16, University of Wollongong Archives.
10 University of Sydney Archivist, Personal communication, 8 May 2023.
11 Francis Neville Arkell, 'Appointments', *NSW Government Gazette*, No. 35, 6 April 1956, 947; Richard Sydney Bruce Arkell, 'Appointments', *NSW Government Gazette*, No. 124, 16 November 1956, 3376.

mentioned a development in Dapto by L.J. McPhail, claiming Arkell must have known about it four years before it became public. The McPhail family were recipients of the original land grant in the area and, later, dairy farmers and landowners from the old Central Illawarra Municipality. Like the O'Donnells, some in the McPhail family had made the transition into real estate, commercial development and local government. The Arkells, O'Donnells and McPhails mixed in the same circles. 'It is impossible to resist the conclusion that Alderman Arkell and Mr McPhail,' claimed Petersen, 'had worked together, not in the interests of the people in the area, but in the financial interests of Mr McPhail.'[12]

It is difficult to assess Petersen's claim and there is little detail beyond an assertion made under parliamentary privilege, but Arkell had clearly already come to the attention of the local Labor Party and its parliamentary powerbrokers. As noted in Chapter 3, Arkell stood against Petersen at the 1971 state election, so it was possibly not merely a concern about the probity of local government that motivated Petersen to name Arkell in parliament in 1973. Local Labor members would not hesitate to use parliamentary privilege to mention Arkell adversely. Indeed, Petersen's remarks in 1973 foreshadowed the events of 1994 and 1996 when two Labor members used NSW Parliament to imply that Arkell was a paedophile and to reveal that he was a person of major concern in evidence given before the Wood Royal Commission.

When in 1974 WIN TV journalist Paul Bongiorno asked Arkell a pointed question about managing the relationship between business interests and politics, as noted in Chapter 3, Arkell simply ignored the question and replied with general comments about the good calibre of election candidates and the council working effectively with the business community. In 1975 Wollongong feminist activists met with the lord mayor about the nature and content of the International Women's Day events planned for that year, but they were also renting offices in Kenny Street, Wollongong, from Arrow Real Estate, one of the key businesses Arkell shared with his mother, Marcella.

Bill Knott, the Labor member for Kiama, criticised Arkell in NSW Parliament in late 1982. In a motion condemning the Fraser Coalition government's economic policies, including its refusal to act on the crisis in the Australian steel industry, Knott noted the absence of the lord mayor at

---

12 George Petersen, in NSW, *Parliamentary Debates*, Legislative Assembly, 11 September 1973, 715–20.

a rally to welcome the striking coalminers from the Kemira Colliery who had come to Wollongong. But Knott also criticised Arkell's approach to the city's economic rejuvenation: 'To talk about attracting industries from Sydney and elsewhere, as Frank Arkell proposes, is blowing in the wind and attempting to sell people a dream.'[13] Always keen to present his main rival in a negative light, Eric Ramsay, state Labor member for Wollongong (1971–1984), in March 1983 raised a constituency matter in parliament involving Wollongong City Council agreeing to changes to an apartment complex allegedly without the approval of the owner. Ramsay suggested that council officers had acted illegally, called for an inquiry and, for good measure, made available to the parliament 'copies of the company's advertisements in the Wollongong Mercury [sic] which refer to that great pretender, the Lord Mayor of Wollongong, Mr Frank Arkell'.[14]

The Smiles report, 1983

In 1983 a major formal inquiry touched on Arkell's business interests. Peter Smiles, the chief inspector of local government accounts, conducted the inquiry, which investigated a range of matters relating to Wollongong Council.[15] After Ramsay raised the issues, detailed below, in parliament, they were referred to the state's Local Government Inspectorate. As always, Labor was chasing Arkell and looking to discredit him. Having first raised the allegations in parliament in September 1982, Ramsay successfully moved a motion on the eve of the 1983 council elections for the Legislative Assembly to record 'its deep concern at the findings of the report of local government inspectors into a series of allegations of graft, corruption and financial maladministration levelled against [the] Lord Mayor'. He further recommended that the minister for local government refer relevant matters to the police and 'consider whether in the light of the findings of scandalous conduct the public interest would be best served by suspension of next Saturday's election for the Lord Mayoralty'. If Ramsay could not dent the popularity of Arkell through public and parliamentary criticism, removing him from office and sacking the council would surely discredit him as an

---

13   Bill Knott, in NSW, *Parliamentary Debates*, Legislative Assembly, 2 November 1982, 2049–55.
14   Eric Ramsay, in NSW, *Parliamentary Debates*, Legislative Assembly, 8 March 1983, 4394.
15   'Report of an Inspection of Wollongong City Council under Section 212 of the Local Government Act, 1919', VI, no. 89, and 'Report of a Special Investigation of Wollongong City Council, 15 April, 1983', VI, no. 90, in *Votes and Proceedings of the Legislative Assembly* (Sydney: NSW Government Printer, 1984).

opponent at the upcoming election. Perhaps the 51-vote margin from 1981 weighed heavily on Ramsay's mind as he sought, by any means possible, to discredit and remove Arkell.

The independent member for South Coast, John Hatton, spoke against Labor's urgency motion in the Legislative Assembly in September 1983:

> I cannot regard this matter as urgent. That decision does not mean I do not regard the allegations as serious, or that I defend or attack the actions of Alderman Arkell. It is simply that I regard the Government's timing in raising the matter, its political tactics, and its way of handling the whole matter, as extremely dubious.[16]

Premier Neville Wran weighed in on the debate, saying in the Legislative Assembly that these were 'grave and alarming allegations' and that the 'proper and decent thing for Lord Mayor Arkell to do is to stand aside. All honourable members know there is plenty of precedent for that.'[17] Arkell found some support among the Liberal and Country party members. The brother of alderman Harry Schipp, Arkell's Ward 5 independent running mate, was Joe Schipp, the Country Party member for Wagga Wagga. Joe interjected when Wran indicated Arkell should stand aside. Wran fired back: 'The honourable member for Wagga Wagga should not say "ah" for his brother is in it up to his neck.' the premier's familiarity with the Wollongong Council's independent aldermen and their relatives is startling. In the Legislative Council, Liberal member Ted Pickering noted the government had taken the unprecedented step of releasing a minority report by a second inspector, G.R. Mercado, which was far more critical of Arkell. 'But it is written by a man,' claimed Pickering, 'who wishes to hatchet a political opponent without providing substantive evidence. That is an incredible action by the Government.'[18] The Opposition made much of Mercado's background as a former Labor Party candidate in the Upper Hunter region.

Despite Eric Ramsay's political intent as the Labor member for Wollongong, the main report written by Chief Inspector Peter Smiles is a model of careful, evidence-based assessment. Among other things, Smiles found that on several occasions companies associated with Arkell had been given

---

16   John Hatton, in NSW, *Parliamentary Debates*, Legislative Assembly, 22 September 1983, 1113.
17   Neville Wran, in NSW, *Parliamentary Debates*, Legislative Assembly, 21 September 1983, 1018.
18   ibid.; Ted Pickering, in NSW, *Parliamentary Debates*, Legislative Council, 21 September 1983, 986–87.

favourable treatment by Wollongong Council. Some of the claims raised by Ramsay in NSW Parliament were found to have substance. These concerned the council's treatment of a series of land transactions with companies of which Arkell was a director. In these cases, the council had waived legal fees or, in one case, agistment fees on land in which Arkell had an interest at Figtree. Companies of which Arkell was a director were found to be in arrears with rate payments and the chief inspector found little evidence of any attempt by the council to follow up on these outstanding amounts. Figtree was, as we have seen, an important base for two of the Arkell family businesses and was the location of the Cobbler's Hill Service Station and neighbouring lockup.

By the time the chief inspector's report was finalised and presented to parliament in September 1983, most of these matters had been resolved internally at Wollongong Council and the payment of monies owed expedited, so there were no police inquiries or charges followed up on. Eric Ramsay's claim that Arkell had used his council vehicle while campaigning for the 1981 state election (when Arkell narrowly lost to Ramsay) was found by Inspector Smiles to be 'without evidence'. Tony Bevan, who had worked with Cabinet minister Rex Jackson and Ramsay in gathering the evidence, was exasperated. In mid-1983, he told Jackson: 'All the [council] reports have come forward, they've all been endorsed, they've all been adopted and [inaudible] unscrambled the bloody egg, but I don't know how you can do that. I don't think they can do that legally.'[19]

The Masters Road deviation

The inspector's report also went into some detail on the Masters Road deviation. Concern over Arkell's role in this matter has persisted in regional memory and several respondents mentioned this issue in off-the-record conversations about possible illegal activities by Arkell. The Masters Road deviation was a major piece of road infrastructure planned to connect the then-new Wollongong bypass with the Five Islands Road. These two major roads, Five Islands Road and the Wollongong bypass (which the Department of Main Roads called the F6 Southern Freeway after 1978), were the major routes south and the subject of increasing holiday, commercial, industrial and commuter traffic. The Five Islands Road ran from the southern end

---

19 Transcripts of the Bevan Tapes, No. 17.

of the Wollongong CBD, skirting the Port Kembla inner harbour, south to Warrawong. As we have seen, George Petersen first raised this issue in parliament in 1973 and Eric Ramsay repeated many of the same claims in 1982 and 1983.[20] Three Arkell family companies were said to have both delayed the construction of this crucial road and benefited from the rezoning and subsequent sale of land to the Department of Main Roads (DMR). The delays, it was claimed, provided a significant boost to the final sale price of the land. This was a complex project as the road had to pass over several local roads, the new freeway and the South Coast rail line. The project was finally completed by December 1978.[21]

As we have already seen, the Arkells and the O'Donnells owned large parcels of land in this general area, between Figtree, Unanderra and Port Kembla. With planning beginning in 1966, the Masters Road deviation would have cut off 5.5 hectares of land owned by Herne Estate Proprietary Limited, an Arkell family company. The DMR agreed to provide road access to this land at its own cost. Other land in the vicinity was sold either to the DMR or to another Arkell company, Marcelle Securities. A section of land was rezoned light industrial after some complicated back and forth between the Wollongong Council and the State Planning Authority. The Labor members alleged that the Arkell family company had obstructed the entire process, forcing the DMR to build the road access, securing a favourable rezoning of their land that benefited them to the tune of $250,000 (Petersen claimed) and then enjoyed the higher land values after the delays, which also benefited them financially. Both Petersen and, later, Ramsay alleged that the Arkell companies had secured preferential treatment from the state Coalition government that was in power until 1976. It was part of Labor's overall strategy to discredit the so-called independent Arkell by suggesting that he benefited from Liberal Party favours.

Inspector Smiles found no evidence that the provision of road access, land rezoning or subsequent land sales were inappropriate or unreasonable. But the city's lord mayor being involved in the significant and complex land sales and management that came with large infrastructure projects was on face value a very concerning prospect. What's more, Arkell's role in these family

---

20   George Petersen, in NSW, *Parliamentary Debates*, Legislative Assembly, 11 September 1973, 719–20.
21   Department of Main Roads, *Annual Report 1971–72* (Sydney: Roads and Traffic Authority of New South Wales, 1972), www.opengov.nsw.gov.au/publications/16108;jsessionid=D58927032234A24C62 E82E8CEB1C8505, and *Annual Report 1977–78* (Sydney: Roads and Traffic Authority of New South Wales, 1978), www.opengov.nsw.gov.au/publications/16102;jsessionid=B8724FC7B4F5AFFD5BD34 015FC17697D.

companies was not transparent. He was a company co-director with his mother and his brothers. While all indications were that he concentrated on his political career, he made no public statements about leaving the family's business affairs to other family members. In this climate of uncertainty, it was inevitable that questions would be asked about whether Arkell's influence with senior council staff had affected the outcome of particularly sensitive decisions.

The inspector did find that two Arkell family companies, Herne Estate Proprietary Limited and Marcelle Securities, were in substantial arrears on payment of council rates on the land that was at the centre of the Masters Road project. In 1982 the rates charges for the property were $14,331.20 while another $4,971.74 was in arrears. There were also other outstanding charges adding up to $1,021.14 in total. Despite four separate payments of $1,000 in 1983, $17,407.68 remained owing to the council, which equates to approximately $68,980 in 2022 dollars.[22] The track record of missing or being behind on payments dated back to 1973. In this case, the inspector recommended that the council 'systematically proceed to recover outstanding rates'.[23]

Another complex matter concerned land owned by Herne Estate Proprietary Limited on the eastern side of the planned new southern freeway. The council entered into a land swap agreement in 1962 that allowed the company to develop a portion of this land while transferring the remainder to council ownership. It was subsequently found that the DMR would need this land for its freeway extensions. After many years of letters, legal demands and meetings between parties, the matter was finally resolved in 1978, but even as late as 1981 cattle belonging to Dembollie Proprietary Limited (another Arkell family company) was found grazing on the land in question. There were no agistment fees being paid despite a 1978 council–company agreement on fees. In this case, the inspector found that the council's 'administration was not diligent' and recommended that legal and agistment fees as well as rates pertaining to this matter be recovered.[24]

---

22 Reserve Bank of Australia, *Pre-Decimal Inflation Calculator*, [Online] (Sydney: Reserve Bank of Australia), www.rba.gov.au/calculator/annualPreDecimal.html.
23 'Report of an Inspection of Wollongong City Council under Section 212 of the Local Government Act, 1919'; 'Report of a Special Investigation of Wollongong City Council, 22 September, 1983', in *Votes and Proceedings of the Legislative Assembly*, 46.
24 'Report of an Inspection of Wollongong City Council under Section 212 of the Local Government Act, 1919, 22 September, 1983', in *Votes and Proceedings of the Legislative Assembly*, 49.

What all these cases from the 1983 report reveal is a pattern of differential treatment by the Wollongong Council towards Arkell family companies. There was no finding of corruption in the report and it is impossible to discern the precise mechanisms working within the council that helped create these outcomes. Was there an informal back channel between Arkell and senior council staff, especially the town clerk? Did senior staff simply act on the assumption that certain outcomes were preferred by the lord mayor and did not need any direction? Was Frank Arkell involved? Whatever the origin of these outcomes, Arkell family companies were allowed to go into substantial rates arrears, avoid paying some legal and agistment costs that would ordinarily be levied on other ratepayers and generally slow council and DMR business to their own financial benefit.

As we have seen, Frank Arkell's sit-in in his lord mayoral office in September 1983 was a successful strategy to force the hand of the state Labor government to allow council elections. The high-profile action had the effect of blurring the specifics of the inspector's report. While there were no charges arising from the report, it was not entirely free of criticism of Arkell and some of its findings suggested a pattern of behaviour in the council that gave favourable treatment to Arkell family companies.

It was not until 1987 that a Labor-initiated reform raised the issue of Arkell's business interests again. The NSW Parliament passed legislation that required MPs to provide a register of their pecuniary interests after a successful referendum on the issue in 1981. Arkell was criticised for listing five properties in his 1986 return but 12 in the return for 1987. Leading the criticism was none other than Laurie Kelly, who would be challenging Arkell at the 1988 state election. The list of 12 properties of which Arkell had sole or joint ownership raised eyebrows in Macquarie Street and in Wollongong.[25]

By the mid-1980s, Arkell had become heavily involved in public campaigns and behind-the-scenes lobbying to attract new business investment to Wollongong. In his mayoral and parliamentary duties, he was privy to a range of information that was not public and could have represented valuable commercial intelligence. I have searched through ASIC records and found numerous companies of which Arkell was a joint director, usually with a family member such as Marcella, before her death in 1979, or his surviving brothers. What is not present is any indication that Arkell formally

---

25   Mark Coultan, 'Pecuniary Disclosures of MP Queried', *Sydney Morning Herald*, 4 February 1988: 5.

placed those directorships in a trust or resigned from them while he was lord mayor or state member for Wollongong. It is possible he effectively left the running of these companies to his family members but, if so, any such arrangement was purely informal.

Assessing Frank Arkell's wealth and income

When I first read George Petersen's 1973 description of Arkell as a 'wealthy landowner' I thought it was political hyperbole. But closer examination reveals the assessment to be quite accurate. Here was another Arkell secret hidden in plain sight. Unlike Bevan, who liked to surround himself with the accoutrements of wealth, Arkell lived a relatively simple life. He did not purchase a penthouse unit overlooking the beach or drive a late-model Mercedes like Bevan. He stayed in the family home with his mother, ostensibly living a utilitarian life. He was well dressed but never showy or ostentatious. He kept the same Ford sedan for many years. This modest public presentation belied his true private wealth. Arkell and the Arkell group of family companies owned extensive tracts of land throughout the Illawarra and elsewhere in New South Wales. They had a portfolio of properties, owned cattle and sheep and had at least six income-producing businesses.[26] In 1963 Frank's brother Richard died of kidney failure in the United Kingdom. Richard Arkell's probate record provides a compelling snapshot of the extensive business interests of the Arkell family, offering more than enough information to show that Frank had valuable shares in at least six family companies and enjoyed income from multiple sources as dividends and profits shared equally with his brothers and mother, except in the case of Arkell Brothers, which, as the name suggests, did not include Marcella.

As probate and ASIC records show, Herne Estate Proprietary Limited was principally a real estate development company formed in 1959 with Marcella and her then-four sons as co-directors. Herne Estate was responsible for residential subdivisions in the Figtree, Unanderra and Farmborough Heights areas. The company made no money in its first year of operation and a loss of £133 in its second year, but in 1962 it made a gross profit of £810 (£677 after tax). The estimated value of the shareholding was £1,806 for

---

26 Probate of the Late Richard Sydney Bruce Arkell, NSW Supreme Court, No. 642257, 11 December 1965, State Records NSW, Sydney.

each director. This value recommended by Wollongong Solicitors Denley & Gargett was given to the NSW Supreme Court to help assess the worth of Richard's estate and was made well before much of the land owned by the company had been subdivided and sold, so there were still strong potential future earnings, though, as Denley & Gargett pointed out, the costs of rezoning and developing the subdivisions were not yet known. By March 1962, 46 lots in Allandale Avenue, Herne Street and Edmund Avenue in Figtree (which was a Herne Estate subdivision) had been completed and were ready for sale or already sold. In 1963 the company still owned approximately 32 hectares of land that was to be part of future residential subdivisions.[27]

If Herne Estate was largely about potential earnings in 1962, other Arkell family companies were already producing income. Arkell Brothers was perhaps the most valuable of their local assets in the period, securing contracts to lease out heavy earthmoving and construction equipment. In 1962 the dividends paid to the four co-directors, including Frank Arkell, was £790 each. In 1963 the dividend rose to a healthy £1,380, while the gross income for the company was more than £48,000 in the year ending 30 June 1962.

Another Arkell family business, Dembollie Pastoral Company, had net assets of more than £18,000 in the year ended 30 June 1963. This company's principal asset was Dembollie Station on the Newell Highway near Coonabarabran in the Central West of New South Wales in addition to the leases held in the Wollongong area. The Central West property covered 2,900 hectares of which 160 were cleared. The land, together with a farmhouse, other buildings and equipment and 65 head of sheep, was valued at just under £4,000 in March 1963. Dembollie returned more than £2,000 for Frank Arkell in the year ending 30 June 1963. NSW Real Estate Institute records also show that Frank secured a stock and station licence to buy and sell in the pastoral sector though it is not clear from what date. There may have been other dealings and business activities about which we do not know. There were certainly other rural assets that are difficult to track. In 1997, facing 29 counts of child sexual abuse, Frank's legal counsel applied to alter his bail conditions because Arkell wanted to visit his two rural properties, one in Coonabarabran and another in nearby Mendooran. One of these

---

27   Valuation documents provided by Denley & Gargett, Wollongong, in Probate of the late Richard Sydney Bruce Arkell.

properties was clearly the Dembollie holding near Coonabarabran, but I have not found any further information on the property in Mendooran. Mendooran is about 80 kilometres south of Coonabarabran.

There were many more sources of income. Kembla Ready Mixed Concrete generated £1,000 for Frank Arkell in the year ending 30 June 1963. Smaller amounts came in from other family companies including the Cobbler's Hill Service Station (£390 in the year ending 30 June 1963), Strathroy Investments (£382), Savoy Sandwich shop (£59) and Stanwell Insurance Consultants (£34). Richard's shareholdings in Dembollie and indeed in all the Arkell family companies were bequeathed to his three surviving brothers and shared equally, further consolidating Frank's financial position.

Converting this reported income for 1963 into 2023 figures gives us at least a broad sense of the financial strength that underpinned Arkell's full-time political vocation. In 1963 Frank Arkell earned £6,055 from the various companies listed above. Using the Reserve Bank of Australia's pre-decimal inflation calculator, we can estimate the value of this income in 2023 figures: an income of £6,055 in 1963 equates to $207,374 in 2023.[28] This amount is approximately $35,000 more than the base salary of a backbencher in the NSW Legislative Assembly earned in the same year and must be considered a minimum since it only captures investments and income that Frank shared with Richard. As we will see below, there were other family businesses that would have added more to this basic annual income. The key point here is that Frank Arkell was indeed independently wealthy, and this scale of wealth gave him great latitude and capacity to be a full-time politician and to be particularly generous when it came to fundraising. The other surprising feature of this financial summary is that the man who made the city of Wollongong the centrepiece of his political program made a sizeable portion of his annual income from a pastoral property in the Central West of New South Wales.

Of course, Richard's probate records do not cover the family businesses that involved Frank but did not include Richard, the main one of which was Arrow Real Estate, of which Frank and Marcella were co-directors.

---

28   See Reserve Bank of Australia, *Pre-Decimal Inflation Calculator*. To arrive at the figure of £6,055, I have added the following amounts: £810 from Herne Estate, £1,380 from Arkell Brothers, £2,000 from Dembollie Pastoral, £1,000 from Kembla Concrete, £390 from Cobbler's Hill Service Station, £382 from Strathroy Investments, £59 from Savoy Sandwich shop and £34 from Stanwell Insurance. We do not have a 1963 income figure for Herne Estate, so I have used the 1962 figure to estimate the 1963 income for this business.

From an office at 300 Crown Street, Arrow owned and managed properties throughout Wollongong and was also involved in the promotion and sale of Herne Estate subdivisions. Only Frank possessed a real estate agent's licence, so he must have worked directly with clients while Marcella worked behind the scenes. There were ambitious projects further afield, too, including an estate at Malua Bay Beach, not far from Batemans Bay, on the state's South Coast. This estate was aggressively marketed in the early 1960s to potential buyers in Canberra looking for holiday homes, with Arrow presenting itself as the 'sole selling agent'.[29] This was a shrewd move, and one wonders whether Marcella's 1941 visit to Canberra on that ill-fated weekend influenced her long-term planning in any way. Heading off from Wollongong on summer holidays to the South Coast in the 1970s and 1980s, we first encountered ACT-plated vehicles in Ulladulla but they were quite common around Batemans Bay. Senior public servants, academics and others could take a reasonably direct road to the coast via Queanbeyan, Bungendore and Braidwood. It is impossible to assess the income from Arrow, but it must have provided an impressive addition to the business income already detailed above.

In 1986 Frank Arkell told *Illawarra Mercury* journalist Paddy Ginnane that his plan was to be independently wealthy by his mid-thirties. Richard's probate record and other records show that Frank had in fact achieved that by the mid-1960s. Arkell turned 40 in 1969, which was the first year he served as deputy lord mayor, and thereafter his round of meetings, openings, fundraisers, parties and media events began in earnest. One of Arkell's contemporaries who accompanied him was Labor alderman John Martin, who observed that this 'was his full-time pre-occupation as Lord Mayor and he was good at it'.[30] In that way, we come full circle from business interests back to politics. Arkell's business pursuits provided the financial basis for his full-time commitment to local government, the financial resources for election campaigns and, later, as we have seen, funding for additional staff in his state electoral office. This was a level of commitment not available to his rivals and allies on the council, all of whom were juggling full-time work and professional careers. Councillors and lord mayors received modest honorary payments and reimbursement of expenses but nothing like an MP's salary to cover a full-time commitment.

---

29   *Canberra Times*, 27 September 1961: 8 [advertising section].
30   John Martin, Personal communication, 23 April 2023.

Plate 6.2 Frank Arkell (centre) stands out from the crowd at the opening and preview of the City of Greater Wollongong Art Competition in 1962

Note: Even before being elected to the council in 1965, Arkell was attending these functions and raising his profile.

Photo: From the collections of the Wollongong City Libraries and the Illawarra Historical Society.

Unlike Richard Arkell's probate, Frank's record is not available to researchers so the value of the estate he left after his death in 1998 is unknown. NSW law provides that records of probate granted after 1977 are only available to those with an interest in the estate such as an executor or a beneficiary or those wishing to legally contest a will. Land title records, however, show that the house and apartment in Reserve Street passed through probate to his two surviving brothers, Bill and Harry. As soon as probate was granted, they sold the house, for $290,000, in November 1999, with the sale completed by late January 2000. A quick sale of the house was understandable given the terrible events that had occurred in the apartment only 18 months earlier. Other properties that Arkell had owned jointly with his brothers now passed into their ownership as well as to other close Arkell family members. The new owners of 1 Reserve Street cleared the site and built a complex of four townhouses. Marcella and Frank Arkell's home is now gone. The scene of his brutal murder—and perhaps the site of other secrets too—has been replaced with townhouses.

7

'Wonderful, wonderful Wollongong'? Arkell's vision for a post-industrial city

In his first speech to the NSW Parliament in 1984, Frank Arkell described Wollongong as a 'city of contrasts': 'It is a city of steel, a city of coal and yes it is an industrial city.' But, he continued, it is also 'a city of beaches, beautiful beaches with its own botanic gardens. Wollongong is a beautiful city and is fast becoming a clean and green city.' Reconciling these two descriptions, he labelled Wollongong 'a beautiful industrial city'. He was always careful to indicate that he embraced the coal and steel sectors of the regional economy. Asked by ABC TV *Four Corners* journalist Mark Colvin what he thought of the view from his mayoral office south towards the Port Kembla steelworks complex and related heavy industries, he said very plainly: 'Oh, that's beautiful. That's a work of art.' For the man who had grown up with the number-one blast furnace towering over his childhood suburb at Steeltown, this is perhaps not surprising. Nevertheless, Arkell was a departure from other twentieth-century political leaders who hailed from the region. In offering a new vision for Wollongong based on something more than just coal and steel, Arkell brought several new issues to regional politics beyond an uncritical acceptance of the centrality of heavy industry to the economy and society. He wanted to clean up the city and address areas that were visually unappealing. He was keen to establish, or re-establish, green areas. Based on his love of gardening, he was a keen supporter of the city's Botanic Garden, but above all, he looked to investment in retail, commercial and tourism development to diversify the city's economic base.

As we have seen, Arkell showed tremendous political discipline when it came to messaging. He kept his main policy ideas simple and stuck to them. There is no evidence of him thinking out loud in public or entertaining possible ideas and indicating that he had yet to make up his mind. He was always certain of what he wanted and what he was advocating for because the basic outlines of the plan were very simple: 'A cleaner greener Wollongong.'[1] Arkell's environmentalism was of the 'Clean Up Australia' kind.

At no stage did Arkell present his concern about pollution as a criticism of BHP's steelworks or the other major industries in the Port Kembla industrial conurbation. This was no extended critique of industrialisation. Rather, he presented a modest, pared-down set of ideas and proposals including green corridors, walking trails, a revitalised Botanic Garden, street plantings and removing rubbish from Lake Illawarra and sewage from Wollongong's beaches. While simple, they addressed everyday concerns and had the potential to make a tangible difference to the lives of locals.

Clean-up campaigns engaged residents and community groups even if they did not shake the foundations of the industrial society and the dominance of BHP. But Arkell's interest in nature and gardening was genuine, so at the heart of these proposals was a real love of plants and trees. The limits of Arkell's environmentalism were nonetheless revealed in 1985 when he suggested that he would rather have the 400 coal trucks and the jobs that came with them than lose the Port Kembla coal loader, despite widespread concerns about coal dust pollution and the safety problems caused by the 25-tonne trucks on Wollongong's roads.[2]

Arkell's role in securing an olive grove behind the Hellenic Club on the Princes Highway in West Wollongong is the best illustration of his approach. Arkell had helped the club during its formative years in the mid-1980s and was a regular visitor in the late 1980s and early 1990s. For the Hellenic Club, like many such clubs, Arkell was a financial supporter, too, using his extensive wealth to buy raffle tickets and participate in fundraising activities. When the club approached the council in 1984 about its desire to build on land between the clubhouse and Byarong Creek at the rear of the property, it was disappointed to learn that development was not possible owing to the flood risk. Local creeks including Byarong had recently flooded, most notably in February 1984. Arkell suggested an olive grove for this area of the

---

1   Michelle Hoctor, 'Arkell Turned City's Blues to Green, Says Historian', *Illawarra Mercury*, 22 June 2007.
2   *Illawarra Mercury*, 29 June 1985.

property and the club's executive welcomed the idea. Arkell even donated the olive trees to assist with the funding and slowly but surely the trees grew and helped create a small private green oasis on otherwise unused land.[3] The grove still stands today.

Unlike no other Wollongong mayor or major state politician before him, Arkell welcomed the new University of Wollongong and became one of its most prominent advocates. The early development of the university was closely linked to the workforce and research needs of the major industries, but it was still something new for the region to have its own provider of advanced education. The University of Wollongong emerged as a proposal from Wollongong City Council in 1959 and, by 1962, the Wollongong University College had been established. Arkell took office as lord mayor in 1974, so the University of Wollongong, with its first year as a fully autonomous institution in 1975, paralleled Arkell's long reign as mayor and grew substantially during his tenure. The new university could not have found a more committed advocate but it was not just advocacy that Arkell provided. He became chair of the Friends of the University in 1981 and was made an honorary fellow in 1985. The whole precinct, which included the new university campus along the northern side of Northfields Avenue and the Wollongong Botanic Garden along a portion of the southern side, was of great interest to Arkell. He devoted his time to its effective development, including ensuring that the historical Gleniffer Brae homestead, on a site overlooking the growing campus, was preserved and a large part of its grounds was incorporated into the Botanic Garden.[4]

Delving more deeply into Wollongong's civic and municipal history indicates that Arkell was not the sole or even the original advocate for a post-industrial Wollongong. This point comes across most strongly in the memories and experiences of a political contemporary to Arkell, Harold Hanson. Hanson was a Wollongong solicitor who worked with other businessmen in Ward 3, based on the Wollongong CBD, to tackle what he saw as the city's drab cultural image and the overreliance on BHP and related industries for its economic health. Starting in 1968, Hanson brought together a team of like-minded men to stand in Ward 3 as independents. What prompted action was the leadership of Tony Bevan, who was mayor from 1965 to 1968. While there was no mention of any concern about

---

3   Interview with Andrew Anthony, 22 October 2022.
4   'History of Gleniffer Brae', [Online], University of Wollongong, documents.uow.edu.au/content/groups/public/@webdev/@webserv/documents/doc/uow129339.pdf.

Bevan's reputation or private behaviour, for many, he was not the kind of committed and visionary mayor who would lead Wollongong into the 1970s. Bevan's term as mayor was unremarkable. It is difficult to discern any initiative, key idea or proposal that was advanced or implemented in those three years. In hindsight, it seems clear that Bevan's energy and his mind were elsewhere.

After the work of Hanson and others to pull together a new Ward 3 independent ticket, they were successful in the 1968 elections. In the 1971 council elections, Tony Bevan was not returned. The Ward 3 independent team was again successful at the 1974 council elections: Hanson was returned along with two other members of the independent ticket. The independents now controlled council numbers and, according to Hanson, there was a close vote among them as to who would stand as lord mayor. Arkell had been on the council since 1965 and naturally gravitated towards the new independents. Arkell's self-confidence and flair meant that he saw himself, and not Hanson, as the natural leader of the independents. Hanson had articulated a series of policy positions that were very close to Arkell's subsequent approach, as revealed during Arkell's tenure as lord mayor from 1974 to 1991.[5]

The Harold Hanson story is important because what initially looks like Arkell pushing a unique and distinctive agenda becomes Arkell taking up one that had been articulated by others. There is no denying that Arkell offered a unique, highly individualised and committed new agenda for Wollongong, but it was not one of his own making.

It was not just Hanson either. Labor alderman John Parker's term as Wollongong mayor from 1971 to 1974 was challenged by rapidly rising inflation and consequent increase in costs for the council. In September 1973 Australia's annual consumer price index was almost 10 per cent and it would continue rising—as high as 17 per cent—until early 1975.[6] Nonetheless, Parker spoke of ambitious plans for a revitalisation of the city centre and the city's cultural infrastructure. Speaking to journalist Terry Moore from the local WIN4 television station in August 1973, Parker mentioned city centre development that needed a:

---

5   Notes of an interview with Harold Hanson, 3 April 2023; Terry Moore, 'Interview with Alderman Harold Hanson', *WIN4 News*, 5 August 1973, Archives Online, University of Wollongong, archivesonline. uow.edu.au/nodes/view/3558.
6   Andrew Glassock, *70 Years of Inflation in Australia*, [Online] (Canberra: Australian Bureau of Statistics, 2018), www.abs.gov.au/statistics/research/70-years-inflation-australia.

'total plan' and noted that the council was: 'considering cultural requirements of the city now ... The city of Wollongong is in need of these amenities ... There is an outstanding need for a cultural centre, a youth centre, and an art gallery'.[7]

Labor and independent aldermen were developing proposals to widen Wollongong's economic base and improve its cultural infrastructure from the late 1960s. But what Arkell brought to these pre-existing proposals was the single-minded determination, distinctive public persona and appetite for media coverage and community engagement that eventually enabled him to craft his 'Mr Wollongong' image. In the shadow of Arkell's energy and determination, the contribution of others is easily lost. Looking back on the 1970s, especially after his election as lord mayor in September 1974, it is clear Arkell made these issues his own, at least in the public mind. This first serious effort to lead an economic and cultural transition out of the challenges of the 1970s recession and inflationary shock was an important context for another, even more challenging economic downturn in the early 1980s. Once again, the national economy struggled as growth declined and unemployment increased, but this time Wollongong's single largest employer, the BHP-owned steelworks at Port Kembla, decided to sack half its workforce.

Diversifying the city's labour market

By the late 1970s, the BHP steelworks and the BHP-owned coalmines employed 22,000 people and dominated the Wollongong labour market. It was a highly vulnerable, narrowly based regional economy. The BHP workforce at Port Kembla would decline from 20,305 in 1981 to 7,700 by 1993. Likewise, the region's coal mining workforce dropped from 5,720 in 1981 to 2,953 by 1991.[8]

The recession of the early 1980s had a major impact on Wollongong's labour market. The steelworks and many of its associated entities and downstream customers had grown to such an extent that Wollongong's economy was

---

7   Steve O'Ferrell and Terry Moore, 'Interview with Mayor John Parker—Mayor 1972 and 1973', *WIN4 TV*, 5 August 1973, Archives Online, University of Wollongong, archivesonline.uow.edu.au/nodes/view/3736.
8   John Wilkinson, *The Illawarra: An Economic Profile*, e-brief 18/2011, December (Sydney: NSW Parliamentary Library Research Service, 2011), www.parliament.nsw.gov.au/researchpapers/Documents/the-illawarra-an-economic-profile/Illawarra%20Region%20An%20Economic%20Profile%20GG2.pdf.

highly exposed to any downturn in the industrial and mining sectors. And that is exactly what this recession brought to the region. In May 1982, BHP announced that 2,500 jobs would be cut at the steelworks. The Liberal–National Coalition government under Prime Minister Malcolm Fraser was less than sympathetic to BHP and refused to provide tariff protection on imported steel, which BHP claimed was undermining its domestic market. But Fraser lost the March 1983 election to Labor's Bob Hawke, and the new federal government under Minister for Industry John Button proceeded to introduce the Steel Industry Assistance Plan. The plan was negotiated between the government, BHP and the relevant industrial unions. In return for investing at least $800 million in plant upgrades, BHP would receive a tariff on imported steel and unions would commit to wage restraint and productivity increases.

It is hard to discern whether Arkell as lord mayor had any impact on the federal government's plans for Wollongong. In an interview with the *Bulletin* magazine in April 1984, Arkell claimed he had seen the problem coming: 'We recognised the problems 18 months ago. We saw this coming and we set out to do something about it.' In that interview, he counted lobbying for the Steel Industry Assistance Plan and new investment more generally as his major responses to the BHP job losses.[9]

'Wonderful, wonderful Wollongong' was the distinctive catchphrase that Arkell made his own in the 1970s. From this vantage point, 50 years later, the power and significance of this catchphrase are not so easily discernible. In the 1950s and 1960s, Wollongong had developed a reputation as a rough industrial city without culture or aesthetic beauty. Its national image came to be dominated by industry: the coke ovens spewing volumes of steam, the newly built inner harbour that tamed the wetlands of Tom Thumbs Lagoon, the hot strip mill opened by Prime Minister Robert Menzies in 1955 and the view south from Bulli Pass and even more so from Mount Keira, dominated by Port Kembla's industrial skyline, the BHP steelworks and the Electrolytic Refining and Smelting Company stack. These were the dominant visual symbols in newspapers, postcards, newsreel footage and later in TV reports, and appeared to represent the new postwar Wollongong. The clarion call of the title music of the *BHP Report*, a public relations TV slot produced by BHP itself, which ran in the five minutes before the local TV news, was the final, and perhaps most sophisticated, purveyor of this ethos of industrial Wollongong.

---

9   David Armstrong, 'A Steel City Sings the Blues', *Bulletin*, [Sydney], 19 April 1983: 27–29.

This environment of rapid industrial and population growth was characterised by a hard-headed, utilitarian approach to Wollongong's development, focusing mainly on industry and infrastructure needs. It was in this context that Arkell's exhortation to celebrate the city and admire its beauty and achievements was a step beyond the world of new industry, new roads and new bridges. He sought loyalty and commitment to place and, in the 1970s, this was a departure from the norm. Amid these national perceptions of Wollongong as an industrial powerhouse, Arkell helped outsiders and locals alike rediscover the beauty of its beaches, its waterways and the Illawarra Escarpment.

In some ways this can be seen as a return to an older vision of Wollongong and not necessarily one of a possible post-industrial future. Wollongong and its northern suburbs, including Austinmer and Thirroul, had a history of catering to Sydney travellers, especially from the late 1880s once the railway line to the Illawarra was completed and, later still, as the road between Sydney and Wollongong gradually improved. Day-trippers on the trains and, after World War I, in motor cars travelled from Sydney to Austinmer, Thirroul and Wollongong, often stopping at the guesthouses there or the garage and café at Sublime Point. One of Thirroul's most famous visitors, who stayed for three months in 1922, was the English novelist D.H. Lawrence and his wife, Frida. Lawrence would complete his Australian novel, *Kangaroo*, during this time. Local historian Arthur Cousins chose the title 'Garden of New South Wales' for his history of the Illawarra region published in 1948: 'The name "Garden" was given,' Cousins explained, 'when some of that rich land had been cleared of its abundantly rich vegetation and turned into fields and meadows in the midst of gloriously beautiful surroundings.'[10] Clearly, the patterns of leisure travel and areas deemed beautiful and worthy of visiting had been established, but these were overwhelmed physically and culturally by the sheer scale of the industrial development that occurred, especially after 1945. Arkell's view of the beauty of the region reactivated some of these older representations but also took on a particular twentieth-century understanding of the desirability and inevitability of progress. Frank Arkell's Wollongong would be beautiful, but it would also be bold, modern and prosperous.

---

10   Arthur Cousins, *The Garden of New South Wales: A History of the Illawarra and Shoalhaven* [First published NSW: Producers' Co-operative Distributing Society Limited, 1948] (Wollongong: Illawarra Historical Society, 1994), 7.

The importance of Wollongong's central business district

In Arkell's vision for a new Wollongong, the CBD played a particularly important role: 'We are trying to establish the central business district in Wollongong as the centre of the city—the capital of the Illawarra region and the service centre for the whole southern part of NSW.'[11] Many of his most ambitious plans focused on the CBD and Crown Street, not Greater Wollongong, which was a complex mix of older villages, new suburbs, the commercial hub of the CBD and the industrial centre of Port Kembla. Crown Street was the heart of the city—a long wide street that ran from the hilly areas near the Wollongong Hospital, past the Wollongong Railway Station to the intersection of Keira Street. Crown Street then took a dog-leg turn and proceeded almost due east towards the sea, finishing at 'City Beach' or, officially, Wollongong Beach (Plate 7.1). The fate of Wollongong's main street shopping centre, most of which was on or near Crown Street, was a major concern. Wollongong Council engaged consultants to make recommendations and Arkell assiduously sought private investors to plan, finance and run new retail developments in the Crown Street area. The council's most important and, in many ways, the most controversial move was the creation of a pedestrian mall along Crown Street between Keira and Kembla streets—something that had Arkell's wholehearted support.

In advocating for major commercial and retail development in the CBD, Arkell courted big developers. Kern Corporation financed and operated the Crown Street Gateway Mall and the council became a joint partner in the management of the site. The Crown Gateway development on the southern side of Crown Street led to the loss of parkland, including the much-loved Rest Park. This small park was established in 1935 and included the Country Women's Association Rest Rooms and significant local memorials: to the 1902 Mount Kembla coal mining disaster; to Stephen Best, who was the first secretary of the South Coast Trades and Labour Council; and to Trooper Frank Andrews, a young Wollongong resident who died in the Anglo-Boer War in South Africa.[12] Only a narrow lane remains with the site now occupied by a large retail development.

---

11 Frank Arkell cited in 'Wollongong: It's a Natural Choice for Manufacturers—NSW: The Premier State', [Supplement], *Sydney Morning Herald*, 27 March 1987: 10.
12 Carol Herben, 'Timeless Wollongong: Little Shopping Lane Once An Attractive Park', *Illawarra Museum*, [Online], 20 August 2012, illawarramuseum.wordpress.com/category/wollongong-rest-park/.

7. 'WONDERFUL, WONDERFUL WOLLONGONG'?

Plate 7.1 The lower end of Crown Street, Wollongong, looking east towards City Beach (officially, Wollongong Beach), 30 July 1981
Photo: *Illawarra Mercury* Image Collection and Wollongong City Library, Image no. P27844.

On the tourism front, Arkell encouraged and welcomed what he called 'international-quality' hotels and he was particularly pleased with the North Beach International development. As part of his major push to sell Wollongong to the rest of Australia, and indeed the world, Arkell hoped that tourism infrastructure including hotels and conference centres would be upgraded to attract more visitors to the region. The Illawarra was rebranded the 'Leisure Coast' to emphasise its tourism potential. By 1989 Arkell was boasting that inbound tourist numbers would rapidly increase as the regional advocacy group the Leisure Coast Tourist Association worked with industry groups and invited their representatives to tour the region. Arkell was the usual guest speaker at these events at which he attempted to sell the city and its virtues. In 1988 the heading on the whiteboard in the mayoral office in the new council building boldly proclaimed: 'Selling Wollongong to the World.'[13]

---

13   Frank Arkell, 'Inbound Tourism Increase', Media release, 29 May 1989, Wollongong City Library.

This view of Wollongong's future was strongly contested. Nick Southal from the local Unemployed Workers' Movement found the 'Leisure Coast' label highly insensitive and inappropriate in an environment of widespread unemployment. Trenchant Arkell critic Paul Matters, from the SCTLC, scoffed at the focus on tourism industry jobs. For him, the Leisure Coast meant 'more people visiting here to have a good time while more of the people living here are having a harder time'.[14] Labor member for Kiama Bill Knott had criticised Arkell in parliament for 'selling people a dream'. Could tourism and major retail and commercial developments really replace the thousands of industrial and coal mining jobs that had been lost in the early 1980s? Beneath the confident predictions of a bright future were the everyday realities of finding gainful employment. In late 1982 when the North Beach International advertised for new workers, 1,000 people expressed interest in the 60 new positions on offer.[15]

By 1987, the gloss of the development boom was wearing thin. A severe global recession and exorbitant interest rates precipitated a stock market crash in October of that year. Thousands of investors including retirees and retail investors lost money. Local retirees joined the other groups, including trade unionists and representatives of the unemployed and Wollongong youth, in questioning the wisdom of big projects and development at any cost. The dream of external investors building world-class retail and commercial developments in Wollongong to replace the jobs lost in the steelworks and the coal mines was beginning to unravel.

It was not only through private investment that Arkell hoped to rejuvenate Wollongong. In his first speech to the NSW Parliament, he complained about the lack of publicly funded transport, saying: 'Wollongong must be the largest city in Australia without a publicly funded transport service.' He noted rather pointedly: 'We in Wollongong subsidize people in Sydney and Newcastle who take trips on public transport.' Arkell welcomed the electrification of the Illawarra rail line (also known as the South Coast line) from Waterfall (at the southern edge of suburban Sydney) to Port Kembla, which was announced by the NSW Labor government just before the 1984 election. However, this service, Arkell argued, had to be connected to a fully

---

14 Paul Matters cited in Cordell et al., 'Labor's Lost Heartland'.
15 Alan Yates, 'Thank Goodness It Couldn't Happen Here', *Canberra Times*, 20 November 1982: 13.

integrated transport system including a new bus network. Even the new rail service was a subject of concern because of overcrowding and constant issues with trains running late.[16]

Plate 7.2 The Wollongong City Council administration building, completed in 1988, photographed in 2008

Note: The lord mayor's suite is on the tenth floor.

Photo: Groggon deYobbo, Wikipedia Commons, en.m.wikipedia.org/wiki/File:Wollongong _City_Council_Admin_Building.JPG.

---

16 Frank Arkell's electoral office summary, 1988–89, Wollongong City Library; Frank Arkell, 'Arkell Demands New Realistic Train Timetables', Media release, 20 June 1989, Wollongong City Library.

POLITICS, PRIDE AND PERVERSION

Plate 7.3 Frank Arkell delivers a speech at the official opening of the Illawarra Performing Arts Centre, 30 January 1988, while Princess Diana looks on and Prince Charles takes notes

Photo: From the collections of the Wollongong City Libraries and the Illawarra Historical Society.

Other major publicly funded projects in and around the CBD included a new council administrative building, a new Commonwealth office block and the Illawarra Performing Arts Centre—all completed by 1988. The Performing Arts Centre was officially opened in late January by Princess Diana and Prince Charles, with the royal guests officially welcomed to Wollongong by Premier Unsworth and Lord Mayor Arkell, replete in his mayoral regalia.[17] In 1988 Arkell was channelling that decade's zeitgeist as he hosted royalty and, later that year, chaired a sold-out business breakfast at the North Beach International. The guest speaker at the breakfast was none other than Alan Bond, who began the 1980s as Australia's America's Cup hero and an increasingly successful business tycoon but was bankrupt by 1992 and in prison for corporate fraud by 1997.[18]

For all its widespread impact on the region and its residents, the 1987 recession did not seem to dent Arkell's confidence even though it financially wounded many of his constituents. There was no change to his approach or modification of his language. Arkell appeared unaffected, even unmoved, by it all. The same could not be said of Arkell's white knight investor Kern Corporation Limited. The Queensland-based property development company, which had built and then co-managed Crown Central with Wollongong Council, went into receivership in September 1991, owing more than $800 million to the Commonwealth Bank.[19]

---

17   'Prince Charles and Princess Diana in the Illawarra, 1988', *WIN Television*, NFSA ID 590255, National Film and Sound Archive, Canberra, www.nfsa.gov.au/collection/curated/prince-charles-and-princess-diana-illawarra-1988. In a side note on the royal visit, Indigenous protestors and their supporters controversially attempted to interrupt Prince Charles's speech by calling for land rights and waving Aboriginal flags. See 'Prince Unfazed by Protestors', *Canberra Times*, 31 January 1988: 1.
18   Sue Neales and Sheryle Bagwell, 'The Nine Lives of Alan Bond', *Australian Financial Review*, 15 September 1989: 12.
19   'Court Orders Wind-Up of Kern Corp Over $65,000', *Sunday Age*, [Melbourne], 13 December 1991: 23.

Plate 7.4 A public relations event celebrating the commercial partnership between Grace Bros, Kern Corporation and Wollongong City Council, 15 October 1984

Note: From left: Grace Bros chairman Michael Grace, Lord Mayor Frank Arkell and Kern Corporation managing director Barry Paul. By 1991, the Kern Corporation had collapsed and Barry Paul had filed for bankruptcy.

Photo: *Illawarra Mercury* Image Collection and Wollongong City Library, Image no. P38987.

Arkell's focus on the Wollongong CBD was an apparent paradox for a man who represented Ward 5, which included many of the older farming centres of Dapto, Unanderra and Figtree but not the city centre. He did not show any bias towards Ward 5 and his view of the older farming towns and farmers looks curiously unsentimental. In 1974 Arkell told journalist Paul Bongiorno:

> I get worried about the people who are running farms in the outlying areas and they are being priced off their farms and they want to run a farm as a farm and in time these people will go of course. But in the meantime these people are being badly treated in that their rates are fairly high.

While concerned about their rates, Arkell's vision simply did not include farmers in the future of the city or the greater Wollongong region.[20] Like the O'Donnells before him, he transcended his rural origins and sought to monetise the landholdings that were once central to the farming economy. As a director of multiple family companies that purchased, rezoned, subdivided and then sold rural land, he apparently saw farmers as an inevitable casualty of the quest for growth and profit.

Unemployment peaked at 15 per cent and rates of youth unemployment were much higher. Arkell was never good at showing compassion for the unemployed and was subject to criticism on that front, but he was an ideal leader to face the uncertain economic times and widespread unemployment that the early 1980s brought to Wollongong. Nonetheless, in Arkell, Wollongong had an irrepressible figurehead who relentlessly talked up the city and its prospects. Arkell's public statements about economic adjustment and regional development never showed any great insight or understanding of the complex relationships between the global and national economies, public policy and regional prosperity but he understood one thing very clearly: perceptions were central to business confidence and investment decisions. He talked up the city, its economy and its people without fail while never engaging in the more substantive end of regional development policy. Arkell was a dogged entrepreneurial booster and shrewd publicist, who gave the people of Wollongong cause for hope amid a severe recession. No regional city mayor could have turned around the patterns of the global and national economies, but at least Arkell provided hope for a better future.

---

20   Bongiorno, 'Interview with Lord Mayor Frank Arkell'.

Frank Arkell was a Wollongong patriot to the bitter end. Walking slowly, almost shuffling, to his committal hearing to face charges of child sexual abuse at Wollongong Court House in February 1998—the final act of his life not too far away—he was mostly silent as the waiting media fired questions his way. But he did answer one question: 'How are you feeling today, sir?' 'Very well thank you,' he replied, 'I'm in Wollongong.'[21]

If we were asked to think of a nickname for Wollongong's number one citizen, a man who was lord mayor for 17 years and state member for seven, 'W1' might be appropriate. But in an astonishing turn, this anonymising coded signifier was coined for a different part of Arkell's life—not the public life of the statesman and energetic city booster, but a secret life submerged beneath the surface of civic commitment and regional enthusiasm. In the late 1990s, 'W1' would enter the public consciousness as a codename not for Wollongong's number one citizen but for the city's most controversial figure yet—a man with a secret the nature of which divides locals to this day.

---

21   'Raw Footage from Wollongong Court House', *ABC News*, 9 February 1998, ID: T352758, ABC Archives, Sydney.

8

'Commander Hook' and the Wollongong paedophile network

Tony Bevan is a central figure in the Frank Arkell story. A real estate agent, developer, alderman and former mayor of Wollongong, Tony Bevan was a man whose life paralleled Arkell's in many ways. We have already seen how Bevan's move into local government in 1961, his term as Wollongong mayor from 1965 to 1968 and his attempt to win the state seat of Wollongong as an independent in 1968 were a template of sorts for Arkell's subsequent actions. From the 1960s, Bevan and Arkell (as well as Wollongong alderman Rube Hargrave) followed a similar path from success in local government to attempts to run in state seats as independents. Tony Bevan established and ran a notorious Wollongong-based paedophile network over many decades and there were allegations that Arkell was involved. To gain an accurate understanding of whether or not Frank Arkell was involved it is crucial to provide background on this network. So, this biography of Frank Arkell takes a detour into the life of Tony Bevan before returning to Arkell in subsequent chapters.

Bevan liked to use nicknames for himself and those in his network. At some point in his long history of grooming and predatory behaviour, he adopted the nicknames of 'Commander Hook', 'Hook' and sometimes 'Mother'. Boys were invariably referred to as 'girls' and given the pronoun 'she'. Commander Hook organised the Wollongong paedophile ring and, as we shall see, he started this kind of behaviour as early as 1958. Even in the dry prose of the 1997 Wood Royal Commission report, Tony Bevan was characterised as 'an evil man', so let us assess the nature of these claims and whether there is substance to them.[1]

'Hook' and 'Captain Hook' are common nicknames for paedophiles, sometimes adopted by paedophiles themselves and sometimes a characterisation used to describe them by police or prosecutors. Once he had fallen out with Arkell over Gleniffer Brae in 1978, as detailed in previous chapters, Bevan called Arkell 'Farkless Arkless' or 'Her Majesty'. 'Hook' and 'Mother' come from J.M. Barrie's children's book *Peter Pan*, in which the 'Lost Boys' are controlled and bullied by Captain Hook, who is also called 'Mother' at times in the text and referred to as 'she'. Some literary critics have suggested that the book has a paedophilic undertone while others have rejected this interpretation.[2] Regardless, there is little doubt that child sex offenders use this much-loved children's book for their own purposes. Bevan's nicknames fitted into, and showed an awareness of, a wider network of paedophile activity and self-identification. Bevan's own nicknames aptly described his role in bullying, controlling and abusing the lost boys of Sydney and Wollongong.

The full extent of Bevan's activities supplying trafficked boys from Wollongong, Sydney and further afield, and subsequently making them available to men who participated in the paedophile network, was revealed through evidence tendered to the Wood Royal Commission. In May 1996 numerous witnesses appearing before the commission detailed the operations of the group and the final report included a section on the Wollongong-based network. The royal commission's focus took its cue from groundbreaking investigative journalism conducted by the *Illawarra Mercury* in 1995. Before that, Tony Bevan was well known throughout Wollongong as an avuncular but sharp businessman who devoted much of his spare time to setting up and running a volunteer shark patrol and sea rescue service from a small airstrip at Windang, just south of Port Kembla. Except for those with personal experience of the paedophile network, Tony Bevan was publicly known as a civic-minded volunteer who had contributed much to the region and the safety of the public who used its beaches and waterways. So, who was Tony Bevan and to what extent did his life and his illicit activities cross paths with Frank Arkell?

---

1   J.R.T. Wood, *Royal Commission into the NSW Police Service. Final Report. Volume IV: The Paedophile Inquiry* (Sydney: NSW Government, 1997), www.opengov.nsw.gov.au/publications/17129;jsessionid=152 611E7FD89AE98D77ADD531D7484DE, [hereinafter Royal Commission, Vol. IV], especially 758–66.
2   Andrew Birkin, *J.M. Barrie and the Lost Boys: The Real Story behind Peter Pan* (New Haven: Yale University Press, 2003).

Tony Bevan and his background

Anthony Frank Bevan, or Tony as he was widely known, was a Wollongong real estate agent, developer and Wollongong Council alderman from 1961 until 1968. Bevan was born in Wollongong on 3 May 1933 and educated at the Christian Brothers High School on Crown Lane, a short walk from his father's office at Frank Bevan's Real Estate in Crown Street, Wollongong. After his father's death in 1960, Tony sold the family business, in 1966, and later managed a series of property developments and other small businesses in the city.

Tony's parents, Frank 'Butts' Bevan and Jessie Jean Adelia Wright, were members of the comfortable Wollongong middle class. Frank Bevan was born on 20 September 1897 in Wollongong, served in World War I with the 55th Battalion and married Jessie in 1924. Jessie was from Cargo in New South Wales and was born in 1904. Jessie and Frank had three children: two boys, Tony and John, and a girl, Ruth. John and Ruth were eight and seven years older than Tony, respectively. The Bevans lived in an impressive brick home on Edwards Street in Smiths Hill, an attractive elevated location to the north of the Wollongong CBD and not far from the harbour and beaches.

Frank built on the work of his father, Frank Bevan Sr (1864–1927), who was a building contractor and then a real estate agent and auctioneer in Wollongong from 1885.[3] After his father's death, Frank Junior, along with his brother Bob, consolidated the family's real estate and auctioneering business into a formidable regional empire. The firm had offices in Crown Street, Wollongong, and branch offices in Corrimal and Warrawong. One of Frank Junior's main competitors in Wollongong was the auction house O'Donnell & Stumbles, so competition between the Bevan and O'Donnell/Arkell families was decades old. This direct rivalry only ended in 1925 with the untimely death of Michael Alfred O'Donnell, who was one of the principals of O'Donnell & Stumbles. In the early 1950s, Frank Junior was beginning to enjoy the fruits of his labour. In 1953, he and Jessie departed on an extensive tour of the United Kingdom.

Frank Senior had also been an alderman on Wollongong Council and was mayor in 1902 at the time of the tragic Mount Kembla mine disaster, which killed 96 men and boys and had a profound effect on the entire

---

3   'The Late Mr Frank Bevan', *Illawarra Mercury*, 15 July 1927: 9.

region. Frank Senior's career in local government is another parallel with the O'Donnell/Arkell family history and that of the inimitable Frank O'Donnell, the great uncle who appeared to have such an influence on the young Frank Arkell. So, another similarity was that both Tony Bevan and Frank Arkell had well-known and highly regarded predecessors who served as aldermen and mayors on the Wollongong Council and the Central Illawarra Council, respectively.

Tony Bevan's father, Frank Junior, was a physically capable, tough man who loved surf lifesaving, billiards and rugby union. The origin of the nickname 'Butts' is not known but it was used often, even in newspaper reports. Frank Bevan was a distinctive presence at auctions, wearing a well-tailored suit, a bow tie and a hat. In the late 1950s, he drove a company car, a late-model Holden. By then his health was still robust for a man in his early sixties although he had a persistent rasping cough, the result of being gassed in World War I, but he was also a heavy smoker. He often said he had been a heavy smoker since he was a child.[4]

Frank Bevan was a proud man who had survived the war and built a successful business empire but something in his family or business life was causing him great emotional turmoil. It was a normal working day, 4 August 1960, when Frank left home in Smiths Hill just after breakfast and drove to the Woronora Cemetery, in the southern suburbs of Sydney not far from Sutherland, where he paid his respects to a deceased relative. The cemetery was about an hour's drive from Wollongong north along the Princes Highway and it is quite common for Wollongong people to have relatives buried or interred at Woronora. My maternal grandmother is interred there. Family members later gave evidence to say that this was a usual morning for Bevan. There was nothing different or unusual in his behaviour that would have led them to believe there was a problem.

On the way home to Wollongong, Frank stopped at Sublime Point, a vantage point on top of the Illawarra Escarpment above Austinmer overlooking the coastline 400 metres below. It is not clear exactly what happened next. There were no witnesses, but Bevan's body was found at the base of the lookout. His back was broken from the fall. His coat was still draped over his left arm. His gold watch, undamaged, kept ticking away until the spring unwound. His car had been left unlocked in the lookout carpark.

---

4   'Inquest held at the Court House, Bulli on 15 September 1960 on the cause of death of Arthur Frank Bevan', AF00288285, State Records NSW, Sydney.

The owner of the Sublime Point kiosk noticed the car had been left in the carpark overnight and found the keys in the ignition, handing them to the police the next day. A police constable searching the lookout area found Bevan's body shortly thereafter. He had fallen some 75 metres to his death.[5]

The coroner returned an open verdict. There were no signs of foul play, but it was not clear whether this was suicide. There was no note. The government medical examiner from Bulli reported scratches and abrasions on Bevan's hands and fingernails. There was a suggestion that this could have been a sign of an attempt to save himself. Counsel for the family encouraged the coroner to deliver a finding of accidental death. The coroner concluded that, while 'the possibility of suicide cannot be disregarded, the evidence adduced does not enable me to say conclusively, that the deceased took his own life'. The coroner believed that the more likely explanation was that Frank had met his death 'purely and simply by accident but the evidence before me does not enable me to say that this was the manner of his death'.

What could have driven a successful businessman who had survived the Great War and the rough and tumble of commercial life in Wollongong real estate to end his life? Or even to take the unnecessary risk of standing on a cliff edge? By 1958, as I shall demonstrate, Frank's son Tony had already perfected his modus operandi as a paedophile. If we look at what Tony was doing in the 1950s, we can gain a clearer picture of a possible reason for his father's suicide or at least for his unnecessary risk-taking behaviour on the precipitous heights of the Illawarra Escarpment.

Tony Bevan was an ordinary student rarely mentioned at the Christian Brothers prize nights with the exception, as we have seen, of that one occasion in 1941 when his participation in a debate on 'Should School Be Abolished?' caused so much mirth among the assembled crowd of parents. By 1953 Bevan was in his early twenties and learning to fly an aeroplane. He had purchased a second-hand Aeronca Chief, a US-built plane that dated from the late 1940s. However, he later said he 'got fed up with flying about for no reason'. He found the hours spent in the cockpit going about in circles frustrating. It was 'like going around and around a lake in a motorboat'. Operating out of a small airstrip at Windang, Tony began flying over the beaches in the Wollongong area trying to warn swimmers and surfers if he saw a shark off the break. The initial warning system—throwing a roll of toilet paper out the cockpit window—was soon replaced

---

5   This information is based on ibid.

with a two-way radio in the plane with radio sets at North Wollongong Beach and at the family home in Edwards Street. From the plane, he could contact North Wollongong Surf Lifesaving Club (where his father was a founding member) or his mother at home. Jessie Bevan would take Tony's calls from the plane if a shark was sighted off one of the beaches with which he could not communicate and would telephone the lifeguards directly.[6]

In 1956 the surf lifesaving clubs formalised this arrangement and the volunteer service began to grow with more pilots and more equipment. Two army surplus jeeps, painted a distinctive red, were purchased and outfitted with two-way radios. The aerial patrol began to watch over Wollongong beaches during the summer months and received funding from the Surf Life Saving Association and Wollongong Council.

By 1958 Tony Bevan had established his method of grooming teenage boys. It is difficult to define the exact date, but we can put together accumulated pieces of evidence and paint a picture that accords with the facts and aligns with what we know more definitely about how he was operating later. In 1957 Bevan purchased a new plane for £1,500, a Cessna 150, reportedly one of the first such Cessnas to arrive in Australia. It was a two-seater—something that was crucial for Bevan's ultimate plan for the plane. The Wood Royal Commission established that Bevan used the plane and the volunteer airbase at Windang as a venue to recruit and groom boys. This was a private location and Bevan could offer inducements that would have been compelling to any teenage boy: a flight in the Cessna soaring high above the spectacular Illawarra coastline was an offer too difficult to refuse.

We know that Bevan was indulging in this form of grooming as early as 1958 because in that year tragedy struck. On closer examination, the details of this event are revealing. On 12 April 1958, Bevan's Cessna crashed into the ocean. Onboard was a 17-year-old passenger, Noel Webster. Rescue craft raced to the ditched Cessna, just off Windang Beach near the mouth of Lake Illawarra, with water swamping the plane and the cockpit steadily filling with water. Both Bevan and Webster were pulled out of the fuselage alive but unconscious and transported to Wollongong Hospital. Webster never regained consciousness and died three days later. Bevan spent three weeks in hospital and finally recovered his health.

6 'Shark Patrol', *Australian Women's Weekly*, 25 October 1961: 7.

8. 'COMMANDER HOOK' AND THE WOLLONGONG PAEDOPHILE NETWORK

Noel Webster was not the last boy to fly with Bevan. We know from later evidence to the royal commission that holding the joystick and steering the plane were indulgences that Bevan offered the boys to gain their trust and establish an obligation. At the hearing investigating the crash, Bevan said the engine had stalled and he had to make an emergency landing on the water, Bevan had five years' flying experience by this stage so a stall was unexpected. Webster himself may have had control of the aircraft. We have no way of knowing what transpired between Bevan and Webster that day but perhaps there was some misunderstanding between the two? Whatever the case, the crash in 1958 showed Bevan flying with young boys from the Wollongong region, and later evidence would show this was one of his primary methods of grooming.[7]

Less than 18 months later, Frank Bevan Jr was dead. The 1958 plane crash and the actions of his son Tony were possible factors behind Frank stepping onto that rock ledge, his coat over his arm, the growing suburbs and the distant, partly shrouded silhouette of the steelworks swathed in smoke and dust far below him. I am suggesting here that Frank Bevan was in a state of emotional turmoil because his son was a compulsive paedophile.

The parallels between Tony Bevan's and Frank Arkell's lives are already apparent. Both Arkell and Bevan were Christian Brothers Old Boys, both were Catholic, both were single and remained so all their lives, and both were involved in real estate and local government. Both had forebears who had excelled in municipal affairs. Both had fathers who committed suicide (this is true of Arkell's father and at least a possibility in the case of Bevan's). If that is not enough, both served as mayors of Wollongong—Arkell for much longer than Bevan. Like Arkell, Bevan stayed living at home with his widowed mother throughout the 1960s and 1970s. He only moved to his penthouse apartment at Creston in Corrimal Street once it was completed in 1983. The two men had this strange pairing with so much about their lives apparently in common, but they were also at times fierce rivals and competitors. Creston apartments was Wollongong's premier address and its tallest building until a spate of high-rise residential developments in the early 2020s. Creston was completed by 1983 and stands almost 50 metres above the site at 22–26 Corrimal Street. It was a signature Bevan development and his penthouse apartment on the fifteenth floor possessed sweeping views of Wollongong Harbour and the coastline to the north and south.

---

7   'Inquiry into a Plane Crash Near Wollongong, 12 April 1958', State Records NSW, Sydney.

Tony Bevan's paedophile network

It was the Royal Commission into the New South Wales Police Service that turned Tony Bevan's secret paedophile network into a commonly known fact that shocked Wollongong residents and, as we will see, had such a profound impact on Frank Arkell's standing and reputation. The commission was formally established by the *Royal Commission (Police Service) Act*, signed into law by the state governor on 1 November 1994.[8] It had been championed by the independent member for the South Coast, John Hatton, who had built a reputation as an anticorruption campaigner and whose vote was crucial in keeping in power the minority Coalition government under NSW premier John Fahey. A NSW Supreme Court judge and former chairman of the Law Reform Commission, James Roland Wood, was appointed as commissioner, hence the commission is commonly given the short title of Wood Royal Commission.

With support from the Labor opposition, Hatton had moved for the establishment of the royal commission against strong resistance from Fahey's government and from then police commissioner Tony Lauer. The terms of reference covered a wide-ranging probe into the 'nature and extent of corruption within the Police Service, particularly of any entrenched or systemic kind'. Paedophilia was covered in the initial terms of reference, including whether police had been impartial in pursuing convictions and whether existing laws were effective and a sufficient deterrent. After the commission's initial terms of reference were established, the state's Independent Commission Against Corruption (ICAC) and other NSW Police inquiries began a more concerted investigation into alleged paedophile networks. Brothel operator Colin Fisk made allegations, subsequently repeated in parliament by Labor MP Deirdre Grusovin, that high-profile paedophiles were protected by corrupt police and that his evidence revealing such networks in New South Wales was subsequently destroyed by corrupt officers. On 1 December 1994, Grusovin moved in the Legislative Assembly for the extension of the royal commission's terms of reference to include:

> Whether any members of the Police Service have by act or omission protected paedophiles or pederasts from criminal investigation or prosecution and, in particular, the adequacy of any investigations undertaken by the Police Service in relation to paedophiles

---

8 See *Royal Commission (Police Service) Act 1994* (NSW), No. 60, legislation.nsw.gov.au/view/html/repealed/current/act-1994-060.

or pederasts since 1983; however, you may investigate any matters you deem necessary and relevant which may have occurred prior to 1983.[9]

The royal commission had sweeping powers to investigate, gather evidence and compel witnesses to appear before it. It was staffed by investigators from every jurisdiction in Australia except New South Wales. The commission's work began in earnest in 1995 and it delivered its final reports to the NSW Government by August 1997.[10]

We know from the Wood Royal Commission transcripts, the recordings that Bevan kept of his own phone calls and, crucially, from the recollections of the victims themselves that Bevan had a farm in West Dapto that also served as a paedophile 'school'. Paedophiles in this period operated these kinds of informal illegal operations to offer boys sanctuary or work and then slowly acculturate them into sex with each other and sex with older men. Apart from being given shelter and work, the boys in these 'schools' were placed under significant emotional pressure and sometimes physical threats to comply. Along with the intimidation, there were gifts and inducements: clothes, money, a ride on one of the farm motorbikes, a trip in the plane and, later, illegal drugs including marijuana and amyl nitrate.[11]

Bevan had placed in charge of the West Dapto 'school' a young man by the name of Peter Foretic, whom he originally met at Albion Park Airport in 1972. Foretic was a 17-year-old who wanted to learn how to fly and gravitated towards the airport. Ultimately, Foretic traded flying lessons from Bevan for sex with the older man. Speaking under the pseudonym of 'John', Foretic would later tell Brett Martin from the *Illawarra Mercury*: 'It was a mutual thing. We used each other. I wanted to fly and he wanted sex.'[12] By the mid-1970s, there were up to a dozen of 'Tony's Boys' at the farm, typically aged between 12 and 16 years. Some were locals from Dapto or Windang who were offered work on the farm in Bevan's turf-cutting business while others were from Sydney, possibly homeless or otherwise estranged and isolated from family and friends.

---

9   NSW, *Parliamentary Debates*, Legislative Assembly, 1 December 1996, 6118.
10 See J.R.T. Wood, *Royal Commission into the NSW Police Service. Final Report. Volume 1: Corruption* (Sydney: NSW Government, 1997), www.australianpolice.com.au/wp-content/uploads/2017/05/RCPS-Report-Volume-1.pdf.
11 This material is based on Wood, Royal Commission, Vol. IV, especially 758–66.
12 Brett Martin, 'Bevan's Double Life Shocks Former Lover', *Illawarra Mercury*, 9 March 1995: 7.

Plate 8.1 Tony Bevan and 'senior flight crewman' Peter Foretic pictured at the Windang base in 1991
Photo: *Illawarra Mercury* Image Collection and Wollongong City Library, Image no. P22609.

Rather than be discarded once he turned 17 or 18, which was the usual practice, Peter Foretic stayed on. The long-term presence of Foretic in Bevan's life marks Bevan out as different to Arkell. Foretic was both a partner of sorts and a participant in the paedophile network. As Foretic recalled, 'Eventually the relationship grew into something more than just sex.'[13] In all the evidence I have reviewed, I have not found any evidence of Arkell having a long-term relationship. There was no-one of his age, as best I can discern, and no engagement with any boy or young man for anything other than sex, so this is one significant point of difference.

Foretic played the role of intermediary, working with the younger boys. This was a common paedophile strategy to help gain the trust of younger boys, to recruit them into the network and to introduce them to sex. The school was designed to produce boys who were pliant, unlikely to complain to police or parents, familiar with what was expected of them and had some sexual knowledge, ensuring an appropriate experience for Bevan and the other men within the network.[14]

---

13 ibid.
14 Wood, Royal Commission, Vol. IV, 758–66; Interview with Ray Leary, 19 October 2022.

8. 'COMMANDER HOOK' AND THE WOLLONGONG PAEDOPHILE NETWORK

Bevan's paedophile network was a multifaceted operation that drew in professional and middle-class men from Wollongong, boys from Wollongong or Sydney who had been groomed, 'schooled' and passed on for sexual services, and even international visitors who desired sex with boys while staying in Sydney. One local man who was heavily involved in Bevan's network was Thomas Emmins Gaun, engineer and owner of Vernier Engineering, who was well known around Wollongong for his Rolls Royce and penchant for very young male chauffeurs, who would drive him to Costellos nightclub in Kings Cross. Gaun's Roll Royce Silver Shadow had personalised number plates, 'TG106'.[15] Living in an impressive home in Mangerton in Woodlawn Avenue—a street that was very much a dress-circle location in the 1960s and 1970s—Gaun had divorced in 1959 but maintained an active public life as pianist and bandmaster for the Wollongong City Brass Band.[16] Vernier Engineering was very successful, growing to more than 80 employees by the 1970s, building railcars for the local coalmines and undertaking other specialist engineering projects for large clients such as the BHP steelworks. There is evidence from Bevan's secret recordings that at least one other senior member of the Vernier workforce was also involved in the paedophile network. Thomas Gaun did not have the charm or the social skills of the other Wollongong paedophiles and was reliant on Bevan for his access to boys. Gaun's codename at the royal commission was 'W9' and he features heavily in the Wollongong evidence.[17]

Bevan's network extended into Queensland. There were trips to that state by men to search for and have sex with boys who were groomed and trafficked there, or new boys from Queensland would be brought down to Sydney and Wollongong to provide sexual services to men. The network had arrangements with a motel in Sydney for meetings between boys and men. Bevan organised what he called 'Royal Parties', groups of men and boys who travelled from Wollongong to Sydney, usually to Costellos nightclub, where they might meet up with other boys. Bevan was always on the lookout for new boys, whether from Wollongong, Sydney or further afield. He told an unnamed associate in the early 1980s, who was himself bragging about the boys he had met on a recent trip to the Philippines:

---

15   'Evidence of W26, Transcript of Evidence from the Wood Royal Commission, 1997, PR251', in J.R.T. Wood, *Royal Commission into the New South Wales Police Service: Public Hearing Transcripts* (Sydney: Police Integrity Commission, 2011[?]), State Library of NSW [hereinafter Wood, *Transcripts*].
16   Electoral Roll for Wollongong 1977; Transcripts of the Bevan Tapes, No. 47.
17   Wood, Royal Commission, Vol. IV, 758–66.

> There's been a bit about up there [in Sydney]. Not so much around the cruising areas, but generally in the Cross there's been a bit of new stuff all round. Long as you get in early.[18]

The 1997 royal commission revealed these details about Bevan and his activities, following up on the *Illawarra Mercury*'s groundbreaking article on Bevan in 1995.[19] At the royal commission, police documents were read into evidence, including a local intelligence file from Wollongong Police Station that stated that 'he [Bevan] is a well known homo and pederast'.[20] After receiving information from an informant, Senior Sergeant Bill King from the NSW Police Special Branch visited the Wollongong station in 1990 to follow up on Bevan's case. In September 1990 he found that the local intelligence file on Bevan was a summary based on several previous allegations made against him dating from 1982, 1983, 1984 and two more recent allegations from 1988 and 1989.

A few months after Senior Sergeant King's report, in November 1990, there was a further allegation of a 13-year-old boy staying at Bevan's apartment and having photos taken. In total, then, there were six allegations of child sexual abuse against Bevan covering the period of 1982 through 1990. None of these allegations were pursued through to charges or an arrest. In preparing a report for the NSW State Divisional Commander, Senior Sergeant King noted that 'Bevan has a local intelligence file at Wollongong Police station in which a number of allegations of sexual assault against boys have been made'.[21] King wrote a lengthy report and included a chart setting out the relationships between the key players. The documents King consulted indicated that Bevan was a known associate of a witness known to the royal commission as 'W1'. King's full report never reached the divisional commander but his cover note and simple chart did. This was one of many instances in which reports were lost or police inquiries never translated into charges or arrest. Bevan, like the well-connected Catholic clergy in Wollongong, appeared to have considerable support from inside the police force in Wollongong.

When I applied to the NSW Police Service for access to copies of the police documents given to the royal commission, or any other police files on Bevan, I was informed that following an extensive search of their databases,

---

18 Transcripts of the Bevan Tapes, No. 48.
19 Brett Martin, 'Former Mayor Ran Child Sex Ring', *Illawarra Mercury*, 9 March 1995.
20 'Evidence of Bill King, Wood Royal Commission, 1997, PR257', in Wood, *Transcripts*.
21 ibid.

the NSW Police had determined that 'the information is not held by this agency'.[22] Crucially, significant parts of these apparently missing documents, including their unique identifying numbers, were read into evidence at the royal commission so we do still have access to some of the material they contained.

Bevan's network also traded in pornography, including photographs, 8-millimetre film and, later, Betamax tapes, which were produced often by Bevan himself and possibly others at the meetings between boys and men. Sex happened in a variety of locations including upstairs at Costellos nightclub in small cubicles with lockable doors designed expressly for this purpose, at the motel in Sydney or in one of Bevan's many properties in Wollongong, including his Creston penthouse and a flat in East Corrimal. Bevan and some of his network participants also indulged in sex tourism, with the Philippines a favoured destination. On at least three occasions boys from the Philippines were brought to Wollongong for sex with men from the network.[23]

It was a characteristic feature of paedophile activity that organisers kept photographs and/or films to use as leverage or blackmail.[24] These could be used against both the men who participated in the network and the boys who were drawn into it. Often if a boy wanted to leave, he was threatened with the release of highly compromising explicit photographs or film. Contrary to the claims of paedophile advocacy groups like the United Kingdom–based Paedophile Information Exchange, which had some Australian supporters in the late 1970s and early 1980s, there was nothing liberating, consensual or enabling for the boys in any of the Wollongong material.[25] None of this material was 'soft-focus' idyllic pictures of burgeoning boyhood sexuality, as those who support paedophilia often claim; rather it was highly explicit and included boys masturbating, boys having sex with men, having sex with each other and, in some cases, having sex with animals. Photographs and

---

22 '*Government Information (Public Access) Act 2009* (NSW) Notice of Decision', NSW Police Information Review Officer, Personal communication, 30 November 2022.
23 Transcripts of the Bevan Tapes, No. 49.
24 *Organised Criminal Paedophile Activity. A Report by the Parliamentary Joint Committee on the National Crime Authority* (Canberra, Commonwealth of Australia, 1995), www.aph.gov.au/Parliamentary_Business/Committees/Joint/Former_Committees/acc/completed_inquiries/pre1996/ncapedo/report/index, s. 3.46.
25 Julie Bindel, 'Gay Men Need to Talk Straight about Paedophilia', *Guardian*, 4 March 2001. On the Paedophile Information Exchange and the Australia-based paedophile advocacy groups, see Parliamentary Joint Committee on the National Crime Authority, *Organised Criminal Paedophile Activity*, especially Chapter 3.

films included material in which boys were hurt, physically overwhelmed and clearly distressed and upset. There is no evidence that any of the boys were ever asked whether they consented to being filmed or photographed.

This material was as disturbing as you could imagine. It did not speak of a love for boys but of a need to dominate them, humiliate them and use them solely for sexual gratification. Survivors speak of their emotional trauma as well as physical pain and many experienced life-long medical issues from the years of abuse. Bevan's role was not simply that of a network ringleader. Bevan and Arkell were also political rivals and there is evidence that Bevan was blackmailing Arkell to secure favourable business outcomes. As we saw from Chapter 4, in 1982 and 1983, Bevan was also collecting material on Arkell and his alleged corruption to assist the state Labor government to compile Chief Inspector Smiles's corruption report on Wollongong City Council. This was done with the participation of local Labor member for Wollongong Eric Ramsay and a state cabinet minister, Rex Jackson, who subsequently resigned and was charged and convicted on unrelated corruption offences.[26] Bevan even boasted at one point that he might run again for public office, but this time as a Labor Party member.

What this means is that some of the claims against Arkell, especially those after 1978 with a direct connection to Bevan, could have been either manufactured or exaggerated to cast Arkell in a negative light. It was widely known in political and media circles in the Illawarra that Bevan taped many of his conversations to secure incriminating material on his co-conspirators should he need it. At the heart of a bitter disagreement between Bevan and Arkell was the council's move to resume Gleniffer Brae in 1978.[27]

Bevan and Arkell fall out over Gleniffer Brae

In Chapter 3 we noted how Arkell's support for the council's purchase of Gleniffer Brae stymied Bevan's plans for a potentially lucrative sale of the property. Wollongong City Council moved to resume Gleniffer Brae just as Bevan was closing in to purchase the property from the Church of England. Gleniffer Brae was an impressive English Tudor-style house, with associated gardens designed by Paul Sorensen, which was completed in 1939. The house and gardens were commissioned by Arthur and Sidney

---

26 Daniel Moore, 'Jackson Guilty of Bribes Plot', *Sydney Morning Herald*, 29 August 1987: 1.
27 Brett Martin, 'Tapes Shame Former Mayor', *Illawarra Mercury*, 9 March 1995: 1–9.

Hoskins, two brothers who first brought the steelworks from Lithgow to Port Kembla in the 1920s. Arthur and Sidney were the first general managers of Australian Iron & Steel until BHP bought out the company in 1935. Both men stayed on in senior roles until 1949. Arthur Hoskins gifted 19 hectares of land to the south of the house precinct to Wollongong City Council in 1954 to be used for a botanic garden. That same year Gleniffer Brae and some surrounding land were sold to the Sydney Church of England Girls' Grammar School. The private girls' school operated on the site until 1975 when a financial crisis and pressure from the Bank of NSW forced an amalgamation with the Illawarra Grammar School. The house was listed for sale on 12 July 1978, but shortly thereafter the council decided to resume the property.[28] The council's acquisition was complete by September 1978 at a cost of $485,000. It was a controversial move but it had the support of the independents and the Labor aldermen.

Tony Bevan's secret recordings of his phone conversations show that the Gleniffer Brae decision created a significant financial problem for his business. There is some evidence that Bevan lost his deposit on the sale, which had been paid when he exchanged contracts with the Church of England.[29] As Foretic later recalled: 'That cost Tony a lot of money and he never forgave Arkell. He used to go into rages over it and he swore he would get him over it.'[30] Deprived of the profits from the sale and subdivision of Gleniffer Brae, Bevan attempted to secure funding from non-traditional sources, including Asian investment banks, for his other investment projects.[31] The growing rift between Arkell and Bevan did not mean they were openly hostile. Bevan had publicly criticised Arkell in the press in 1980, but they had to keep working together on some issues.[32] For example, Bevan was still trying to secure funding for the aerial patrol and had approached Arkell about getting the matter on the council's agenda. So, their rift was not complete, but Bevan was definitely working behind the scenes against Arkell.[33]

---

28   'History of Gleniffer Brae', [Online], University of Wollongong, 2011, documents.uow.edu.au/content/groups/public/@webdev/@webserv/documents/doc/uow129339.pdf.
29   Interview with Brett Martin, 23 May 2022.
30   Martin, 'Bevan's Double Life Shocks Former Lover'.
31   Transcripts of the Bevan Tapes, No. 7.
32   'Prominent Businessman and Former Alderman Tony Bevan Has Slammed Lord Mayor Frank Arkell', *Illawarra Mercury*, 29 July 1980.
33   Transcripts of the Bevan Tapes, No. 28.

Bevan made one recording, which he dubbed the 'Scorpion Tape', sometime between 1978 and 1982. This tape was both instigated and recorded by Bevan, so presumably 'Scorpion' was a reference to a 'sting' or setup designed to ensnare Arkell. Bevan encouraged an associate to call Arkell and elicit a recorded revelation from Arkell that he was involved in sex with boys under the age of 18. In 1995 Arkell told Brett Martin from the *Illawarra Mercury* that 'Tony Bevan set me up' and 'there is no truth in the tape. If the tape was checked I think you will find it has been tampered with.'[34] It was only many years later that the precise circumstances of the production of the Scorpion Tape were revealed. In February 1998, evidence from Arkell's committal trial, which covered the 29 counts of child sexual abuse with which he had been charged in May 1997, revealed that an associate of Bevan's had entered his Crown Street office and told him he had sex with Arkell the previous evening. Bevan immediately set up a call to Arkell with the man in question and taped the ensuing conversation. Bevan had played this tape to *Illawarra Mercury* editor Peter Cullen and other Wollongong political and business leaders in 1983. To discredit Arkell, he told all and sundry that the male voice on the tape talking to Arkell was 16 years old, but evidence at the 1998 committal trial revealed that the man was 21 at the time.[35] Magistrate Paul Johnson threw out that charge.

We do not know how much Arkell knew about Bevan's moves against him. In 1980 Bevan told the local media that he was very disappointed with Arkell's leadership and was seriously considering running against Arkell in the next lord mayoral election and directing preferences to Labor. So, to that extent, Arkell knew that Bevan was now one of his political critics but did he know that Bevan was working with Labor on the Smiles report? And did Arkell know that Bevan had sources within the council who were helping him gather evidence to feed into Labor's inquiry? These are all important unknown factors, such that it is almost impossible to tell whether the deteriorating relationship between the two men in politics and in business affected Arkell's involvement in Bevan's paedophile network.

Given Bevan's confounding role here, accepting the overall truth that Arkell engaged in abusive relationships with boys and young men does not mean accepting every claim of abuse against him. Bevan's role is a complicating factor. Even more than 30 years after Bevan's death, we cannot let his animus for Arkell shape the record so clearly. Bevan traded in real estate, but he

---

34   Martin, 'Tapes Shame Former Mayor', 7.
35   Guilliat, 'City of Secrets', especially 26.

also brought that cold, calculating eye to the young boys whom he desired. While offending clergy satiated their desires in the vestry or at a youth refuge called Eddy's Place, Bevan ritualised and commercialised the practice of child sexual abuse, partaking in it wholeheartedly, then monetised it by charging the men, filming the activities and distributing the pornography throughout Australia and overseas.

Tony Bevan contracted cancer and died in September 1991 after a short illness. Peter Foretic, the young man who had graduated from being one of 'Tony's Boys' to someone with a permanent presence in Bevan's life, was left to clean out Tony's Crown Street office. Foretic destroyed some of Bevan's secret recordings, especially those that he felt were personally incriminating, but some of the tapes survived. These secret recordings, hereafter increasingly referred to as 'the Bevan Tapes', made their way to journalists working for the *Illawarra Mercury* and eventually to the Wood Royal Commission. Foretic also destroyed much of Tony Bevan's pornography collection.[36]

After 1991, Foretic began a new life working as a telecommunications technician in the western suburbs of Sydney. In his newspaper interview as 'John' in 1995 he had conceded that Tony Bevan had been attracted to young men but disavowed any suggestion of his own participation in, or knowledge of, a paedophile network or other illegal activities. In the following year, Foretic's past caught up with him. In 1996 when investigators from the Wood Royal Commission began examining Bevan's history and interviewing men who as youths had been dragged into the network as one of 'Tony's Boys', Foretic started to worry. On 7 May 1996, a subpoena arrived from the royal commission. This was evidently too much for Foretic. The next day, he bought a length of hose from a service station and drove about two and a half hours to a secluded location in the bush outside the town of Oberon, due west of Sydney. He connected the hose to the exhaust pipe and directed the other end inside the vehicle. He turned on the engine. A few hours later Foretic, aged 41, was found dead inside his vehicle with the royal commission subpoena in his top pocket.[37]

---

36   Martin, 'Bevan's Double Life Shocks Former Lover'.
37   Caroline Overington, 'Public Lives and Private Perversions: They Called Him Mr Wollongong, but the City's Favourite Son was Leading a Double Life', *Sunday Age*, [Melbourne], 5 July 1998: 4; Interview with Brett Martin, 23 November 2022.

9

Public and private: The evidence, the allegations, the charges

The question we ask ourselves now is how did Mr Wollongong become 'W1'? The transformation of Frank Arkell from state member, lord mayor and the city's number-one citizen to a public pariah, a shunned figure and, ultimately, a codenamed person of interest at a royal commission occurred over seven years from 1991. At first, it was a loss of electoral support and public office together with a gradual contraction of his public life, but as allegations of child sexual abuse and paedophilia emerged, revelations about Arkell's secret life began to taint and irrevocably damage his once unassailable public image as Mr Wollongong.

The seeds of Arkell's later decline were sown as early as 1984. One of the first issues with which he had to deal as the newly elected state member for Wollongong was the Wran Labor government's plan to decriminalise homosexuality. Beyond the private world of sex and intimacy there is the legal and political regime that frames our intimate world, defines the boundaries between illicit and illegal and excludes or regulates access to the profane world of sex for money. In the 1970s and 1980s, there was a growing movement for homosexual law reform that sought to harmonise the operation of the law for both heterosexual and homosexual relationships. From 1978, there were several unsuccessful attempts to reform the NSW *Crimes Act 1900* by both Liberal and Labor party members, usually operating without party support. Yet, there was still extensive resistance to law reform in this area from across the political spectrum.

The *Crimes Act 1900* included provisions that defined certain kinds of sexual conduct between consenting males as a crime. Before 1984 these provisions included buggery (s. 79) and attempted buggery (s. 80), committing an act of indecency with another male person (or procuring) (s. 81A), indecent assault on a male (s. 81) and acts of indecency with a male person under 18 (s. 78Q).[1] On the Labor side of politics, it was George Petersen from the seat of Illawarra, just on the southern border of Arkell's seat of Wollongong, who attempted to move amendments to government legislation and later introduced a private member's bill to equalise the operation of the law. In other words, in the NSW Parliament, and in other Australian state parliaments, there was a reformist intent to change the law and address ongoing legal discrimination against individuals in same-sex relationships.

While every parliament was seeking to reform the law and the way it interacted with the private domain of relationships and sexuality, Arkell could hardly avoid having to confront a possible disjuncture between his public self and his private self. Instead of maintaining a low profile or keeping away from the issue altogether, Arkell did the opposite. In 1984 he sponsored a petition to condemn the Wran government for the steps it was taking towards decriminalising homosexuality—a move that is explored in more detail below. A small group of powerful men and their former and current boy targets in Wollongong and Sydney must have realised the hypocrisy of such an action. This is where the lines between public and private become blurred. If Arkell had maintained a private life as a gay man who sought the company of young men without making public pronouncements about conservative social mores and statements stressing the primacy of the traditional family, we may have good reason to hesitate to explore his private world. But he did not do any such thing. In fact, he publicly opposed homosexual law reform, presented himself to the electorate as a social conservative, publicly denied being gay, and made active public and political gestures that sided with conservative Christians, especially the Reverend Fred Nile (member of the NSW Legislative Council) and his Call to Australia party. In other words, Arkell's public stance on a range of social and reform issues, and indeed the way he presented himself to the electorate, was diametrically opposed to some of his private behaviours.

---

1   This list was compiled by criminal defence lawyer Jimmy Singh, 'Is Homosexuality an Offence?', *Criminal Defence Lawyers Australia Blog*, 5 September 2017, www.criminaldefencelawyers.com.au/blog/is-homosexuality-an-offence/.

9. PUBLIC AND PRIVATE

The evidence of Frank Arkell's involvement in the sexual abuse of boys and young men is scattered across multiple sources and the following overview represents the first time this evidence has been consolidated and assessed as a whole. In the process of surveying this evidence, we encounter Bevan's Wollongong-based paedophile network, but also other forms of grooming and child sexual abuse allegedly carried out by Arkell separate from the Bevan network. By 1991, once he was out of office at both the state and the council levels, revelations about his private life began to surface. Losing electoral popularity and influence made him a less powerful target. Slowly but surely the allegations and the evidence began to emerge into the public sphere. What was once secret and hidden beneath the veil of privacy was becoming public.

The evidence

The evidence of Arkell's involvement in the sexual abuse of boys and young men is both extensive and diverse in origin. It relates to material gathered through police inquiries and, to some extent, common knowledge in Wollongong and the memories of those interviewed for this book. As noted previously, Arkell was named in the Wood Royal Commission and later charged by police, but he was never convicted. His death cut short the opportunity for the cases to be heard in court and properly adjudicated. In researching this material, I came across evidence that Arkell was having sex with young men. These encounters are not the subject of this chapter except where they may have allegedly involved some duress, intimidation or subterfuge including the use of a stupefying drug.

In May 1996, the Wood Royal Commission spent three weeks interviewing witnesses who had some knowledge of Tony Bevan's paedophile network. Investigators working for the commission had tracked down and interviewed a vast number of police and members of the public who had information to share. There was evidence that Bevan's activities had been reported to police but not followed up, so this activated the particular focus of the royal commission on potential police corruption. It is important to point out that the royal commission was not focused on child sexual offences as such, and the commissioner made it plain that this line of inquiry was pursued only to the extent that it involved or appeared to involve police corruption. Material had been passed to the commission by ICAC, by sources within NSW Police and by outside organisations including the *Illawarra Mercury*, which forwarded its copy of the Bevan Tapes. The commission was exploring the evidence as it was presented to it—not from the perspective of the child 'victims' or even necessarily from the perspective of the perpetrators—but with a firm eye on police corruption or possible police ineffectiveness in pursuing investigations and securing convictions.

In late 1990, as evidence to the commission revealed, Senior Sergeant Bill King from the NSW Police Special Branch received intelligence from an informer about Bevan and visited Wollongong to conduct further inquiries. Counsel assisting the inquiry Patricia Bergin read from King's report, which he wrote in February 1991, and began to explore the basis of the evidence he had pieced together. She read out loud part of his report and then asked about the origin of certain information: 'He is a director of certain companies and he is also an associate of W1.' King replies that 'for the directorship of certain companies I probably received [the information] through having a company search done back here in Sydney'. King continues:

> The person that you refer to as W1, that was something that would have been reinforced by, I'd say, the intelligence officer from Wollongong and it's something that was because there was a sort of a relationship there to start with. Without going any further, I knew what the situation was.[2]

The NSW Police records on Bevan and Arkell were not available at the time of writing despite my request to access this information under the *Government Information (Public Access) Act 2009* (NSW). We do know from police documents that were cited or read into the transcripts of evidence for the royal commission that Arkell was listed as a 'known associate' on Wollongong police's intelligence file on Tony Bevan.[3] Unfortunately, the original documents from which Bergin and the NSW Police witnesses were reading are no longer available. These documents are sealed for 100 years with all the royal commission documentation. Furthermore, NSW Police reported to me that no copies of these documents or any other material relating to Tony Bevan exist within their historical databases. In the case of Frank Arkell, NSW Police reported to me that it would not be in the public interest to release the documentation on Arkell that they do possess.[4]

---

2   'Evidence of Bill King, Wood Royal Commission, 1997, PR257', in Wood, *Transcripts*.
3   ibid.
4   NSW Police Information Review Officer, Personal communication, 30 November 2022.

Journalist Brett Martin had received information from his sources that Arkell was given a 'serious warning' by police in the 1970s.[5] Given that NSW Police rejected my request to access the police files on Arkell, it has not been possible to confirm this. Furthermore, it may have been that any such police 'warning' was not formally recorded. The police evidence that we can access is refracted through the royal commission transcripts and shows that Arkell was mentioned by name in Wollongong police records as a 'known associate' of Bevan and, further, that the NSW Special Branch was in receipt of information such that Senior Sergeant King 'knew what the situation was'.

Four witnesses who were survivors of child abuse gave evidence to the royal commission that referred to Frank Arkell, though always using the codename 'W1'. This evidence was given as sworn testimony under oath. One man, codenamed 'W2', gave evidence that he met Arkell in Tony Bevan's office in 1976 or 1977 when he was aged 13 or 14 years. He was offered a job in return for sex but refused. Another witness, 'G17', testified that he met Arkell and went for a drive and they had sex in the car. This was in 1977 when G17 was 14 years old.[6]

Another witness, 'W13', was born in October 1967 and grew up in country New South Wales. In 1982 he came to Sydney to visit his sister. He was befriended by a boy his age, 'W11', and taken to a motel in the Sydney suburb of Elizabeth Bay. They watched a gay pornographic video. W11 left the motel room and Tony Bevan came in. As W13 recalled: 'I started getting really scared and I thought, "Well, I'm just going to do whatever this man wants so I can get out of here."' W13 continued contact with W11, even visiting him in Wollongong, where contact with Bevan also resumed.

According to testimony provided to the royal commission, in 1983, W13 decided to stay in Wollongong, with Bevan placing W13 and W11 in a Wollongong apartment. They became involved in Bevan's 'Royal Parties', which visited Sydney on weekends. Both W13 and W11 along with several of 'Tony's Boys' had sex with Bevan and other men in Wollongong and in Sydney. W13 said that this was part of what Bevan called 'earning our allowance'. According to W13, the men never paid the boys; they always

---

5   Interview with Brett Martin, 23 November 2022.
6   Wood, *Transcripts*, PR248. I have not named or identified any of the individuals who were given codenames and provided with legal suppression orders by the royal commission except in the case of W1, where the suppression order was lifted. I have made every effort to avoid possible re-identification of the codenamed individuals even though some of those individuals later chose to make their details public.

paid Bevan beforehand. The boys who were already part of the network were also expected to 'break in' new and usually younger boys so they could become familiar with sexual activities.

On one occasion W13 was asked to go to an apartment on the fifteenth floor of a large modern apartment building with spectacular views of the coast and the ocean to the north and south of Wollongong. This is clearly a reference to Bevan's then-new penthouse at Creston in Corrimal Street. In early to mid-1983, Bevan introduced W13 to a man without giving his name. W13, who was by this time 16 years old, had sex with this man. The following night, W13 was watching the television and saw this man on a news report. He told Bevan that he had seen the man whom he met the previous day and that it was Frank Arkell, but Bevan denied it was Arkell. W13 never met Arkell again.[7]

In considering W13's evidence, it is clear he had detailed knowledge of Bevan's network and how it operated. He described Creston perfectly and his description of the anonymous interactions between men and boys also accords with other evidence to the commission. The connection to Arkell hinges on the identification of him from a TV news report. Certainly, Arkell featured heavily in the TV news around this time as major job losses were announced at the BHP steelworks and the regional economy was in crisis.[8] If W13's year and identification of Arkell are correct, this would indicate that, despite the major disagreement over Gleniffer Brae, Arkell still participated in Bevan's network. We do know that Bevan was working against Arkell in 1982 and 1983, however, as we saw in previous chapters, it is not clear from the available evidence whether Arkell knew the full extent of Bevan's plotting.

W26, who was born in May 1959 and grew up in Wollongong, first met Arkell in the Wollongong CBD. W26 was already involved in Bevan's paedophile network but he happened on Arkell purely by chance. He told the royal commission that when he was aged 13, in 1973, he was riding his bike in Wollongong and had an encounter with Arkell in the public toilets near the IMB Building carpark. As W26 recalled: 'I saw a black LTD with, I think, personalised plates parked just near the men's toilet and I encountered the person who I now know as W1 in one of those cubicles.'

---

7   'Evidence of W13, Wood Royal Commission, PR248', in Wood, *Transcripts*.
8   ibid.

According to W26, Arkell paid him $20 for a sexual act. The IMB Building is a well-known landmark on Crown Street in Wollongong. The impressive three-storey building was completed in the early 1970s, so it was certainly in existence at that time. Counsel for Arkell at the commission, Mr McIllwraith, requested access to W26's real name, which was not provided during the evidence. Arkell's counsel also queried whether the material contained in the Bevan Tapes represented admissible evidence—a question the commissioner dismissed based on the existing case law and the nature of the relevant legislation at the time Bevan was making the tapes. According to his evidence, W26 was followed by W1 in his car 'on a couple of occasions' in the following weeks but did not have any subsequent meeting with W1 until many years later.[9] The *Illawarra Mercury* published W26's story and Arkell began defamation proceedings in March 1998 against the paper and journalist Lisa Carty.[10] At the 1998 committal hearing, Arkell's defence team offered an extended critique of W26 and his character with what Magistrate Paul Johnson characterised as 'a considerable deal of persuasion'. The length of time since the offence (in 1973) and the lack of corroborating evidence also weighed on the magistrate's decision. W26's case was discounted at the committal hearing and would not proceed to trial.[11]

W26 was, according to the *Illawarra Mercury*, 'shattered' when the three charges for which he was listed as the victim were dropped, telling the paper: 'They've all got away with it—Bevan, Tobin, and now Arkell.'[12] Arkell's defence team had emphasised W26's criminal convictions, including his conviction for child sexual abuse, to undermine his credibility as a witness. But looked at another way, the fact that W26 had a subsequent criminal history of child sexual abuse was an explicable path into adulthood since at least some victims of child sexual abuse are so badly affected they become offenders as adults.[13] The magistrate needed to make a judgement that a jury, if properly instructed, would likely find the defendant guilty of the offence beyond reasonable doubt and these charges did not clear that high threshold. This must have been a bitter blow to W26.

---

9   'Evidence of W26, Wood Royal Commission, PR307', in Wood, *Transcripts*.
10 Liz Hannan and Anna Patty, 'Child Sex MP Slain', *Sun-Herald*, [Sydney], 28 June 1998: 7.
11 Lisa Carty, 'Arkell Goes to Trial—Wollongong Magistrate Decides: Former MP Faces 11 Sex Charges', *Illawarra Mercury*, 13 February 1998: 1.
12 Lisa Carty, 'Victims Wanted Their Day in Court', *Illawarra Mercury*, 29 June 1997: 2.
13 Ashley F. Jespersena, Martin L. Lalumièrea and Michael C. Seto, 'Sexual Abuse History among Adult Sex Offenders and Non-Sex Offenders: A Meta-Analysis', *Child Abuse & Neglect* 33, 2009: 179–92.

Overall, the royal commission featured three witnesses who testified that they had sex with Arkell between 1973 and 1983 when they were between 13 and 16 years of age. A fourth witness rejected an offer of sex from Arkell when he was aged 14, in 1977. After considering the evidence that emerged in the royal commission, we can move on to consider the police evidence and charges. We can then recount the details that emerged with the initial charge sheet or at least the parts of it we can reconstruct from media reporting. The Wood Royal Commission passed evidence covering Arkell's alleged activities to the newly formed Police Child Protection Enforcement Unit (CPEU). The formation of the CPEU was in fact one of the recommendations of the royal commission. Following the investigation, on 1 May 1997, Arkell was arrested and charged with 29 sex offences by officers from the CPEU.

Unfortunately, NSW Police rejected my request to view the Arkell file so it was not possible to see a list of the entire charge sheet. The police statement indicated that the offences dated back to 1973; however, some of the 'victims' involved in these charges were prepared to make their experiences public by talking to the media so we can piece together details of at least some of the 29 charges against Arkell (see Appendix 9.1).

David Potbury had been recruited into Bevan's network and had sex with a man in Bevan's flat in East Corrimal. He reported to police that he later recognised that man on television as Frank Arkell. There were four other occasions when he had sex with Arkell at the flat. He also had sex with Bevan at the Windang aerial patrol base. In part of his evidence, he said he had sex with Arkell at Bevan's penthouse at Creston, but he later revealed that he had mistaken the location.[14] In Potbury's case, Arkell was committed to stand trial on one count of buggery, while 11 other charges involving Potbury were dropped at the committal hearing in February 1998.

Frank Stansbury reported that he was undressed and assaulted by a man he knew to be Arkell at Bevan's farm in West Dapto in the early 1980s. He had already been recruited into Bevan's network of boys, but he was never told the names of the men who assaulted him. Stansbury approached officers from the CPEU after Arkell's arrest on 1 May 1997, but the case never went forward as police considered the details to be 'too flimsy'.[15]

14 Carty, 'Arkell Goes to Trial'.
15 Lisa Carty, 'Old Wounds Still Raw', *Illawarra Mercury*, 28 June 1998: 2.

9. PUBLIC AND PRIVATE

The evidence provided by both David Potbury and Frank Stansbury is compelling. Their recollections of the way Bevan's network operated and of places and events were mostly reliable. Given the nature of many such allegations, they are often difficult to prove in a court of law because there are typically no witnesses and often no physical evidence. The cases of Potbury and Stansbury place Arkell as an active participant in Bevan's paedophile network on at least six occasions across four separate and typical Bevan venues: Bevan's flat in East Corrimal, the aerial patrol base at Windang, the farm at West Dapto and Bevan's North Wollongong apartment. The specific claim from W13 that he met and had sex with Arkell at the Creston penthouse, with his identification of Arkell via a television news report, adds credence to the reality that Arkell was an occasional participant in Bevan's network.

Ray Leary's experience provides further confirmation that Arkell participated in Bevan's network in the 1970s. Leary was born in 1961 and was dragged into the Sydney and Wollongong paedophile networks after a difficult childhood in Sydney and periods when he was a ward of the state living in different institutions. Ray said he was driven in a motor vehicle to Wollongong by an abusive social worker who had already assaulted him and had begun trafficking Ray and other boys to paedophiles in Sydney and Wollongong.

Ray recalls being driven to Wollongong three or four times in the summer of 1974. He was in the company of a couple of other boys. They were taken to hotels, given lunch, sometimes bought presents such as clothes and then driven to an apartment. He recalls the apartment was elevated and had a view of the ocean. Before the completion of Creston, Bevan owned another apartment on Corrimal Street just across the road and close to North Beach. One evening several men turned up at this apartment, including Arkell and Bevan.

Ray recalls that he had sex with Arkell three or four times in the summer of 1974 when Ray was 14 years old. During these evening sessions, Bevan was often present with a film camera, but the boys were never asked for their consent to be filmed. Ray's social worker would pick them up the next morning and drive them back to Sydney. Sometimes the boys were given $20 or even $50 but often his social worker would take the money Ray earned for sex, photographs and pornographic films, claiming he had a special bank account for Ray with all his money in it. Ray never saw any of the money. Ray's recollections are sourced both from an interview conducted by the author and from his own memoirs, which he published in 2016.[16]

The children who were trafficked into these networks faced multiple barriers in pursuing police charges and claims against their abusers. On the challenge of corroborating his story, Ray noted: 'Most of my friends are dead so I couldn't get them to support my evidence.'[17] Another challenge for Ray, and indeed all the other boys involved, was that real names were never used for the perpetrator or the victim. Those boys who were deemed 'unsafe' because they showed signs of telling others—by complaining to police or parents, for example—were blackmailed into silence through the threat of releasing illicit photographs, videos or films, or simply excluded from the network and never contacted again. When Ray was trafficked to Wollongong by the Bevan network, Arkell entered the beachside apartment, but he was not named, nor did he introduce himself. Ray was told to use a different name and, as the royal commission evidence showed, swapping details including names and phone numbers between perpetrator and victim was strictly forbidden by the organisers of paedophile networks. This is important context for a case such as Frank Stansbury's, for example, in which, as we noted, police considered the evidence 'too flimsy'. In a secretive illegal organisation carrying out criminal practices, evidence was systematically and ruthlessly suppressed. The odds of a successful conviction were deliberately stacked high against the victims.

Allegations not linked to the Bevan network

There are further allegations against Arkell that reach beyond Bevan's network. These come from a different kind of engagement by Arkell with victims. There are two basic methods of recruiting 'victims' for child sexual abuse though abusers often utilise both. One form of recruitment, which matched the Bevan network's mode of operation, targeted homeless, desperate children who were vulnerable to grooming, duress and intimidation and was often organised in groups or networks. The other form was one-on-one grooming between perpetrator and 'victim' that could

---

16   Interview with Ray Leary, 19 October 2022; Ray Leary, with Kate Shayler, *A Beautiful Boy: Ray's Story* (Hazelbrook: Moshpit Publishing, 2016), www.scribd.com/read/307228103/A-Beautiful-Boy-Ray-s-Story.
17   Interview with Ray Leary, 19 October 2022.

involve duress and intimidation, but the grooming phase was often about developing a good reputation and establishing a rapport with the child's family. For perpetrators, these targets were much more of a challenge as they were not isolated from family networks of protection and support but there seems to be a special attraction for paedophiles in grooming and then abusing children who are new to sexual activity.[18] This is shown by the way in which boys in Bevan's network who were abused by paedophiles were often passed on to other paedophiles after the novelty of having sex with them had worn off.

There is evidence that Arkell engaged in one-on-one grooming. In this case, Arkell allegedly attempted to build a relationship of trust with the parents alongside a long-term relationship with the child. In 1998 Rene Mori told the ABC's *Background Briefing* program that he had met Arkell at a family function at the age of 12 and regarded him 'as a second father, a mentor'. Mori, who grew up in Dapto, noted how Arkell 'would mentally manipulate me into believing that what I was doing was right'.[19] Aged 17, he met with Arkell in the lord mayor's office, they shared an alcoholic drink and began talking about sex. The drink made him drowsy and he soon fell asleep. When he awoke, he found Arkell was sexually assaulting him with two objects. The assault left him physically injured and emotionally traumatised. In 1997 Arkell was charged with administering a stupefying drug (alcohol) so as to commit an indecent assault and intercourse without consent, with the incident occurring between 1 January and 16 June 1984.[20] After Arkell's death, the *Illawarra Mercury* reported the same story, initially without naming Mori and, two days later, Mori agreed to go on the record.[21] Mori's case survived the 1998 committal hearing with Magistrate Paul Johnson calling Mori 'a witness of credit'.[22] These charges would have been heard in September 1998 had Arkell been alive. Mori's case includes the damning piece of evidence that directly links Arkell's public role with his secret perversion. Apart from the incident occurring in the lord mayor's

---

18   See, for example, Georgia M. Winters, Leah E. Kaylor, and Elizabeth L. Jeglic, 'Toward a Universal Definition of Child Sexual Grooming', *Deviant Behaviour* 43, no. 8, 2022: 926–38, doi.org/10.1080/01639625.2021.1941427; Parliamentary Joint Committee on the National Crime Authority, *Organised Criminal Paedophile Activity. A Report by the Parliamentary Joint Committee on the National Crime Authority*, 1995, especially Chapters 2 and 3.
19   Rene Mori quoted in 'Wonderful Wollongong', *Background Briefing*, [ABC Radio], 1 October 1998, C100, 1286175, National Archives of Australia, Canberra.
20   Lisa Carty, 'New Arkell Victim Speaks Out', *Illawarra Mercury*, 30 June 1998: 1; Rene Mori quoted in 'Wonderful Wollongong', *Background Briefing*.
21   Carty, 'Victims Wanted Their Day in Court'; Carty, 'New Arkell Victim Speaks Out'.
22   Carty, 'Arkell Goes to Trial'.

office—which is troubling enough in itself—at the hearing, Mori said Arkell told him that he could be trusted 'because he was the Lord Mayor'.[23] This was no separate private obsession of Arkell's, locked away from his public world, but a practice that was enabled through his public office and standing in the community.

Across multiple interviews for print, radio and television, Rene Mori described the process of grooming that occurred over five years. The specificity of the allegations and the long lead-in time characterised by careful grooming behaviour and encouragement and normalisation of specific feelings, behaviours and emotions are typical of other cases of child sexual abuse.[24] In such cases, rather than target the isolated, vulnerable child, the abuser gets close to the child and their family, building a relationship of trust and respect that makes an excellent cover for an eventual move towards inappropriate intimate behaviour. As Mori himself notes, 'I believe that he had prepared me for what he wanted to do. He would quite often say "I love you" … amongst other things.'[25] Again, there is no mutual love and respect of equals here, but a careful and deliberate cultivation and manipulation of a young person over many years with the aim of securing sexual gratification. That the alleged offence occurred in the mayor's office also shows an offender using the accoutrements of power to impress or intimidate a teenage boy.

Both Arkell and Bevan were real estate agents (as was Arkell's political ally, Brian Tobin from Woonona) and their access to apartments and flats was a useful resource to cultivate obligations among boys and young men and, ultimately, even provide a venue in which to have sex with boys. Bevan had access to vacant properties around Wollongong. He could offer accommodation for struggling boys or young men or even host parties at which older powerful men had sex with boys or young men at these premises. Narelle Clay, the former director of a homeless shelter in Wollongong, reported to the ABC's *Background Briefing* in 1998 that it was well known that Bevan offered properties to desperate young men: 'We believed that

---

23 ibid.
24 See, for example, Georgia M. Winters, Leah E. Kaylor, and Elizabeth L. Jeglic, 'Toward a Universal Definition of Child Sexual Grooming', *Deviant Behaviour* 43, no. 8 (2022): 926–38, doi.org/10.1080/01639625.2021.1941427.
25 Rene Mori quoted in 'Wonderful Wollongong', *Background Briefing*.

[Bevan targeted] homeless young people who needed to rent properties thus beginning a cycle of grooming, which sought to create obligations and dependencies.'[26]

Arkell was the subject of an allegation that he offered a job in return for sex to a 16-year-old boy whom he had met at Bevan's real estate office. In this case, the business provided an opportunity to dispense favours in the form of a job and Bevan's office provided a venue in which to make the offer away from the public eye. Arkell was also known to have used his own real estate agency for his personal benefit as was the case in 1975 when he offered the Women's Committee for the International Women's Year rental premises in an office managed by his family company Arrow Real Estate. Networks of abusers found ways to control, manage and facilitate their abuse, and owning a real estate agency provided a source of jobs, office space and residential accommodation to enable grooming behaviour and private sex.

The details of the second case against Arkell that was to proceed to trial in September 1998 are known only in broad outline. A man spoke to the media but did not give his name. From the charge sheet published by the *Illawarra Mercury* in 1997, we know this man was 19 when the alleged offence occurred and that, like Mori, it involved Arkell using a drug to overcome and then assault him. In this case, the venue was Arkell's apartment in West Wollongong and the incident occurred between 1 May and 31 May 1978. In relation to this man, Arkell was charged with administering a stupefying drug (alcohol) to commit an indecent assault and buggery.[27]

This was not the only allegation for which the venue for Arkell's abuse was his apartment. After Arkell's death, another man came forward offering a story similar to Rene Mori's. This man grew up in Wollongong but moved to Queensland as an adult. He told the Brisbane *Courier-Mail* that Arkell abused him in the Reserve Street apartment for a period of three years, starting when he was aged seven. This man also gave evidence before the royal commission. He was first abused by a male relative and then introduced by that relative to the Wollongong paedophile network.[28] This was also the first public allegation of abuse with a prepubescent child and, in that sense, stands out as different from the others.

---

26 Narelle Clay quoted in ibid.
27 Carty, 'Victims Wanted Their Day in Court'.
28 Fynes-Clinton and Ware, 'Shadowland'.

Arkell may have had links with Queensland-based paedophile networks. He was certainly a regular visitor to Queensland in his capacity as lord mayor. In the early 1980s, 'Grant', then an 18-year-old, was involved in the Brisbane-based paedophile scene. As a slightly older boy, he was often asked to drive younger boys to network clients. He told *Courier-Mail* reporters he drove an Asian boy, who he believed to be 13 or 14 years old, to a client in Wollongong for the weekend. From Brisbane, they drove south all day on a Friday:

> By twilight on Friday, he had arrived at the destination: an address in Wollongong where a man was waiting. Invited inside briefly, Grant says he can still remember the fine details of the house's interior. At the time, he was unaware of the identity of the man awaiting the Asian boy. But the address—1 Reserve St—was that of disgraced Wollongong mayor Frank Arkell.

He dropped the boy off for the weekend and drove him back to Brisbane a few days later.[29] The boy was reportedly injured and in pain from his weekend ordeal.

Beyond the evidence given to the royal commission, the personal testimony of witnesses and stories from interstate media, there was also evidence that was put before the NSW Parliament. In 1994 Deirdre Grusovin was the Labor member for Heffron and shadow minister for housing. That year she read a statutory declaration from Colin Fisk into the parliamentary record (or Hansard). The declaration alleged that John Marsden, a prominent NSW lawyer and police board member, and Frank Arkell, were pederasts. Reading Fisk's statutory declaration, Grusovin told the Legislative Assembly:

> I … [Colin Fisk] sincerely declare and affirm that five weeks after I was arrested on March 31, 1989 I made a series of records of interviews with the NSW police Internal Security Unit (IPSU) in which I named a number of prominent people I knew to be pederasts, including the solicitor John Marsden, MP Frank Arkell and other leading members of the community.

This was the first major public revelation that Arkell may have been leading a double life. There was general outrage inside and outside parliament about a potential abuse of parliamentary privilege. Grusovin endured widespread

---

29 'Grant' cited in ibid.

criticism for her actions and the then-leader of the Labor opposition, Bob Carr, asked her to resign her shadow ministry. Carr apologised to Marsden and Arkell.[30]

Fisk later reneged on his statement regarding Marsden although he never said anything further about Arkell. Other researchers have found that Fisk was an unreliable witness. Born in 1948, Fisk was known to be operating brothels in the 1970s and 1980s that allegedly featured underage boys. In 1998 he was charged with multiple child sex offences that dated from the 1970s and 1980s and spent 12 years in prison. In 2018 he pleaded guilty to further child sexual offences that occurred in 2015 and 2016.[31] Chief Inspector Ken Watson, who was asked by police minister Ted Pickering to investigate Fisk's statutory declaration, claimed before the royal commission that 'unless what he [Fisk] told me was able to be corroborated, it could not be relied upon'. Watson's material provided to the royal commission indicated that, as summarised by counsel assisting Patricia Bergin, 'in relation to the matter relating to Mr Arkell, you said that the information that you had was unconfirmed intelligence and you believed in many instances that they were assumptions made by Fisk. Do you remember saying that to us?' asked Bergin. 'Yes, I certainly do,' answered Watson.[32]

Despite losing her shadow ministerial portfolio and causing general outrage by reading Fisk's statutory declaration into Hansard, Grusovin doubled down on her comments the next day, telling the assembly:

> We sometimes suffer some travail when undertaking our commitments in this House. In the past 24-hour period I have clearly accepted responsibility for my actions in the House yesterday. In this closing session of Parliament I want to advise the House that I am now in possession of a recording of a conversation between Frank Arkell and an under-age boy in which that boy was offered sex.[33]

Grusovin clearly now had access to the infamous 'Scorpion Tape', recorded at the behest of Tony Bevan and circulated in Wollongong and Sydney to discredit Arkell. As we now know, the tape involved a 21-year-old man phoning Arkell at Tony Bevan's behest, so the most it could have proven

---

30   Quentin Dempster, *Stateline*, [*ABC TV*], 18 April 1997, ID: T336611, ABC Archives, Sydney.
31   Jessica Clifford, 'Known Paedophile Pleads Guilty to Fresh Charges', *ABC Illawarra*, 7 August 2018, www.abc.net.au/news/2018-08-07/known-nsw-paedophile-pleads-guilty-to-fresh-charges/10083596.
32   'Evidence of Chief Inspector Ken Watson, Wood Royal Commission, PR309', in Wood, *Transcripts*.
33   Deirdre Grusovin cited in NSW, *Parliamentary Debates*, Legislative Council, 29 November 1994, 'Special Adjournment'.

was some moral criticism of Arkell's behaviour and not child sexual abuse as such. Arkell specifically denied all the allegations in Fisk's statutory declaration and indicated that Fisk had confused him with Tony Bevan.[34]

On 31 October 1996, Franca Arena, a Labor member of the Legislative Council, asked a series of questions that, much like the Grusovin incident in 1994, caused uproar inside and outside parliament. When discussing the possible extension of the terms of reference of the royal commission into police corruption and the role of suppression orders in particular, Arena asked: 'What about former member of Parliament Frank Arkell, known to the commission as W1, who was summoned and did not attend as his lawyers said he was too ill?' Arena suggested that the application of suppression orders was far too common and rather at odds with the commissioner's initial view when he said, 'I do not intend to make suppression orders, save where necessary.' She continued:

> Instead, with due respect to the commissioner, the community's perception was that the commission found the task too difficult and concentrated its effort on overseas or dead paedophiles while those loose in the community continued to get away with it.[35]

Arena's actions in naming Arkell in parliament breached the suppression order imposed by the royal commission. From Arena's point of view, the commission needed to extend its terms of reference to cover child sexual abuse. She claimed she had not made allegations in parliament, merely asked questions: 'I asked the questions because victims had come to see me, they showed me evidence, they told me their stories, I could not ignore it.'[36]

Both Grusovin and Arena were strong parliamentary advocates for the victims of child sexual abuse. They already had a track record of speaking out about alleged offences before referencing Arkell in parliament. For speaking out, the two suffered considerable setbacks in their political careers, with Arena threatened with expulsion from the Labor Party before resigning her membership in 1997. Grusovin arguably lost a chance to make a bid for the Labor leadership before losing a bitter preselection battle to a Labor rival, Kristina Keneally. While their methods were unorthodox, both women were concerned that corrupt police were protecting powerful, well-connected

---

34   'NSW: Arkell Denies in Commission He Is a Paedophile', *AAP* [*Australian Associated Press*], 7 November 1996, Access global NewsBank, National Library of Australia, Canberra.
35   Franca Arena cited in NSW, *Parliamentary Debates*, Legislative Council, 31 October 1996, 'Royal Commission into the New South Wales Police Service Paedophile Investigation'.
36   Franca Arena cited in *ABC TV News*, 9 February 1998.

9. PUBLIC AND PRIVATE

individuals who were engaged in child sexual abuse. Their interventions, along with the support of the Reverend Fred Nile in the Upper House, ensured that the Wood Royal Commission received extended terms of reference to investigate child sexual abuse. But to this day Arena and many survivors of child sexual abuse remain disappointed with the outcome of the Wood Royal Commission, suggesting that it failed to tackle the true extent of the problem. As Arena wrote in 2012:

> The Wood royal commission was about police corruption and only attached itself to paedophilia if police were corrupted by paedophiles. Former Labor MP Deirdre Grusovin and I lobbied the premier at the time, Bob Carr, to have a royal commission on paedophilia because we knew of so many cases … but he refused.[37]

For Arena and other critics of the royal commission, a deceased regional mayor was a much safer target compared with senior NSW judges or other possible high-profile, living targets.

While Grusovin and Arena were the main parliamentary critics, Frank Arkell had his supporters inside parliament. Nothing is ever cut and dry with Arkell. In the NSW Parliament as in the community, he had his critics who thought he was a sinner and supporters who thought he was a saint. Perhaps the most high-profile supporter was the highly respected member for the South Coast, John Hatton, who said in the assembly:

> Mr Frank Arkell, with whom I sat on the back bench, is a man of high reputation. He lives and breathes Wollongong. He is one of the city's best ambassadors and he has done much for the image, industry and business, and greening, of that city.[38]

The final type of evidence against Frank Arkell relates to claims that he frequented known gay beats in Wollongong and Sydney to solicit boys. There were several sites around Wollongong where gay men could meet up and either have anonymous sex on the premises or leave to go elsewhere. These sites arose because there were no gay bars in the city where they could socialise, with the partial exception of the front bar at the Wollongong Hotel. This hotel on the corner of Kembla and Crown streets was demolished in

---

37 Franca Arena, 'We Must Deliver On Important Promises', *Daily Telegraph*, [Sydney], 14 November 2012, www.news.com.au/national/nsw-act/we-must-deliver-on-important-promises/news-story/baff1 c87f18db93961804ead6885912e.
38 John Hatton cited in NSW, *Parliamentary Debates*, Legislative Assembly, 29 November 1994, 'Debate on Defamation Bill (2nd reading)'.

the early 1980s. Rod Stringer did not open Kennedy's until 1983. Located at the top of the Piccadilly Centre near the Wollongong Railway Station, Kennedy's became the city's first gay nightclub. There were two key gay beats in Wollongong. One covered the public toilets at Fairy Meadow Beach, the carpark area and the reserve behind the beach to the south. There was thick, woody scrub there that could hide a quick liaison. The other site was MacCabe Park in Wollongong.[39]

'Cruising' carried out by adult men meeting up with other adult men is not the focus here. Even if Arkell encountered adult men at these sites this is not a major concern except to the extent that it contradicted his public stance on the family, morality and sexuality and possibly made him vulnerable to blackmail or intimidation in carrying out his public duties. The real question of concern is whether Arkell used gay beats to pick up boys under 18 years of age. Eighteen was the legal age of consent for homosexual sex in New South Wales until 2003. Older men picking up underage boys through cruising was a form of child sexual abuse that posed the highest risk for the offender and a result was not always guaranteed. The risks were both mundane and potentially dangerous. It may not have been possible to find a suitable partner, but there were also cases of violence directed towards homosexual men at these sites or elsewhere in the city, including the unsolved murder of Bill Rooney, who was found beaten and unconscious not far from MacCabe Park in February 1986. Rooney died in hospital six days later.[40] Despite the clear risks, the evidence suggests that, as Arkell found success and could carry on without retribution, he became more emboldened and began to take greater risks. Perhaps he also found some thrill in this riskier form of abuse?

Regarding his actions in Sydney, I have been told that Arkell cruised 'The Wall' in Kings Cross, asking his chauffeur to take him there on numerous occasions after parliamentary sittings. The Wall was a notorious spot on Darlinghurst Road where men and boys offered themselves for sex. Journalist Brett Martin alleged that Arkell had an apartment in Sydney

---

39 'Park Toilets Not for Homosexual Antics', [Letter to the Editor], *Illawarra Mercury*, 30 December 1986; 'MacCabe Park: It's No Solution', *Illawarra Mercury*, 18 March 1987. MacCabe Park was named after Thomas MacCabe, the first bishop of the Wollongong diocese, who served from 1952 to 1974. See Neil Dwyer, 'Diocese Celebrates 70th Anniversary of its Foundation Decree! (Pt 2)', [Online], 24 February 2022, Catholic Diocese of Wollongong, www.dow.org.au/diocese-celebrates-70th-anniversary-of-its-foundation-2/.
40 Tim Fernandez, 'Police Criticised for Bungled Investigation into Possible Gay Hate Death in Wollongong', *ABC Illawarra*, 18 May 2023, www.abc.net.au/news/2023-05-18/lgbtiq-inuiry-hears-evidence-of-bill-rooney-death/102361452.

9. PUBLIC AND PRIVATE

that was another potential site for grooming and child abuse. Colin Fisk's allegations had included the claim that Arkell co-rented an apartment in Kings Cross with a Sydney lawyer who was a known associate of Fisk's and a person who visited Costellos and the K Roo underage brothel in George Street, Sydney. Both establishments were alleged to sell access to underaged boys for sex. Arkell specifically denied this claim in his submission to the royal commission.[41] I attempted to contact Arkell's former chauffeurs, without success. In one case, there was no reply and in another the person acknowledged my message but did not wish to participate in the research for this book. Whatever secrets these men are keeping will remain hidden for now.

There is one incident, told to me in great detail, in which Frank Arkell was quite brazen and open in his attempts to seduce a young man. The incident itself revealed for the first time here, shows that Arkell was prepared to pursue his goals in a relatively public, open environment. There was an arrogance to his actions that is strongly suggestive that he felt above reproach.

The story also reveals much about the nature of Arkell's desire—the strong and unabashed impulse for sex but the overall lack of interest in any form of longer-term relationship. In 1984 Antonios Tziolas and his friends, which included my older brother Peter Eklund, visited HMAS *Wollongong*, which was moored in Port Kembla harbour as part of Wollongong's 150th anniversary celebrations. Antonios was 20 years old. He had attended Keira Boys High School and was at the time doing a Bachelor of Science degree at the University of Wollongong. Antonios and Peter were in a band and had a friend, also in the band, who was a crew member of HMAS *Wollongong*.

Antonios was the very opposite of the homeless, desperate boys and young men often targeted by paedophiles. He had a circle of good friends and he was a confident young man—confident enough to front a Wollongong postpunk band variously called 'Casualty' and 'A Family' as the lead singer. On the ship, they met Frank Arkell and, as Antonios describes it: 'It was clear from the start that he wanted my ass.'[42]

The brazen public nature of Arkell's attempted seduction of Antonios is noteworthy. It suggests that by 1984 Arkell was less concerned about showing his true sexual desires in public than we might otherwise imagine.

---

41   Malcolm Brown, 'Pedophile Claims "Confused": Arkell', *Sydney Morning Herald*, 9 November 1996: 11.
42   Interview with Antonios Tziolas, 13 November 2022.

It was not uncommon for Arkell to partake in edgy flirtatious behaviour in public, especially at parties and commemorative events, where he would invite women to sit on his knee and he would reach around and try to unhook their bra straps with a twist of his fingers. I was told by one source that he became quite proficient at it. However, there were dangers to showing homosexual desire in public and the brutal murders and bashings of gay men in the period show that all too clearly. But there was, simultaneously, a quiet acceptance of difference. Many knew or suspected Frank Arkell was gay, but this never became a political or public liability. In fact, after Kennedy's nightclub opened in 1983, I started frequenting that spot with my friends, in July 1984. My friends from Keira Boys High School—all typical Wollongong boys aged 17 or 18—accepted the reality of a gay subculture, even as we sampled its music and dancing. I recall watching a drag show one night at Kennedy's in late 1984. My sense of the response from some of the crowd was not violent rejection but curiosity. Without downplaying the homophobic violence around us, in the bubble of the nightclub, there was also a quiet acceptance of difference.

Arkell's attempts to seduce Antonios did not stop on the ship. One of his friends invited Arkell to a party that night held in the garage of a Mount Ousley house, where Antonios's band was playing. Much to the amusement of Antonios and his friends, Arkell turned up chauffeured in his council car and continued his obvious display of lust for the young, confident man of Greek heritage:

> He was really, really pushy and persistent. Again touching, arm around me, saying I really like Greeks, tell me about your Greek heritage, that kind of stuff. But I remember he had his arm around me and he was like just there in my presence for the whole night.[43]

We have seen from his involvement with the Hellenic Club how Arkell was especially attracted to Greek culture. As Antonios recalls, Arkell was relentless:

> It was just him touching me and feeling me and cuddling me and whispering all these sexual allusions, or speaking all of these sexual allusions to me. I wasn't fearful. I just found it really funny and a little bit shocking that this was the Lord Mayor of Wollongong behaving so openly like this. You've got to consider the time. It was 1984. It was the time of gay men being pushed off the cliffs in Sydney. Being bashed,

---

43   ibid.

being arrested. It was just a really, really different time. Again, if you view those events through the lens of today you would be mortified and horrified by how overt and predatory his behaviour was.

Towards the end of the night, the novelty of having the lord mayor attend a garage party had worn thin:

> I do recall there was a point reached for me that it was really just fucking annoying. It was like you are not going to get anywhere with me. It was kind of fun for a while but then it just dragged on. And I think he got the message and he left, so I don't think he stayed at the party particularly long.

It is also significant that Arkell never made any further contact. The point of the behaviour was to secure sexual gratification and any idea of getting to know Antonios and trying to establish a relationship with him was not considered. In this case, we see Arkell pursuing a fleeting, impulsive encounter driven entirely by the desire for sexual gratification. I have found no evidence of any other kind of interest in longer-lasting relationships that might go beyond sex. I have been in receipt of vague off-the-record allusions that Arkell may have had gay lovers, but at this point, these are secret matters that await further research or perhaps an individual may come forward. Alternatively, they may remain hidden forever.

Antonios and his friends were well prepared for Arkell's advances as they knew his reputation. This information was circulating through Keira Boys High School and through the adjacent Wollongong High School in 1978 and 1979—the years when Antonios completed fifth and sixth forms. As Antonios recalled:

> It was common knowledge amongst the high school cohort, as well as your brother ... [W]e all knew that Frank was gay ... So, the rumours were out there. So, there was no mystery about his sexual preferences ... I can't remember where I, firstly, heard that he was gay and, secondly, that he also liked young boys as well. These rumours were circulating through my generation, through my cohort. As far as I could tell, it was quite common knowledge.[44]

This is very similar to the type of general rumour that was apparent during my final two years at Keira Boys High in 1983 and 1984. There are other recollections cited in this book, including those of Mark Richmond,

---

44   ibid.

showing that among groups of boys across at least three local high schools, there was knowledge of Arkell and some inkling about his sexuality and his preference for boys and young men.

This kind of behaviour by Arkell could hardly go unnoticed. Among some of the city's journalists, too, there was a growing disquiet about Arkell. In 1986 Janine Cullen interviewed Arkell at the opening of the city's new Crown Street pedestrian mall, between Flinders and Kembla streets. Cullen found Arkell's attention barely focused on her questions. Arkell's gaze kept wandering over her shoulder to a group of 14 and 15-year-old boys sitting nearby. Arkell finished the interview quickly, walked over to the group and invited them back to the council chambers for a tour.[45]

Plate 9.1 Lord Mayor Frank Arkell watches as NSW Premier Barrie Unsworth officially opens the Wollongong City Mall, 20 October 1986
Note: After this event, ABC journalist Janine Cullen attempted to interview Arkell only for him to cut the interview short to speak to a group of teenage boys who were standing nearby.
Photo: *Illawarra Mercury* Image Collection and Wollongong City Library, Image no. P27872.

---

45   Interview with Janine Cullen, 20 October 2022.

Arkell had a habit of issuing such invitations. The opening shots of Mark Colvin's *Four Corners* report on the NSW independents and the 1988 state election showed Arkell mixing with a group of high school art students at Wollongong Art Gallery. He approaches a group of three boys, who tell Arkell they are Keira Boys High students, and Arkell says: 'You want to come and see me one day. One afternoon I'll put it all together. I'll make sense of it all.'[46] For child sexual abuse, for which evidence and proof were notoriously difficult to secure, 29 counts from the multiple allegations against Arkell reached the threshold of warranting police charges (see Appendix 9.1). Five of those charges, involving four victims, were passed on from the committal hearing and were due to be heard in a Parramatta court in September 1998. The date range of these known cases extends from 1973 through to 1984. One final point to make when discussing the known allegations against Arkell is that past studies have estimated that only 2 to 10 per cent of all child abuse incidents are reported,[47] so we can reasonably assume that there are many more names, details and memories that are not mentioned here.

There are many judgements that can be made about a life and not all of them are made in a court of law. Historians gather and assess evidence and make judgements to the best of their ability. Based on the cases that have been surveyed and analysed here, the evidence against Arkell is very strong. The long-term and consistent evidence that Arkell was engaged in sex with boys between the ages of 13 and 18 is incontrovertible. It comes from multiple sources and it has internal consistency and credibility. The case against Arkell is represented not by a single complaint or a series of rumours but by a multitude of survivors who have spoken up. At the edges of this wealth of cases and the diverse collection of survivors are allegations that are less certain. We simply do not know whether Arkell and Bevan had ceased all contact in the paedophile network after their rift over Gleniffer Brae in 1978. These allegations await further research to determine the true extent of Arkell's offending, but the available evidence shows he was an occasional participant in Bevan's paedophile network in the 1970s and possibly in the early 1980s. It also shows that he pursued other instances of child abuse as a lone actor throughout the 1970s and early 1980s.

---

46 Colvin, 'Independents' Day'.
47 See, for example, Ben Mathews, Xing Ju Lee and Rosanna E. Norman, 'Impact of a New Mandatory Reporting Law on Reporting and Identification of Child Sexual Abuse: A Seven Year Time Trend Analysis', *Child Abuse & Neglect* 56, 2016: 62–79, doi.org/10.1016/j.chiabu.2016.04.009; Ben Mathews, Leah Bromfield, Kerryann Walsh, Qinglu Cheng and Rossana E Norman, 'Reports of Child Sexual Abuse of Boys and Girls: Longitudinal Trends over a 20-Year Period in Victoria, Australia', *Child Abuse & Neglect* 66, 2017: 9–22, doi.org/10.1016/j.chiabu.2017.01.025.

Appendix 9.1

A summary of the 29 charges against Frank Arkell.

Alleged Victim A:

- Three charges of indecent assault at Wollongong between 1 July and 30 September 1973.

Alleged Victim B:

- Four charges of buggery at Wollongong between 1 May and 31 May 1978.
- Indecent assault at Wollongong between 1 May and 31 May 1978.
- Unlawfully administering a stupefying drug (alcohol) to commit an indictable offence at Wollongong between 1 May and 31 May 1978.

Alleged Victim C:

- Four charges of indecent assault at Wollongong between 1 August and 31 December 1983.
- Three charges of having sexual intercourse without consent at Wollongong between 1 August and 31 December 1983.
- Unlawfully administering a stupefying drug (alcohol) to commit an indictable offence at Wollongong between 1 August and 31 December 1983.

Alleged Victim D:

- Two charges of indecent assault at East Corrimal between 1 May and 31 May 1984.
- Buggery at East Corrimal between 1 May and 31 May 1984.
- Two charges of indecent assault at East Corrimal between 1 June and 31 August 1984.
- Indecent assault at East Corrimal between 1 September and 31 October 1984.
- Indecent assault at Windang between 1 September and 30 November 1984.

- Sexual intercourse without consent at East Corrimal between 1 March and 31 May 1984.
- Two charges of sexual intercourse without consent at East Corrimal between 1 June and 31 August 1984.
- Sexual intercourse without consent at East Corrimal between 1 September and 31 October 1984.
- Sexual intercourse without consent at East Corrimal between 1 September and 30 November 1984.[48]

---

48   Lisa Carty, 'Arkell Sex Case Held Next Year: Preliminary Hearing', *Illawarra Mercury*, 10 September 1997.

10

A wide and diverse network of abuse

For many decades Frank Arkell was surrounded by a wide and diverse network of individuals who had some relationship to the sexual abuse of young people, especially boys. This is a theme that reoccurs throughout Arkell's life, from his father's experience as a juror in 1934 through to his school colleagues, many of whom became notorious abusers, and later to his business and political associates. The Wood Royal Commission found that paedophiles tend to group together in small secretive networks to share their preferences and support one another[1]. Even putting aside the evidence of Arkell's alleged personal involvement in Bevan's paedophile network, his grooming of Wollongong boys and his trawling of the city's gay beats, Arkell's networks were already connected to, or associated with, such practices. The spectre of gossip, suspicion, charges and occasionally convictions hangs over the wider personal, business, religious and friendship networks of Frank Arkell. We cannot assume guilt by association, but it seems well beyond mere chance that so many of his schoolmates, business associates, council colleagues, friends in the clergy and other acquaintances were involved in the sexual abuse of minors.

The first sign is a tentative one and comes from his father. Before his suicide in 1941, Sidney was involved as a juror in a sexual assault case, in 1934. The case heard at Wollongong Quarter Sessions Court concerned an 11-year-old girl from Nowra, 80 kilometres south of Wollongong, who was

---

1   J.R.T. Wood, Royal Commission into the NSW Police Service. Final Report. Volume 4: The Paedophile Inquiry (Sydney: NSW Government, 1997), www.opengov.nsw.gov.au/publications/17129; jsessionid=152611E7FD89AE98D77ADD531D7484DE, especially 758–66.

allegedly assaulted. 'I did not go to school that day because I did not want to,' the girl had told the court. 'I was supposed to go to school but I did not. When my mother found out she gave me a hiding. It was then my mother found out what had happened.'[2] The girl had identified the accused, George Henry Phillips, standing among a group of men in the cell yards at the Nowra Police Station. Phillips was working as a gardener in Nowra though he was usually employed as a truck driver in Port Kembla. The girl's story was backed up by evidence from a doctor and a nearby witness, who helped her. As we covered in Chapter 2, Sidney was part of a 12-man jury who found the defendant not guilty and there is circumstantial evidence that Sidney knew the defendant.

Brian Tobin was a long-serving Wollongong Council alderman politically aligned with Arkell's independent team. Tobin was born in 1934 in Thirroul, a key railway town and popular tourist site in the northern suburbs of Wollongong. He was a Christian Brothers Old Boy four years behind Arkell at school. He married his wife, Rita, in the late 1950s and they lived in various places throughout the Wollongong region. Brian described his occupation variously as a fitter, a painter and a storekeeper. By the 1960s, the family had moved to Woonona and, by the 1970s, Brian was working as a real estate agent. An active Rotarian with the Bulli Rotary Club, Tobin had been secretary of the Woonona Chamber of Commerce and chairman of the Combined Northern Chambers of Commerce before being elected to the Wollongong Council in 1984 after several unsuccessful attempts.

Tobin, a key ally of Arkell, was an alderman in Ward 1 in the northern suburbs; he served from 1984 to 1991. In 1987 Brian Tobin stood as an independent at the by-election for the state seat of Heathcote, which included the northern suburbs of Wollongong. He secured 6.1 per cent of the primary vote.[3] On 18 April 1996, investigators from the Wood Royal Commission interviewed Tobin in connection with the then-emerging evidence of Tony Bevan's Wollongong-based paedophile ring. That interview reportedly covered two specific allegations of child sexual abuse against him. Two hours later, Brian Tobin connected a hose to the exhaust pipe of his vehicle, turned on the engine and succumbed to carbon

---

2   'Evidence of an Eleven Year Old Girl Given before Wollongong Quarter Sessions Court', *Illawarra Mercury*, 22 June 1934: 1.
3   Antony Green, *Changing Boundaries, Changing Fortunes: An Analysis of the NSW Elections of 1988 and 1991*, Occasional Paper No. 7, October (Sydney: NSW Parliamentary Library Research Service, 1998), www.parliament.nsw.gov.au/researchpapers/Documents/changing-boundaries-changing-fortunes-an-analysi/op07-98.pdf, 45.

monoxide poisoning.[4] Journalist Richard Guilliat suggested that Tobin was a regular at Bevan's sex parties.[5] No charges were laid against Tobin and the allegations against him were never tested or legally proven.[6] A number of sources indicated to me that it was common knowledge in the northern suburbs and indeed throughout Wollongong that Tobin was an associate of Bevan's and that he had also picked up teenage boys from the beaches at Thirroul and Woonona.[7] These sources also indicated that Brian Tobin, like Bevan, used the resources and opportunities afforded him by being a real estate agent to facilitate his abuse. While Tobin indulged in sex with teenage boys in secret, he lived a public life as a married man with children. He was a regular churchgoer with his wife, Rita, at St Joseph's Catholic Church in Bulli. Indeed, his respectability was central to how he presented himself at council elections. In 1980, the 'Let's Go Independent' election pamphlet with Frank Arkell on the front cover presented Brian Tobin as 'a family man born at Thirroul with many dedicated years behind him of activity in community affairs'.[8]

In 1996 T.K. Tobin, Brian's brother, who lived in the southern suburbs of Sydney, took a complaint to the Australian Press Council against the *Sydney Morning Herald* for publishing claims about Brian, including the subheading 'Brian Tobin, Whose Respectable Facade Concealed a Life of Paedophilia'.[9] In defence against the claim, the newspaper stated that it had information that 'was wholly persuasive and which was corroborated from several, and separate, sources', and that the Wood Royal Commission was aware of Brian Tobin's paedophilia.[10] T.K. Tobin strongly asserted that Brian was innocent of the accusations and argued that the paper made claims in the article but had failed to provide any supporting evidence. The Press Council complaint was upheld on the basis that the paper had failed to publish the supporting evidence.[11]

---

4   Peter Newell, 'Long Struggle to Expose Evil Abuse of Children in the Illawarra', *Illawarra Mercury*, 17 November 2012, [Updated 20 February 2017], www.illawarramercury.com.au/story/1126599/long-struggle-to-expose-evil-abuse-of-children-in-the-illawarra/.
5   Guilliat, 'City of Secrets', 23.
6   Anna Patty and Linton Besser, 'Tough Tactics Forged in the City of Steel', *Sydney Morning Herald*, 21 May 2010, www.smh.com.au/national/nsw/tough-tactics-forged-in-the-city-of-steel-20100520-vpd8.html.
7   Notes from an interview with Janine Cullen, 23 November 2022.
8   'City of Wollongong Council Elections, Independent How to Vote Leaflet, Ward 1', 20 September 1980, Item ID C1/19/01, University of Wollongong Archives.
9   'Shamed to Death', *Sydney Morning Herald*, 5 October 1996.
10 'Adjudication No. 901', *Australian Press Council News*, February 1997: 14.
11 ibid.

Plate 10.1 Wollongong Bishop William Murray, left, with Luigi Barbarito, the Pope's personal representative in Australia, and Lord Mayor Frank Arkell, sometime between 1978 and 1984
Photo: Stuart Piggin: Faith of Steel Collection, University of Wollongong Archives, ID: D158/3/105.

Arkell's Catholicism, his networks through the church and his relationship with priests in the Wollongong diocese also brought him into close association with child sexual abuse. Research by the 2017 Royal Commission into Institutional Responses to Child Sexual Abuse found that between 1950 and 1997, 11.7 per cent of all parish priests from the Diocese of Wollongong were reported to be alleged perpetrators. This was significantly higher than the national average of 7 per cent, giving Wollongong the fifth highest rate in the country, with the highest in the Sale diocese in Gippsland, Victoria. Stephen Jones, federal member for Whitlam (which includes the city of Wollongong) and a former student at Edmund Rice College, said in parliament that students there 'knew what was going on' and his own father had later apologised for sending him to the school.[12]

Arkell was a member of the Catholic Church. Marcella received home visits from the parish priest and she and Frank attended church together at St Therese's in West Wollongong. Frank's attendance dropped away and

---

12   Nick McLaren, 'Wollongong MP Speaks of Sadness as Edmund Rice College Apologises over Historical Abuse of Student', *ABC Illawarra*, 16 June 2016, www.abc.net.au/news/2016-06-16/mp-opens-up-on-child-sex-abuse/7515624.

10. A WIDE AND DIVERSE NETWORK OF ABUSE

became irregular after his mother's death in 1979.[13] The O'Donnells and the Arkells were central figures in the Catholic Church in Wollongong and its suburbs. One of Frank's many uncles, Philip O'Donnell, was the first Christian Brothers Old Boy to become a Catholic priest. Michael O'Donnell, Frank's grandfather, was a strong supporter of the Christian Brothers from its foundation in 1926. The two major figures who were charged with child sexual abuse and who stand out are Father Peter Lewis Comensoli and Brother Michael Evans, though, as we shall see, there were many others. Comensoli was charged and later convicted. The following individuals were all active in Frank Arkell's world of the church and Catholicism.

Peter Lewis Comensoli was born in Corrimal in March 1939.[14] A Christian Brothers College student from the late 1940s until the mid-1950s, he received an A grade in Christian doctrine for the third form in 1954.[15] He was ordained as a priest in 1965 and served in the Wollongong diocese in the 1970s and 1980s. Comensoli was convicted of assaulting two altar boys, aged 10 and 17. One of these assaults occurred in the vestry at St Therese's. These assaults were prefigured by a period of grooming with the use of alcohol and pornographic material, as was common practice among paedophiles. The offences occurred between 1979 and 1983. He was sentenced to 24 months in prison on 18 October 1994.[16]

Comensoli was subsequently charged with further historical offences dating from 1966 and 1968. The first involved multiple assaults of a boy from Ingleburn, where Father Comensoli would visit the family's home and wrestle with the boy, touching him inappropriately. The second involved the assault of a boy from the Shellharbour parish after he had become close to the priest through church activities.[17] Comensoli was removed from the priesthood in 2015 and died in 2019.[18]

---

13 Interview with Peter Bahlmann, 8 July 2023.
14 *South Coast Times*, [Wollongong], 7 February 1941: 10.
15 *South Coast Times*, [Wollongong], 13 December 1954: 4.
16 'Father Peter L. Comensoli Was Jailed but Was Allowed to Remain "Reverend"', *Broken Rites*, [Online], Updated 3 September 2019, www.brokenrites.org.au/drupal/node/194.
17 'This Priest Assaulted Boys in Wollongong NSW, Police Allege', *Broken Rites*, [Online], 15 May 2015, www.bishop-accountability.org/news2015/05_06/2015_05_15_BrokenRites_ThisPriest.htm.
18 'Statement by Bishop Brian Mascord on the Death of Mr Peter Lewis Comensoli', Press release, 20 March 2019, Catholic Diocese of Wollongong, www.dow.org.au/resource/statement-from-bishop-brian-mascord-on-the-death-of-mr-peter-lewis-comensoli/.

Was there a link between Comensoli and Arkell beyond shared Catholicism? There is one source that suggests there was. A senior Wollongong City Council official told journalist Brett Martin that he saw Father Comensoli on at least four occasions deliver a group of boys to Frank Arkell's mayoral office on the tenth floor of the then-new council administration building in Burelli Street, sometime between 1988 and 1991.

Brother Michael Evans was appointed in the late 1970s as a teacher at Edmund Rice College, which had until 1962 been known as Christian Brothers College and had moved from its Crown Lane location to a new site in West Wollongong. From 1975, the school operated solely from the new site on Mount Keira Road.[19] Despite rumours and concerns about inappropriate conduct at his previous school—St Patrick's in Strathfield, Sydney, where he taught from 1974 to 1979—Brother Evans was seen as a suitable candidate for the most senior appointment at the Wollongong school. He became principal in 1982, once again showing how the assortment of Wollongong paedophiles in this period included apparently successful, high-performing individuals who thrived in the public spotlight. Evans was well-liked, confident and, soon, very well-connected in the Wollongong area.[20]

There is evidence that Brother Evans was close to Arkell. Senior ABC reporter in the Illawarra region Julie Posetti told Ellen Fanning on ABC Radio's *AM* program in 1996 that Brother Evans had been 'a regular companion' of Arkell's.[21] Posetti, an award-winning and highly credentialled journalist, was certainly well placed to make these observations. In the late 1980s, she had worked in local commercial radio and for WIN4 TV news, before joining ABC Illawarra in 1990. From 1992 to 1996 she served as ABC regional news editor while maintaining her base in Wollongong.

By the late 1980s, Evans was impossible to miss, becoming a local celebrity of sorts. He was not just a high school principal but also a high-profile cleric, a regular on local radio, the author of a column in the *Illawarra Mercury* and the kind of active, engaged clergyman whom Arkell respected. Evans was close to some senior police officers in Wollongong and Corrimal and was a member of the Wollongong Police Community Consultative Committee

---

19 'Our History', [Online], Edmund Rice College, Wollongong, www.edmundricecollege.nsw.edu.au/our-college/our-history/.
20 Richard Guilliat, 'Brotherly Love', [*Spectrum*], *Sydney Morning Herald*, 22 July 1995: 1A–4A.
21 Ellen Fanning, 'Interview with Julie Posetti', *AM*, [*ABC Radio*], 6 November 1996, R67432, ABC Archives.

10. A WIDE AND DIVERSE NETWORK OF ABUSE

in 1988 and 1989.[22] Inspector Dooley, commander at Corrimal Police Station between 1990 and 1991, told the Wood Royal Commission that his children went to Edmund Rice College and he attended parent–teacher interviews, sporting events and school association meetings with Evans. He said he had known Brother Evans 'I suppose for a total of 10 years and I had regular contact with Brother Evans during the time they [his children] attended school there'.[23]

However, there were emerging reports of child sexual abuse by Evans from the period 1979–1982. In 1989 a local priest, Father Morrie Crocker from Berkeley, reported Evans's behaviour to the Catholic hierarchy in Wollongong and to the police, but there was no serious attention given to the matter.[24] Father Crocker ran a gym in Berkeley and had extensive contact with troubled youth. Three young men who were abused by Evans had confided in Crocker. Their stories were heartfelt, consistent and plausible. After taking formal statements from these three men at Corrimal station, police were given assurances that Evans was receiving counselling and put aside their investigation, with one senior Wollongong officer telling the district commander that there was 'insufficient evidence'.[25] Evans was quietly removed from the principal's post in late 1991.

In the case of Brother Michael Evans, there is evidence of an informal network of knowledge apparent before major public revelations. Brett Martin was captain of the Vikings rugby union first-grade team in the late 1980s when Brother Evans, who was an experienced rugby union coach, applied to join the club as manager of the first-grade team. Several of Martin's teammates spoke to him, indicating that they would not stay with the club if Evans joined, hinting at a dark side to the brother's past behaviour. Many of these players had been through the Catholic school

---

22 See 'Evidence of J. Dooley, Wood Royal Commission, 1997, PR238', in Wood, *Transcripts*. Dooley was Wollongong police patrol commander from 1988 to 1989 and Corrimal patrol commander from 1990 to 1991. He had been stationed in the Wollongong area since 1976.
23 See ibid.
24 'Brother Michael Evans', [Online], Moody Law, Sydney, 2020, www.moodylaw.com.au/brother-michal-evans.
25 See 'Evidence of Patrick Cassidy, Wood Royal Commission, PR238', in Wood, *Transcripts*. Cassidy had been with NSW Police all his adult life and was district commander of the Wollongong patrol area in 1988 and 1989. A senior Wollongong police officer told Cassidy that one of the city's crown prosecutors had informed him that there was 'insufficient evidence' against Brother Evans. In evidence given to the royal commission, P. Conlon, one of the three crown prosecutors based in Wollongong, indicated: 'No, I don't have any recollection of the conversation.' See 'Evidence of P. Conlon, Wood Royal Commission, PR240', in Wood, *Transcripts*.

system in the Illawarra, including Edmund Rice College.²⁶ In a little-known but crucial aspect of the Evans story, it was the information Brett Martin gleaned from his teammates at Vikings, passed on to Peter Cullen, that first activated the *Mercury* editor's interest in the case.

Despairing at the lack of action from local police and the Wollongong diocese, Father Crocker went to see Cullen. Now Cullen had access to the three witness statements that had been taken by the police in Corrimal. There were further reports of alleged offences and, in October 1993, the *Illawarra Mercury* published allegations against Evans from six 'victims'.²⁷ Police resumed their investigations. However, in late 1994, the day after he was served with an arrest warrant for one count of indecent assault, Evans committed suicide by gassing himself inside his car.²⁸

Father Crocker had a clear-eyed sense of the mind of a paedophile and a burning desire for justice for the boys he saw dragged into their orbit.

He wrote:

> If the young, vulnerable and innocent are not protected by the law then all of us become potential victims and we are all vulnerable. There is one universal trait associated with sex abusers and that is their arrogance. They act as if they are immune to retribution and, tragically, too often they are. That these men are still in positions of trust and responsibility is of real concern.²⁹

As a whistleblower who called out the inaction of his church, Father Crocker was ostracised by his peers. In March 1998, the burden of grief and injustice, and the death of a close friend, saw Crocker take his own life in the church hall that had served as his gymnasium and a haven for the boys of the region.

Brother Michael Evans and Father Peter Lewis Comensoli were the most high-profile examples of offending clergy but there were, unfortunately, dozens of other alleged or convicted offenders who taught at Christian Brothers, or who were parish priests in the Wollongong area on a long-term basis or who had served in the area and moved on. Brother John

---

26 Interview with Brett Martin, 23 November 2022.
27 *Illawarra Mercury*, 27 October 1993.
28 Guilliat, 'Brotherly Love'.
29 'Fighting Priest Loses Last Round: Fr. Morrie Crocker, Australian Whistle-Blower, Apparently Commits Suicide', *New Zealand Herald*, 7 June 1998, www.bishop-accountability.org/news/1998_06_07_NewZealandHerald_FightingPriest.htm.

Vincent 'Chris' Roberts had been the subject of multiple complaints while teaching at Christian Brothers. He was ultimately convicted and sentenced to 10 years imprisonment in 1996 for repeated rape in the early 1980s of a 13-year-old boy whom he had met at the school.[30]

Brother Roberts was born in 1942 and ordained in the early 1960s in the Christian Brothers order. There were complaints while he was teaching at a Catholic high school in the Sutherland Shire, in southern Sydney, so he was transferred to Canberra. There were complaints made against him at the Canberra diocese before he was moved to Edmund Rice College in Wollongong in 1983. The practice of transferring paedophile priests and brothers to new parishes or schools rather than addressing their behaviour was well established by the 2017 royal commission and was a phenomenon seen in other jurisdictions internationally. Roberts was convicted of repeatedly molesting, assaulting and raping a 12-year-old from Edmund Rice College in the late 1980s and pleaded guilty to 11 of the 21 charges. He was sentenced to 10 years in prison in September 2016. The sentencing judge found that Roberts had 'betrayed him [his victim] and he betrayed himself as a Christian Brother. The assaults were planned, they were persistent and they were degrading.'[31] In other cases involving Roberts, the church had already paid compensation and these matters were not brought to trial. The survivor support group Broken Rites alleged a coverup of Roberts's alleged crimes committed in Sutherland and later in Canberra.[32]

Father Kelvin Gerald Sharkey was a parish priest in the late 1960s at Fairy Meadow, a suburb 3.5 kilometres north of Wollongong and at the time a feeder area for the high school I attended in the early 1980s. Sharkey was transferred to Batemans Bay in 1971 and retired from the ministry in 1988. He was convicted of 11 counts of child sexual assault, including cases where the abuse occurred in the vestry. The offences occurred between 1968 and 1976 and the victim was 10 years old when they began.

---

30   Shannon Tonkin, 'Former Edmund Rice Brother John Vincent Roberts Jailed for a Decade for Child Abuse', *Sydney Morning Herald*, 30 September 2016, www.smh.com.au/national/nsw/former-edmund-rice-brother-john-vincent-roberts-jailed-for-a-decade-for-child-abuse-20160930-grspxz.html.
31   This information is sourced from the support and advocacy group Broken Rites. See 'Christian Brothers Harboured This Criminal, Brother Chris Roberts, but Now He is in Jail', *Broken Rites*, [Online], Updated 8 October 2016, www.brokenrites.org.au/drupal/node/395.
32   ibid.

Christian Brother Peter Nicholas Lennox, a teacher at Edmund Rice College from 1982 to 1983, was jailed for offences against boys committed at schools in Manly and Goulburn, where he worked in the 1970s.[33] None of these priests or brothers had heeded the advice of Bishop MacCabe, the first Bishop of Wollongong, who did so much to establish the new diocese on a firm footing, when he advised the men of the diocese in the following terms: 'I ask that you all live your Catholic faith every moment of your lives.'[34]

By the late 1980s and early 1990s, the abuse of boys by the Catholic clergy in Wollongong extended beyond the church and schools and included a youth refuge called Eddy's Place, on Mount Keira Road, opened by Brother Michael Evans in 1988. Arkell had been strongly supportive of the proposed refuge as it accorded with his belief that the churches should take a more active role in the provision of social and youth welfare services.[35] Homeless and troubled youth were targets for paedophiles as they could be psychologically manipulated and did not necessarily possess protective family and friendship networks. Bevan had shown this by consistently targeting isolated youth who had already been exposed to sexual abuse or who had troubled relationships with the police. In 1992 Brother William 'Bill' Hocking, who oversaw the refuge, was convicted of sexually assaulting a 14-year-old boy at Eddy's Place. Hocking was also a youth counsellor at Edmund Rice College and a former head of the Wollongong diocese. After receiving only a non-custodial sentence, he was removed from any contact with boys.[36]

In the case of Evans and Hocking, other survivors made statements to the police and even public comments to the effect that these two men targeted them in the early 1980s in Wollongong. The weight of evidence suggests that the successful convictions represent only a small percentage of the total offences committed. This occurred for a variety of reasons: survivors died, they received less than sympathetic treatment from police, they felt disempowered and unable to speak up or police made mistakes or took resourcing decisions that meant their case was not followed up. More than this, the courts and the legal system itself represent a complex, expensive

---

33 This information is sourced from the support and advocacy group Broken Rites Australia. See 'A Christian Brother is Jailed for Offences He Committed 40 Years Ago', Broken Rites, [Online], Updated 2 January 2020, brokenrites.org.au/drupal/node/340.
34 Dwyer, 'Diocese Celebrates 70th Anniversary of its Foundation Decree!'.
35 Stuart Piggin, 'Interviews with Kathleen Skipp and daughter, and Frank Arkell: Saint Michael's, Wollongong (Anglican)', 1983[?], D158/04/13a, Archives Online, University of Wollongong, archives online.uow.edu.au/nodes/view/3050.
36 'Brother William Hocking', [Online], Moody Law, Sydney, 2020, www.moodylaw.com.au/brother-william-hocking.

10. A WIDE AND DIVERSE NETWORK OF ABUSE

and forbidding process. Journalist Louise Milligan in her book *Witness* has poignantly detailed the harrowing experience for female 'victims' who pursue sexual assault cases.[37] Given all these factors, it is a small miracle that any cases secured a conviction.

The long list of cases involving Catholic clergy in Wollongong shows some connections to Frank Arkell. Child sexual abuse was occurring in his church, of course, but more specifically, there was evidence of a friendship between Brother Michael Evans and Arkell and there was the recollection of a senior council officer, who saw Father Peter Lewis Comensoli taking boys to Arkell's mayoral office. What this long list also shows is that Arkell's old school, Christian Brothers College (renamed Edmund Rice College in 1962), was a damaged institution with entrenched sexual abuse dating back many decades.

In some cases, the links between Arkell and sexual abuse were once removed and manifest in relatives, political allies or even the siblings of political allies. Arkell's friend and political ally Brian Tobin was interviewed by investigators from the Wood Royal Commission with two specific allegations of child sexual abuse. His suicide could be seen as further evidence of the reality of his secret life as a paedophile since he chose a path common to many child sex offenders on the verge of being uncovered. Harry Schipp was a long-serving Wollongong councillor from an influential Dapto family and a key Arkell ally in the independent camp, elected from the number-two position on the ticket for Ward 5 in 1974. Harry Schipp's son, Murray, was charged with and convicted of several counts of indecent assault and aggravated indecent assault of girls in 2010.[38]

In another extraordinary coincidence, Arkell's successor as lord mayor, David Campbell, made the transition from local government to state member for Keira and then police minister in a state Labor government, but resigned on the eve of the broadcast of a Channel 7 news report showing him visiting a gay sex club in Sydney. Campbell's actions sparked a debate about media ethics and his right to privacy.[39] By 2010, such clubs and gay

---

37 Louise Milligan, *Witness: An Investigation into the Brutal Cost of Seeking Justice* (Sydney: Hachette, 2020).
38 Michelle Tydd, 'Murray Schipp's Sex Assault Appeal Fails', *Illawarra Mercury*, 21 April 2011, [Updated 6 November 2012], www.illawarramercury.com.au/story/635019/murray-schipps-sex-assault-appeal-fails/.
39 Andrew Norton, 'The Minister, the Gay Sauna and the Seven Reporter', *Crikey*, 21 May 2010, www.crikey.com.au/2010/05/21/the-minister-the-gay-sauna-and-the-seven-reporter/.

sex itself were no longer illegal. Rachel Evans in the *Green Left Weekly* argued that Campbell's resignation was a sign that 'Labor governments around Australia have capitulated to homophobia to varying degrees' and it 'was this entrenched prejudice that kept this ambitious politician in the closet for 25 years'.[40] It is not clear how Evans gained access to Campbell's innermost personal motivations and choices. Others, however, questioned the wisdom of a minister travelling to the club in his ministerial vehicle and noted the contradiction between his public persona as a committed family man and his apparent private preferences. As police minister, this was especially high-risk behaviour, making him potentially vulnerable to blackmail or duress. Adam Walters, the Channel 7 reporter who broke the story, argued that it was 'a question of integrity, character and deception'. Were we comfortable with a member of parliament and police minister who had led a double life for 25 years, which even his family and closest friends knew nothing about?

There are no easy answers regarding Campbell's choices and the validity of Channel 7's broadcast, but the question of how much of a politician's secret life is a matter of public interest, and in what circumstances, is strongly reminiscent of the issues in Frank Arkell's life. Successive lord mayors of Wollongong, and their actions, kept delivering ethical conundrums for residents and media commentators alike. If that was not enough, Campbell's successor as lord mayor, George Harrison, a Labor and later independent, from 1999 to 2002, often described as 'colourful' and 'controversial', was forced to resign after being declared bankrupt. A long-running legal battle had triggered Harrison's bankruptcy and he was required to resign under section 234 of the *Local Government Act 1993* (NSW).[41]

The final type of evidence against Arkell comes not from inquiries, police charges or personal, political or religious associations with known paedophiles but from the widespread awareness in the Illawarra that there was something up with Frank Arkell. My school friend in Year 7 in 1979 associated Puckeys Estate, a known gay beat, with Frank Arkell. In the late 1970s through to the 1990s, the students from Keira Boys High School and adjacent Wollongong High School and possibly many other high schools knew about Arkell's homosexuality and had even heard rumours indicating he preferred younger males. In 1991, a student friend from the University

---

40 Rachel Evans, 'David Campbell "Scandal" Reveals Gay Bigotry', *Green Left Weekly*, [Sydney], 29 May 2010, no. 839, www.greenleft.org.au/content/david-campbell-scandal-reveals-gay-bigotry.
41 Lisa Carty, 'He's Gone: Harrison Quits as Mayor', *Illawarra Mercury*, 26 July 2002: 1, 4. See section 234, *Local Government Act 1993* (NSW), as amended, www5.austlii.edu.au/au/legis/nsw/consol_act/lga 1993182/s234.html.

10. A WIDE AND DIVERSE NETWORK OF ABUSE

of Wollongong spoke to me about a paedophile network in Wollongong. The final reports of the Wood Royal Commission, published just six years later, proved her right.

This amounted to tacit local knowledge about Frank Arkell passed among family and friends. As much as Arkell's illicit activities were a secret, for many in Wollongong, it was an open one. Some of those people knew because they heard from friends, from relatives or from the boys and young men who were drawn or dragged into that world. Mark Richmond, who was born in 1963 and grew up in Keiraville, Figtree, Dapto and West Wollongong, recalled that there were places you did not go as a boy, including the toilets at Fairy Meadow Beach and at MacCabe Park. He was also aware as a young man in the late 1970s and early 1980s that there were certain vehicles that cruised around town of which you had to be aware.

Richmond also recalled that it was 'common knowledge' that Tony Bevan 'wasn't a very nice man', and he could list the names of many of Bevan's paedophile associates. Richmond had a close friend who had worked at the Market Street Bistro in the late 1970s. At closing time, Bevan and many other Wollongong businessmen would congregate hoping to offer rides or late-night drinks to young male patrons, many of whom were under 18 years of age.[42] Some of 'Tony's Boys' had friends who were not happy with the behaviour of the older men. The secret recordings made by Tony Bevan included at least three prank calls to his office in Crown Street. They all followed a similar pattern to the one transcribed below, which was taken by Bevan's secretary:

> Richard: Hello?
>
> Speaker 2: 5475.
>
> Richard: Is Tony there?
>
> Speaker 2: No, I'm sorry. He's not.
>
> Richard: Richard here. I was wondering if I could borrow one of Tony's motorbikes tomorrow.
>
> Speaker 2: I don't know if he has any motorbikes. Has he?
>
> Richard: Yeah.
>
> Speaker 2: Who's Richard?
>
> Richard: Richard. You know the one that gives head jobs all the time?[43]

---

42 Interview with Mark Richmond, 13 October 2022.
43 Transcripts of Bevan Tapes, No. 37.

That Bevan was the target of prank calls offering oral sex in return for riding his motorbike shows clearly that information about his network as well as what was happening at the West Dapto farm, at the Windang aerial patrol base and elsewhere was filtering out into the wider community.

Andrew Anthony is a lifelong Figtree resident whose family came to know Frank Arkell in the early 1980s. Their association with Arkell was very positive. Arkell was a keen supporter of and a regular visitor to the Hellenic Club in West Wollongong. Andrew's father was one of the original signatories to the club's first constitution, signed in 1989, and he maintained a healthy respect for Arkell, including speaking at his funeral in 1998. As we have seen, the olive grove behind the club was Arkell's idea and he donated the trees—a fitting contribution from a man who loved gardens and Greek culture. Andrew recalls that:

> when the club was established, he [Arkell] donated money, and he attended functions that the club had as fundraising events to buy the club [building] … I have pretty fond memories of Frank coming there quite regularly—at least, you know, like once a week to have dinner at the club. My family would be there.[44]

A Figtree High School graduate in 1995 with an interest in politics, Andrew talked to Arkell about politics and Greek culture, in which Arkell showed a particular interest. Arkell lent Andrew his copies of the Greek epics by Homer, the *Iliad* and the *Odyssey*. As he recalled: 'I never felt that it was inappropriate. But he certainly seemed to take a liking to me because I had a big interest in politics during high school. He encouraged me a lot to take an interest in politics.'

But Andrew was told to be wary of Frank Arkell and watch out for him around younger children:

> And I have got two younger brothers. People would often say to me, 'Oh, just be careful leaving them alone around Frank.' People would say that to me. You'd get cautions and warnings. People quite often [say,] 'Just be careful. Frank's a bit different.' No-one labelled him a paedophile. But just that he could get too familiar with young kids. That was what was implied.[45]

---

44 Interview with Andrew Anthony, 24 October 2022.
45 ibid.

Andrew's family had a positive association with Arkell, yet they had also heard rumours and stories of illicit and troubling behaviour. They live with this essential paradox, which only became stronger after the allegations were made public and formalised into police charges. This paradox is almost a central feature of Wollongong culture as many have tried to reconcile their experience of a Frank Arkell who gave so much to Wollongong with the emerging picture of a persistent child sexual abuser. Gordon Bradbery, who visited Arkell in the last few months of his life and served as lord mayor from 2011 to 2024, called this Wollongong's 'cognitive dissonance that we are all suffering'—a dissonance that speaks to the difficulty of remembering and making sense of a man of such terrible contradictions.

Many people were, of course, shocked when the allegations came into the public sphere, but others felt as though these allegations, and the nature of Arkell's death in 1998, merely confirmed their suspicions or even their own experiences of him. Rumour and innuendo are a treacherous guide for the historian but the widespread and persistent nature of these concerns, and their ongoing grounding in the culture and way of life of the city, make common knowledge and local understanding in this case factors that further confirm the reality of Arkell's systemic and long-term child sexual abuse. What appeared to be rumour and innuendo were also informal networks of shared vernacular knowledge passed around to minimise risk and give the lost boys of Wollongong a chance to avoid known abusers in a region that possessed a wide and diverse network of abuse.

11

The University of Wollongong and its paedophile past

Frank Arkell's rise to prominence coincided with a formative period in the evolution of Wollongong's post-secondary education institutions. As a growing regional city, there were hopes and plans for a local university but these took some time to mature. When a new institution did emerge it was finding a place in the city and seeking autonomy from its parent institution, the University of New South Wales, which was based in Kensington, a suburb of Sydney. By the 1960s, new academic leaders were moving to Wollongong and the city's well-to-do middle class was seeking to get involved in the life of the university and influence its direction.

Frank Arkell was very interested in, and committed to, the new university for Wollongong. The site proposed for it was on Northfields Avenue in Keiraville, about 3.5 kilometres north-west of the Wollongong CBD. The Hoskins' homestead of Gleniffer Brae sits on the slopes of Mount Keira overlooking the future university site, while the future Botanic Garden, which did not open to the public until 1971, was immediately to the south. The setting, nestled in the shadow of Mount Keira, is quite spectacular and, in the 1950s and 1960s, this area had tremendous potential as a site for civic, educational and greenspace usage. Having a university for the region was also a common aspiration for many of Wollongong's middle-class civic leaders. It matched their call for a better-educated, more refined and more cultured city. That the University of New South Wales (and its predecessor organisation) controlled post-secondary education in Wollongong in the 1950s also activated a desire for greater regional autonomy and neatly tapped into a growing sense of civic pride.

From the immediate postwar period, an outpost of the NSW Institute of Technology delivered post-secondary education in Wollongong. The institute would eventually transform into the University of New South Wales, in 1958. The idea for an autonomous and comprehensive university in Wollongong arose formally through support from the Wollongong Council, which, in 1959, inaugurated a mayor's appeal to raise money to advance the idea. Wollongong's move followed that of Newcastle, which had formed a committee for an autonomous university in 1958. As with other regional centres such as Armidale in New South Wales and the Latrobe Valley in Victoria, acquiring a local university was a way to mark towns and cities as coming of age as well as having achieved a level of sophistication not always accorded to them by wider society. It spoke to civic pride as much as being an entrepreneurial move to attract, secure and retain high-income professionals in the region.[1]

The Wollongong University College, a branch of the University of New South Wales, was officially opened in 1962. The first courses it offered were closely tied to the workforce and research needs of the steelworks and the coalmines, which were also the major corporate donors. The earliest disciplines were engineering, science and metallurgy with arts and commerce gaining a tentative foothold only from the mid-1960s. Its structure and method of operation closely followed the model set by Newcastle, which also secured a branch campus of the Sydney-based university in 1951. When the Wollongong University College held its formal opening ceremony at the Northfields Avenue site in 1962, all the students were male, enrolled in engineering, science or metallurgy, and most were part-timers who worked in the local industries by day.[2]

Widespread support for a new university was shared across political party lines and by key independent aldermen. We noted in Chapter 7 that Harold Hanson had articulated the city-based independent platform in 1968 and this, too, covered the development of cultural and educational institutions

---

[1] See, for example, Nancy Cushing, Katrina Quinn, and Caroline McMillen, 'University of Newcastle: Recasting the City of Newcastle as a "Univer-City"—The Journey from "Olde" Newcastle-Upon-Tyne to the New Silk Road', in *Univer-Cities: Strategic View of the Future. From Berkeley and Cambridge to Singapore and Rising Asia. Volume II*, ed. by Anthony S.C. Teo (Singapore: World Scientific Publishing, 2015), 93–118, doi.org/10.1142/9789814644457_0006, especially 101–7; Matthew Jordan, *A Spirit of True Learning: A Jubilee History of the University of New England* (Sydney: UNSW Press, 2004), especially 18–38; Vincent Lyn Meek, *Brown Coal or Plato? A Study of the Gippsland Institute of Advanced Education*, ACER Research Series No. 105 (Melbourne: Australian Council for Educational Research, 1984).
[2] Josie Castle, *University of Wollongong: An Illustrated History* (Wollongong: University of Wollongong, 1991), 17.

11. THE UNIVERSITY OF WOLLONGONG AND ITS PAEDOPHILE PAST

including a university and an art gallery. Labor members of Wollongong Council, such as former mayor John Parker, and of state parliament, including Laurie Kelly, were also very supportive. Kelly became a member of the University Council in 1976 and deputy chancellor in 1978.

But no one in this period made the university such a key part of their public platform as Frank Arkell. It helped that when Arkell became lord mayor in 1974 the university was on the cusp of dramatic change as it gradually came out from under a long period of control by the University of New South Wales. The subsequent year, 1975, was of course the university's foundation year—the first year of full autonomy. There were key ceremonies to mark these occasions. A building program, inaugurated to cater for growing numbers of students and staff, offered many more public engagements and media opportunities. Arkell became mayor at exactly the right time to be heavily involved in the life of the new institution.

Plate 11.1 The first University of Wollongong graduation ceremony, held in Wollongong Town Hall, 11 June 1976
Photo: University of Wollongong Archives, Collection U25/n2b/31/10.

In April 1976, Arkell officially opened the third stage of the University of Wollongong Union building, unveiling a plaque that featured his name as the man who did the honours.³ The unveiling featured one of Arkell's more compelling speeches. He said it was a great honour as he was the first Wollongong mayor to open anything on a university campus. He went on to say:

> This University of Wollongong can be said to be, I think, closer to the community than its mother and its older sisters. There is more identification with the city and its citizens at Wollongong than can be said of other universities. This Union building will be the soul of the University. It combines students and staff. It brings together all the hopes, all the yearnings, and all the aspirations of the students— our future generation of citizens—and the intellectual drive and enthusiasm of the staff. The combination of these two segments of our society is bound to have a tremendous impact on the growth and development of our city.⁴

Plate 11.2 Lord Mayor Frank Arkell unveils the plaque commemorating the official opening of the stage three extensions of the Wollongong University Union building, 2 April 1976
Photo: University of Wollongong Archives, Collection U25/n2b/14/09.

---

3 *University of Wollongong Campus News* 2, no. 4 (21 April 1976): 1–2, Call no. 378.94405/WOLL/26, Archives Online, University of Wollongong. More details on the official opening are on pp. 6–7. All editions of the *Campus News* were accessed through the University of Wollongong's Archives Online, at archivesonline.uow.edu.au/.
4 ibid.

This was Arkell at his rhetorical best. The speech had a clear and strong message and none of the usual twists and turns that sometimes limited the impact of his rhetoric. And he was right to predict a central role for the University of Wollongong in the years to come.

In 1981, Arkell accepted an invitation from the newly appointed vice-chancellor Ken McKinnon to be chairperson of the Friends of the University membership committee. The Friends of the University was a registered company with three main arms: a consulting service called Uniadvice, a project committee and a membership committee. By 1982, there were 212 members of the last and the list was a who's who of Wollongong in the early 1980s. The Friends included members of the legal profession, businesspeople, senior staff from the coalmines, steelworks and associated industries, as well as corporate members such as Metal Manufactures, John Lysaght (Australia) Proprietary Limited and Vernier Engineering, and cultural members such as Theatre South.

In 1982 Robyn Slater, a local media personality and active member of the Friends, conducted an oral history interview with Arkell in which he noted that the rationale for the Friends group was to 'promote better understanding within the community of Wollongong of the University. And I do hope— and a better understanding of the University in the city and vice versa, in the city of the University.'[5] This is more characteristic of Arkell's phrasing, in which he often overly complicated the simplest of ideas.

During his long term as lord mayor, Arkell had also officiated at graduations for the Wollongong Institute of Education in the 1970s, with the formal ceremonies held at the Town Hall and including a 'civic address' by the mayor. The institute was co-located with the university at the Northfields Avenue site and had yet to secure an appropriate venue for its graduations. The institute amalgamated with the university in 1983. From 2,300 students at the institute in 1976, numbers at the university grew to almost 6,000 by the second semester of 1985.[6] Arkell made the university his own. It was one of the few places where he was able to forge a role separate from that of his political twin, Tony Bevan. The beaming pride on his face when he was made one of the first of four new fellows of the university in 1985 was very clear.

---

5   Robyn Slater, 'Interview with Professor Ken McKinnon and Mr Frank Arkell', Friends Session on the FM Test Broadcast, 24 March 1982, U59/03/03a, Archives Online, University of Wollongong, archivesonline.uow.edu.au/nodes/view/3259?keywords=Friends+Session+on+the+FM+Test+Broadcast &type=all&highlights=eyIwIjoiZnJpZW5kcyIsIjciOiJzZXNzaW9uIiwiOCI6ImZtIiwiOSI6InRlc3Q iLCIxMCI6ImJyb2FkY2FzdCJ9&lsk=c735464575a768a8cab0413bf2aed3f8.
6   *University of Wollongong Campus News*, 16 August 1985: 2.

There were other Wollongong professionals who were heavily involved in the formation, development and governance of the university. As it happens, all of them had close working and personal relationships with Frank Arkell. Wollongong solicitor and local historian Edgar Beale became an important figure in the formation and development of the university. James Edgar Osborne Beale was a major Wollongong identity, often featuring in newspaper court reports in his role as a solicitor. He was a member of Wollongong Rotary, a member and past president of Legacy, a member of the Illawarra Historical Society from 1946, sometime president of the Wollongong Symphony Orchestra management committee and honorary secretary of the Illawarra Grammar School Council.[7]

Like Arkell, Beale traced his family's origins to the 'founding fathers' of the Illawarra. In Beale's case, this was embodied in his middle name: Henry Osborne was a pioneering landowner and coalmine owner of the area, though many Australians may better know the name Octavius Beale, the Sydney-based piano manufacturer. Octavius, who was Edgar's grandfather, brought good-quality upright pianos into the living rooms of Australian families. Beale was also related through his mother's family to Charles Throsby Smith, who secured one of the first land grants in Wollongong, in 1820, so his Illawarra colonial credentials were impeccable. As *University of Wollongong Campus News* put it in 1989, Edgar Beale was 'connected with Illawarra's oldest colonial families'. Born on 8 October 1916 in Sydney, Beale had enlisted in Wollongong in 1939 and served in the 34th Battalion of the Second Australian Imperial Force. After the war, he qualified as a solicitor, set up a practice in Corrimal Street in Wollongong and was secretary of the 34th Battalion Veterans' Association by the early 1950s.[8] Beale married Margery Mouton (nee McPhee) in late December 1952, whom he first met when he acted for her in a probate matter after her first husband, J.L. Mouton, died at just 35 years of age.[9] Beale's small though influential Wollongong practice comprised just himself as a solicitor and his sister, Jean, who was the office administrator.

---

7   *University of Wollongong Campus News*, 7 April 1977: 3; 'BEALE, Edgar (1916–1989)', *Bulletin*, [Illawarra Historical Society], June 1979, www.illawarramuseum.com/page/beale-edgar-1916-1989.
8   James Edgar Osborne Beale, Service Number NX125047, National Archives of Australia, Canberra; *University of Wollongong Campus News*, 8 May 1989: 4, call no. 378.94405/WOLL/26, Archives Online, University of Wollongong.
9   On Beale's legal work representing Margaret Mouton, see *Illawarra Mercury*, 14 July 1950: 6. On their subsequent marriage, see *Sydney Morning Herald*, 17 January 1953: 40.

11. THE UNIVERSITY OF WOLLONGONG AND ITS PAEDOPHILE PAST

Plate 11.3 Edgar Beale and Frank Arkell at an Illawarra Historical Society event in 1983

Note: Beale and Arkell are holding a letter of thanks from the Queen Mother written to a Wollongong family who cared for a child evacuee from England during World War II.

Photo: *Illawarra Mercury* Image Collection and Wollongong City Library, Image no. P26238.

Edgar Beale knew Arkell very well through the Illawarra Historical Society of which Beale was a long-time president, a life member from 1978 and a highly influential and well-published historian. Margery was also very active in the society. Edgar was on the initial Wollongong University College Advisory Committee from 1962 and was elected to the university's council, serving a term from 1975 to 1978. He was deputy chairman of the council and chaired several of its committees. He was a key member of the University Union including a member of its first board of management in 1965. He served variously as president and vice-president of the union board and remained on the board until 1977 as a University Council nominee. He was honoured with an invitation to give an occasional address at a graduation ceremony in that year.[10] Also in 1977 the university conferred on Beale an honorary Doctorate of Letters for his extensive contributions to general and regional history and the university.[11] After his death in 1989, *Campus News* described Beale as 'a founding father of the University', who 'belongs in the University honour roll'.[12] It is hard to imagine a more favoured member of the university community; he was offered every honour imaginable.

This 'founding father' was, however, also the subject of a sexual abuse allegation. In late 1978, an 18-year-old male made a complaint to Wollongong police that he had been picked up by Beale in a motor vehicle at Figtree in October. Beale was subsequently charged with 'attempt to commit an act of indecency on a male' (listed under s. 60L of the NSW *Crimes Act 1900*) as well as 'common assault' relating to the same incident. The young man was due to give evidence at Wollongong Court of Petty Sessions in early March 1979 but was threatened by unknown persons outside the courthouse. The alleged victim was given $1,000 and told to disappear to Queensland or his life would be in danger.[13]

Brian Pullen was another important figure in the Friends of the University group. Born in 1948, Pullen was a sociable, well-connected businessman who managed the Normandie Motor Inn and Function Centre in North Wollongong. The Normandie was a two-storey, blond-brick hotel with a penthouse built in 1948. In 1955 it was extensively renovated and redesigned, with the addition of a third floor by Sydney-based architect Cyril Christian Ruwald (1895–1959).[14] In the 1970s and early 1980s, the French restaurant at the Normandie was considered one of the better eateries in Wollongong, the blond brick now painted white. After a steady decline in more recent years, the Normandie was demolished in 2024, but back in the early 1980s, as Normandie's manager, Pullen cut a dashing figure driving a Triumph TR6 open-top sports car and later a Jaguar. He was elected a life member of the Friends of the University in 1982. In 1981 and 1982 Pullen was chairman of the Leisure Coast Convention and Tourism Bureau and took on the role of general manager of the new North Beach International.[15]

---

10 *University of Wollongong Campus News*, 7 April 1977: 3.
11 *University of Wollongong Campus News*, 7 July 1980: 11.
12 *University of Wollongong Campus News*, 9 May 1989: 4; Illawarra Historical Society *Bulletin*, 'BEALE, Edgar (1916–1989)'.
13 NSW Police File on Edgar Beale, CNI Number 3013464; Brett Martin, Unpublished manuscript.
14 'Diazo Print Normandie Hotel Wollongong', Object no. 90/317-350, 1955, in *Architectural Plans and Drawings by Cyril Ruwald and Others* (Sydney: Powerhouse Museum Collection, 1990), collection.maas.museum/object/104303#ixzz2uc5OBZBh&gid=1&pid=1.
15 *Canberra Times*, 7 March 1982: 6. See also Yates, 'Thank Goodness It Couldn't Happen Here'.

11. THE UNIVERSITY OF WOLLONGONG AND ITS PAEDOPHILE PAST

In 1984 Pullen offered to host a welcome home event for Lauchlan Chipman and Robyn Slater at the Normandie. Chipman was, at the time, a professor of philosophy at the University of Wollongong, while Slater was a well-known media identity in the region. The newly married couple had spent a semester at Harvard University. In one report, *Campus News* editor Giles Pickford described Pullen as 'Lord Pullen'—a testament to his outgoing, flamboyant character.[16]

Brian Pullen was very close to Arkell. He was Arkell's campaign manager for the 1981 state election campaign and a key advisor on the successful 1984 campaign. But Pullen was to become an embarrassment to the Arkell camp in 1987 when he was charged and convicted of inappropriate dealings with a 16-year-old boy at a shopping centre in Sutherland Shire in Sydney. His name quietly disappeared from the Friends group. The university never made a formal statement about Pullen and never publicly revoked his life membership of the Friends. In February 1998, when Arkell's charges were being heard at the committal hearing, the *Illawarra Mercury* reported that he was being publicly supported by two friends—'most notably by his former political advisor Brian Pullen'.[17] Pullen later moved to Queensland and died in 2004.[18]

Engineering remained an important field for the university and, in the 1980s, Vernier Engineering was a corporate member of the Friends group and was involved in a series of projects with the Faculty of Engineering.[19] We know that the owner and managing director of Vernier Engineering was none other than Tom Gaun. As we saw in Chapter 9, Gaun was a central participant in the Bevan paedophile network and was recorded on the Bevan Tapes. He also used employment opportunities at his own firm to attract boys into his orbit and groom them, and he was a regular visitor to Costellos nightclub in Kellet Street, Kings Cross. Gaun's flashy Rolls Royce was well-known around Wollongong. Several sources have told me that boys and young men knew enough to be wary of the vehicle and the man who sat in the backseat, for Gaun always had a chauffeur.

---

16 *University of Wollongong Campus News*, 10 June 1986: 4.
17 Carty, 'Arkell Goes to Trial'.
18 'Brian Christopher Pullen Death Notice', *Illawarra Mercury*, 14 April 2004: 47. See also *Sydney Morning Herald*, 8 April 2004.
19 *University of Wollongong Campus News* 6, no. 4 (1988): 8; *University of Wollongong Campus News*, 8 November 1988: 1.

In the cases of Arkell, Beale, Pullen and Gaun, we see highly successful, sometimes flamboyant individuals who were associated with child sexual offences drawn to the university. In the process of setting up the funding, governance and support structures for the university, individuals who had an association with child sexual abuse managed to secure a number of key positions on the University Council and the Friends of the University. It is important to emphasise that there is no evidence that the university or the Friends group was in any way involved in illegal or illicit activities. The evidence simply suggests that several Wollongong paedophiles were active across a range of groups and organisations in the Illawarra and the university was not immune to their obvious capacity and desire to be involved. A characteristic feature of the Wollongong paedophiles was that they were not leading quiet private lives pursuing their illicit plans. Instead, they were living in plain sight, using their charm, wealth and organisational networks to be publicly engaged wherever possible.

While a series of individuals connected with child abuse participated in the life of the university, on a separate level altogether, Arkell appears to have influenced university staff to become more heavily involved in local politics. This was an unusual development and begs the question of whether it was Arkell's persuasion that convinced staff to do so or whether the university had an unofficial policy of securing staff representation on Wollongong Council to ensure its interests were effectively represented. Frank was able to convince several well-placed senior university officials to stand for the council as Arkell-aligned independents. The private actions of staff should legitimately be separate from their work roles but when such high-profile senior staff were standing for council election, it does raise the question of whether the university was allowing itself to become an Arkell-aligned political force. Whatever the precise origin, the University of Wollongong provided several of the personnel who subsequently joined Arkell's independent group as candidates or campaign managers.

One such figure was Giles Pickford. As the university's public relations manager, he provided, among other things, administration and support for the Friends group. He was the interface between the university and the public and edited the weekly *University of Wollongong Campus News* until his departure for The Australian National University in 1988. He worked with Arkell quite closely and, within a few short years of Arkell's appointment as chair of the Friends, Pickford stood as an independent candidate for Wollongong Council. Pickford served one term, from 1985 to 1988.

University staff should be able to have a life beyond their workplace, including a politically active one, but this general principle is complicated by Pickford's senior community-facing role at the university and the fact that one of the key organisations with which he was liaising was Wollongong Council. Then there was the overlap between Arkell's deep engagement with the Friends and Pickford's subsequent successful move to stand as an Arkell-aligned independent on the council. One wonders how Pickford managed his potential conflicts of interest on the council when a matter related to the university came onto the agenda. Likewise, at the university in his community relations role, how did he separate his work and council roles and to what extent did he disclose any potential conflicts of interest? At the 1988 state election, Pickford stood as an independent candidate for the northern suburbs seat of Keira, so his political engagement with the 'Arkell Independents' was a wholehearted one.[20] We saw with Brian Tobin and now with Pickford that the Arkell Independents were looking to broaden their electoral base and they fielded candidates in the 1987 Heathcote by-election and in the 1988 state elections. Another university staff member, Phillip Laird, a transport expert from the Department of Mathematics, also ran on the Arkell ticket in 1983. There were of course exceptions to this pattern, including Bill Mowbray from the School of Education, who stood for the council in Ward 2 under the Labor Party banner, but Pickford's central and senior role in community relations at the university and his subsequent move onto the council aligned with Arkell raise questions about whether this was a university strategy approved at the most senior level or whether Pickford's political ambitions were driven entirely by his life outside the university and not endorsed (or at least tacitly encouraged) by its management.

Another figure was Ethel Hayton, an English migrant from Durham, who was born in 1913. Her father, W.J. Hayton, had moved to Australia in the 1920s while Ethel and her mother, Elizabeth, followed in 1930. Ethel's father died in 1931 after a short illness and her mother continued working in a bookshop.[21] As a young woman, Ethel also worked in the bookshop at the lower end of Crown Street. After World War II, she began working as a journalist and became the social affairs reporter for the *Illawarra Mercury* in the late 1960s. She led a busy civic and social life and was known to be close to many of the key identities in Wollongong politics and professional

---

20 Peter Stewart, 'Interview with Giles Pickford—Academic Manager and Epicure', July 2011, The Australian National University, Canberra, openresearch-repository.anu.edu.au/bitstream/1885/12924/2/giles_pickford.html.
21 'Late Mr W.J. Hayton', *Illawarra Mercury*, 23 October 1931: 8.

life. Living in an apartment on Crown Street, she was herself a Wollongong identity and could be found at many charitable and fundraising events. In 1959 she was one of the founding members of the committee established to raise funds for the new university.

Hayton's agenda matched those of Harold Hanson, John Parker and Frank Arkell, all of whom supported the idea of improving the cultural tenor of Wollongong. There was a pervading sense among the well-off Wollongong middle class that the city needed improving and a healthy dose of high culture would help. Wollongong's image as a grimy steel city weighed heavily on the shoulders of these residents as they sought to advance and refine (as they saw it) regional culture and education. Hayton was a founding member of the Committee for the Wollongong Conservatorium of Music, helped raise money for the purchase of a Steinway piano for the Town Hall and was heavily involved with the Wollongong Art Gallery. It was almost inevitable that Hayton would end up on the Friends of the University and, indeed, she was made a life member in 1982.[22] Frank Arkell was very close to Hayton. When Wollongong celebrated the 150th anniversary of the gazettal of the town, Arkell commissioned Hayton to write a commemorative history—a hardcover coffee-table book with colour photographs.[23]

The Friends evinced this cultural sensibility in their very first function in 1981 at which local writers, and one member of staff, read selected Australian poetry. Guests of honour included eminent historian Professor Russel Ward and renowned Australian composer Peter Sculthorpe. Sydney musician David Pereira performed a selection of Sculthorpe's work.[24] Reflecting on the legacy of Ethel Hayton many years after her death, research by a University of Wollongong academic underpinning a University Library exhibition celebrated Hayton's life while also pointing out that some people found her a difficult, often-irascible character. Wollongong Council named a short street near her old Crown Street apartment the 'Ethel Hayton Walk'. Hayton remains a key figure in university life, with her name gracing a generous visiting fellowship.

---

22 'Ethel Hayton: Avid Arts Advocate or Social-Climbing Busybody?', Media release, 9 April 2019, University of Wollongong, www.uow.edu.au/media/2019/ethel-hayton-avid-arts-advocate-or-social-climbing-busybody.php.
23 See Ethel Hayton, *Wollongong 150 Years: The City of Greater Wollongong, 1834–1984* (Port Kembla: South Coast Printers, 1984).
24 *University of Wollongong Campus News* 7, no. 3 (25 March 1981): 1.

11. THE UNIVERSITY OF WOLLONGONG AND ITS PAEDOPHILE PAST

In the 1990s, Wollongong Council commissioned the University of Wollongong to produce another history of the city—an update of Hayton's 1984 publication. It was published by the University of Wollongong Press in 1997 and featured the work of university staff and other local scholars. The book was edited by Jim Hagan, then a recently retired professor of history and former dean of the Faculty of Arts, along with Andrew Wells, a member of the Department of History and Politics and later a senior research leader. Hagan was an active and long-serving member of the Labor Party's Thirroul branch and, in 1967, had secured membership on the powerful NSW Labor administrative committee.[25] The book was published the year after the Wood Royal Commission had heard evidence on the Wollongong paedophile network and the activities of Tony Bevan and others.

The collection includes valuable historical scholarship written in an accessible way. The chapter 'Local Government since 1947' by Peter Sheldon makes general reference to the concerns about potential conflicts of interest regarding Arkell and his family businesses, noting: 'It was easy to point out potential conflicts of interest involving Arkell's family property holdings and developments and business interests as a real estate agent.' However, he argues that 'it was harder to mobilise these claims into successful electoral campaigns'. The reference to the emerging evidence of Arkell's secret life is coyly referred to only as 'Labor's repeated allegations'. The chapter suggests it was Arkell's vision for a post-industrial Wollongong that was especially effective at the electoral level. This contrasts with the argument presented here in Chapter 7 that this vision was articulated by other Labor and independent aldermen (most notably Harold Hanson) and effectively coopted by Arkell to become part of his irrepressible media presence.[26]

These are matters of interpretative difference but there are other more disturbing aspects of Sheldon's chapter. Tony Bevan is mentioned in the text as the first mayor to hold both the mayoralty and a ward seat but there is nothing about his alleged paedophile activities, which were made public in 1995. The role of Bevan in encouraging the state Labor government to pursue Arkell as part of his vendetta over Gleniffer Brae is not mentioned nor is the way in which Bevan used his council contacts to gather material for his personal and financial benefit. The 1983 Smiles report is also a significant absence.

---

25 Malcolm Brown, 'James Seymour (Jim) Hagan (1929–2009)', *Obituaries Australia* (Canberra: National Centre of Biography, The Australian National University, n.d.), labouraustralia.anu.edu.au/biography/hagan-james-seymour-jim-16951.
26 Sheldon, 'Local Government since 1947'.

The author of the local government chapters, Peter Sheldon, confirmed to me that the editors altered his draft chapter without his approval. Subsequently, material was removed or added that he did not have a chance to approve. He was a former student of Jim Hagan's, having secured his PhD from the University of Wollongong in 1990, and was at the time of publication a senior lecturer in industrial relations at Griffith University. Sheldon recalls that he learned, after publication, that then council general manager, Rod Oxley, had insisted on the inclusion of a photo of himself in the chapter. Furthermore, the council was clearly responsible for inserting a photo of then-mayor David Campbell to conclude the chapter—a different, standard public relations photo to the one that appeared in Campbell's foreword.

Additional material lauding the council's plans for the future was added without Sheldon's approval. In the concluding section, there are sentences that seem out of place in the scholarly register of the chapter. We are told that: 'Led by Lord Mayor David Campbell, the Council elected in 1991 developed environmental policy much further.' And a few paragraphs later: 'By helping Wollongong's environment to regain its pristine beauty, Council had sought to reduce the City's reliance on its traditional export industries and remake the area into one which would attract post-industrial commerce, tourism especially.'[27] These two sentences praised the current council and contrasted with the even-handed synthesis that Sheldon had offered in the rest of the chapter.

Peter Sheldon cannot recall whether references to Tony Bevan's paedophile network or more details about Frank Arkell's growing reputational problems were removed from his draft.[28] By the early 1990s, Wollongong was swirling with rumours and allegations about both Bevan and Arkell. Journalists working for the *Illawarra Mercury* had passed material on to the police as early as 1988, again in 1990 and once more in 1995. Arkell had been referred to in parliament in 1994, when Deirdre Grusovin read Colin Fisk's statutory declaration, and again in 1996, when Franca Arena identified Arkell as the 'W1' referred to in evidence to the Wood Royal Commission. In 1995 the *Illawarra Mercury* featured a front-page story about the paedophile past of former mayor Tony Bevan and included denials from Arkell that he was in any way involved. The Bevan story was unequivocal, with the second paragraph reading 'Bevan led a secret life as a pederast and pimp', followed by

---

27 ibid.
28 Peter Sheldon, Personal communication, 30 March 2023.

four pages of details from the Bevan Tapes and an editorial.[29] In April 1996 a former Wollongong Council alderman, Brian Tobin, committed suicide. In November, the *Sydney Morning Herald* reported the substance of sworn testimony from three witnesses at the Wood Royal Commission claiming that Arkell was a paedophile.[30] Certainly, by early 1997, the year the book was published, there was a clear and widespread belief that Arkell too was in a lot of trouble, with child sexual abuse allegations raised at the Wood Royal Commission by survivors and widely reported in the print, radio and television media. And by May of that year, Arkell was formally charged.

Yet the 1997 edited collection is mostly silent on the allegations against Arkell and makes no reference at all to Bevan's dark past. Arkell was especially litigious so this may have been legally prudent, but Bevan had died in 1991. In its content and form of production, the book reveals the historically close and ongoing links between the university and Wollongong Council. The editors wrote in the foreword that 'Wollongong City Council provided generous funding for the research and the editing'. The editors also noted that the current lord mayor, Labor's David Campbell, showed 'respect for our independence as historians'. Both Campbell and Jim Hagan were stalwarts of the local Labor Party and had worked together on Labor campaigns.

As a collaborative product, the collection shows the benefits but also the possible dangers of such a close working relationship. The collaboration enabled funding for university researchers to research, write and edit a major work on Wollongong history. However, the gaps in the narrative regarding Bevan and Arkell, the celebratory tone in the final pages of the local government overview and the absence of any critical assessment of the role of the council in past child sexual abuse show the downside of scholars working so closely with the funding body. At the very least Bevan's paedophile network was an unequivocal fact, Brian Tobin's suicide was clearly bound up in the whole affair and allegations about Arkell were gaining wider currency. Therefore, three Wollongong Council aldermen, including two former mayors, were caught up in the issue of child sexual abuse. This was an uncomfortable truth but one that demanded investigation or at least some acknowledgement. In this sense, this University of Wollongong

---

29   Martin, 'Former Mayor Ran Child Sex Ring'.
30   *Sydney Morning Herald*, 5 November 1996: 7.

publication stands in the shadows of the *Illawarra Mercury*, which fearlessly reported these matters. In contrast, the approach revealed in this university publication could be seen as timid and compromised.

Paedophiles operate in ways that control and influence important organisations in civil society. The University of Wollongong was an obvious target and those who were known or alleged to be involved in child sexual abuse were represented on its council and in the Friends organisation. Despite the extensive evidence of Frank Arkell's activities, including from the royal commission, the rumours and common knowledge around the city, the university continued its association with Arkell. Even after his tenure as lord mayor and state member, he was still attending functions at the university. In 1995 he attended an alumni function at the Gleniffer Brae campus to farewell a senior staff member.[31] The university's Child Protection Policy, first adopted in December 2016 and amended in 2020, notes that the university 'is committed to ensuring the safety and well-being of children under the care and supervision of University staff, students, volunteers, contractors, subcontractors and affiliates' and that they 'must be mindful of their position of authority with respect to children and must ensure that their interactions with children are ethical and do not amount to an abuse of that position'.[32] Universities have a duty of care to young men and women, many of whom are aged 17 or 18 in their first year as students, yet those who were alleged to be involved in child sexual abuse were allowed to participate in the governance of the University of Wollongong, officiate at its important ceremonies and continue to visit campus.

More than 25 years after Arkell's murder, after the allegations of child sexual abuse against him had been aired in extensive media coverage and in evidence before the Wood Royal Commission, the university's relationship with Frank Arkell's legacy remains unresolved. Arkell is still listed as one of the first cohort of four fellows of the university appointed in 1985.[33] Yet, the plaque commemorating stage three of the Union building, which featured Arkell's name and was officially unveiled by him in 1976, has curiously disappeared. In 2022, a search by myself and another by the university archivist failed to locate it. At some point during the many extensions and renovations of this section of the university, the plaque had been removed.

---

31 *Wollongong Outlook: The University Alumni Magazine*, Autumn–Winter (1995): 13.
32 *Child Protection Policy*, [Online], University of Wollongong, policies.uow.edu.au/document/view-current.php?id=159&version=1.
33 *University Fellows*, [Online], University of Wollongong, www.uow.edu.au/alumni/honorary-alumni/fellow/.

12
'People don't wave anymore': The diminishing years

The year 1991 marked a turning point in Frank Arkell's political career. In May Arkell lost the seat of Wollongong at the state election and, despite close confidants encouraging him not to run in the September mayoral election, he lost that vote, too. After the 1991 losses Arkell harboured plans for a return to politics and turned his characteristic energy and discipline to that task. There were even continuing honours after his electoral defeat. In 1992 he was made a member of the Order of Australia General Division (AM) 'for services to local government, the New South Wales parliament and to the community'. This joined his 1977 award and his Knighthood to the Order of Merit of the Italian Republic in May 1987.

But from this distance—more than 30 years later—1991 was also a turning point in Arkell's life. In hindsight, we can see that his halcyon days were over. He began the year as state member and lord mayor and finished it out of office altogether. His political message was now less popular. There were several controversies that had accumulated that had clearly eroded his electoral support. There was a sad addendum to his political career in 1995 when he stood as an unaligned independent for the NSW Legislative Council and came last in the ballot with only 1,824 votes. Also in that year, he ran for the lord mayoralty and this time was soundly beaten by Labor's David Campbell, who won a second term of office.[1] In the next few years before his death in 1998, allegations of child sexual assault and paedophilia

---

1   See Antony Green, *NSW Legislative Council Elections, 1995*, Background Paper, 1996/2 (Sydney: NSW Parliamentary Library Research Service, 1996); 'Local Council—The Verdict Local Elections '95: How We Voted', *Sydney Morning Herald*, 11 September 1995: 4.

would emerge into the public realm to taint his once unassailable public image as Mr Wollongong. For Frank Arkell, the crisis emerged as his public and private worlds began to overlap. What was once a secret, if known to a small number very acutely and perhaps to larger numbers in a general sense, was finally coming into the light of day.

Frank continued some of his civic activities after losing office. He attended meetings at the Illawarra Historical Society where he had old friends and much support. He had been a member since at least 1960 and patron since 1985. The society voted him patron again in 1993 and 1994 but thought better of it by 1995 when Dr H.C. Maldon was nominated and elected.[2] At the society's fiftieth anniversary dinner in August 1994, Frank presented an address to launch the republication of a 1948 regional history classic, Arthur Cousins's *The Garden of New South Wales*. The reissuing of this book was a special golden jubilee project.[3] In the middle of 1995, Arkell attended a farewell function for a university staff member at Gleniffer Brae.[4] In August he attended another historical society event, the launch of the 'War on the Homefront' exhibition at its museum in Market Street, Wollongong.[5] Arkell maintained his membership until his death but he disappears from the pages of the society's *Bulletin* after the August 1995 exhibition.

Even after Deirdre Grusovin had put on the public record Colin Fisk's allegations that Arkell was a paedophile in December 1994, Frank continued to attend public meetings.

There was always a question mark over Labor Party attempts to criticise Arkell as its accusations of political bias introduced an element of doubt and there had been, as we have seen, a long history of Labor using parliament to further its own agenda with respect to Arkell. The Grusovin revelations could be explained away, at least for now. Arkell had phoned Grusovin and demanded she repeat the allegations outside parliament.[6] In early 1995 he even claimed he was looking forward to the Wood Royal Commission,

---

2   See 'Annual General Meeting', *Bulletin*, [Illawarra Historical Society], 6 May 1993, and 1 February 1995: 6, Call no. ARC 994.405/1, University of Wollongong Archives.
3   *Bulletin*, [Illawarra Historical Society], December 1994, Call no. ARC 994.405/1, University of Wollongong Archives.
4   *Wollongong Outlook: The University Alumni Magazine*, Autumn–Winter 1995: 13.
5   *Bulletin*, [Illawarra Historical Society], September 1995, Call no. ARC 994.405/1, University of Wollongong Archives.
6   Mark Coultan, 'Outrage over Paedophile Accusation', *Sydney Morning Herald*, 2 December 1994: 3.

telling the *Sydney Morning Herald*: 'I have spoken to my solicitor and, when notices are issued calling for submissions, we will speak to the investigators. I am looking forward to it.'[7]

In March 1995 the first major public revelation regarding Bevan's paedophile network was published in the *Illawarra Mercury*. The story included an alleged link to Arkell via Bevan's Scorpion Tape, however, it was an easily overlooked although compelling sideline to the entire imbroglio that was so dominated by the incredible revelations about Bevan's network. But the steady stream of revelations simply did not let up. In May 1996 the Wood Royal Commission heard evidence covering Bevan's paedophile network and four witnesses who were 16 years old or younger had identified 'W1' as a participant. In late October 1996 Franca Arena identified Arkell in parliament as 'W1', asking why he was not being required to give evidence before the Wood Royal Commission. As we know, Arkell was subpoenaed but claimed he was unwell and his legal counsel tendered statutory declarations to that effect. Arkell's erstwhile political ally the Reverend Fred Nile, in defending Arena's comments in parliament, argued that everyone in the NSW Parliament, and indeed in the Illawarra, had known that 'W1' referred to Frank Arkell for more than two years. By the middle of 1996, Arkell had withdrawn from civic life. His world was shrinking.

Every revelation diminished Arkell. On 4 November 1996, the royal commission lifted its suppression order on the identity of W1 as Justice Wood thought it now meaningless given Arkell had been identified in NSW Parliament. Lifting the suppression order also allowed Arkell to issue a public statement in the form of a statutory declaration in which he denied all the charges made against him.[8]

The lifting of the suppression order had an immediate effect. On 5 November 1996, the *Illawarra Mercury* ran a front-page story by journalist Lisa Carty with the chilling headline 'Wollongong Man Tells: "I Had Sex with Frank Arkell"'. Arkell was livid. He phoned Carty and told her she was now on his 'list' and he would 'get' her. Arkell said to her: 'I thought Peter Cullen was the biggest bastard in the world until I met you.' Until that day Carty had a good relationship with Arkell. She later recalled in an opinion piece: 'That story changed my relationship with Arkell. The pressure was well and truly

---

7   Lisa Price, 'MP Vows to Fight Pedophile Claims', *Sun-Herald*, [Sydney], 5 February 1995: 23.
8   'NSW: Arkell Denies in Commission He Is a Paedophile', *AAP*.

on him, and for that he hated my guts.'[9] Once crossed, Arkell was a great hater but in this case, the stakes could not have been higher. On the same day as the *Mercury*'s story, 5 November 1996, the *Sydney Morning Herald* reported the allegations of three witnesses at the Wood Royal Commission who had claimed that Arkell was a paedophile.[10] Kate McClymont began her story plainly and pointedly:

> As of yesterday, it is no longer a criminal offence to reveal publicly that former local and State politician Frank Arkell is the W1 of royal commission fame or that his codename in a Wollongong pedophile ring was 'Farkless Arkless'.

The steady stream of allegations was now an avalanche.

Arkell's mental health suffered, as he became isolated and withdrawn from public life. Arkell's submission to not appear before the Wood Royal Commission in August 1996 included statutory declarations indicating that he had significant mental health issues.[11] There was the question of his risk of suicide. At face value, the concern appeared genuine. His friend Brother Michael Evans had taken his life in December 1994 and his friend and political ally Brian Tobin followed in May 1996. After the suppression order was lifted, he somewhat disturbingly showed journalists his wrists and said, 'Look see. No slash marks.' Asked whether he had considered suicide, Arkell replied, 'No, never. The last thing on my mind. That would mean leaving Wollongong. I would never leave Wollongong. Not in a thousand years.'[12] Arkell was still fighting but there was a slightly manic, desperate edge to his defence.

On 1 May 1997, Frank Arkell went to the shopping area in Unanderra. He was approaching people to say hello and chat and, to his great distress, people avoided him or were cold and guarded. 'I hope you haven't moved to Unanderra', was one woman's response when Arkell tried to talk to her. She later told journalist Lisa Carty: 'He went crazy—he chased me down the street and accused me of calling him a paedophile. He said he was going to sue me.'[13]

---

9 Lisa Carty, 'The Day Frank Turned from Kiss to Hiss—'96 Cup One to Remember: My View', *Illawarra Mercury*, 1 July 1998: 8.
10 *Sydney Morning Herald*, 5 November 1996: 7.
11 Fanning, 'Interview with Julie Posetti'.
12 Greg Bearup, 'I'm No Pederast, Says Former Mayor', *Sydney Morning Herald*, 5 November 1996: 2.
13 Lisa Carty, 'The Day Frank's World Came Crashing down—The Arkell Murder', *Illawarra Mercury*, 29 June 1998: 2.

12. 'PEOPLE DON'T WAVE ANYMORE'

Unanderra was home turf for the Arkells. It was just 2 kilometres down the road from the Cobbler's Hill Service Station and the Arkell Brothers yard and surrounded by land that they owned and, in some cases, had subdivided and sold. It is significant that Arkell returned there in these last days desperately seeking the public acceptance he had formerly enjoyed. That afternoon after lunch with a friend who lived in Mount Keira Road, Arkell went home to Reserve Street. Police officers from the Child Protection Enforcement Unit were waiting. He was arrested at 4.30 pm, escorted to a waiting police vehicle by Inspector Gordon Ball and later charged with 29 counts relating to child sexual offences. He was released on bail from Wollongong Police Station just after 8 pm.[14] On 27 May the charges were subject to a preliminary hearing at Wollongong Court before Magistrate Paul Johnson. Arkell did not enter a plea at this stage. Leaving the court, he made a short statement: 'I've said it before, I'm not guilty. I will defend the charges.'[15]

On 1 July 1997 Arkell's legal team applied to have his bail conditions relaxed. He had to report to Wollongong Police Station once a week and he had surrendered his passport. His solicitor and long-time friend Peter Daly told the court that Arkell was being treated by a team of doctors: 'Mr Arkell has had a bit of difficulty in timing with reporting to police. And that is due to his poor health.' It was also apparent that Arkell wanted to visit his two rural properties in the Central West of New South Wales. The weekly check-in at Wollongong Police Station made that impossible. The magistrate refused to alter the bail conditions. Outside the court, Arkell told waiting journalists: 'I'm a winner. I never lose. And I'll win this one.'[16]

Further widespread media coverage followed Arkell's arrest and application to revise his bail conditions. Arkell was now the subject of regular stories in the Wollongong print and TV and statewide media. By the end of 1997, 1 Reserve Street was becoming a target for those who felt compelled to make a statement about its sole inhabitant. Graffiti was painted on the fence. The front light was smashed. Obscenities were yelled from passing cars and, in a few cases, burnouts were performed on the driveway or at the front of the property. Arkell refused to speak to an *Illawarra Mercury* journalist—his

---

14 Kate McClymont, 'Former MP Frank Arkell Faces 29 Child Sex Charges', *Sydney Morning Herald*, 2 May 1997: 1.
15 Frank Arkell cited in Michael Lawson, 'Former Mayor Faces Sex Charges', *Sydney Morning Herald*, 28 May 1997: 6.
16 Michael Lawson, 'Doctors Treat Sick Arkell—Bail Too Tough on Frank, Claims Lawyer ... but Magistrate Stands Firm', *Sydney Morning Herald*, 9 July 1997: 1.

relationship with the major regional newspaper now irreversibly broken—but he was photographed showing a police constable the graffiti,[17] which read: 'W1 You are a wanker.'[18] Arkell's identity as W1, the codename adopted for him by the Wood Royal Commission, was now widely known. In the photograph published in the *Sun-Herald*, Arkell looked dishevelled and underdressed by his standards. These were his darkest days as even his highly curated dress sense and flawless public presentation appeared to be slipping.

His neighbour from across the street Michael D'Souza witnessed Arkell walking up and down Reserve Street or sitting in Gilmore Park next to his home, seemingly in a daze. A haze of depression, which some have suggested may have been a form of dementia, descended on Arkell. His behaviour was strongly reminiscent of his mother's path into dementia in the last few years of her life in the late 1970s.

At this time Frank Arkell would turn up in the D'Souzas' backyard, sitting on a garden seat or doing some gardening. (On visiting the D'Souza house in England Street, just opposite Arkell's, I was shown a cactus in the front garden—a gift from Arkell that was still alive after 25 years.) Coinciding with the last few months of Arkell's life, Michael D'Souza experienced the distressing suicide of a close friend, so he returned to the family home for a few weeks of respite. One morning he got up early while his father was still asleep and made coffee. Arkell was sitting in their back garden. Michael said hello and he vividly recalls Frank looking at him directly and saying: 'You can call me poofter, you can call me faggot, you can call me gay, I'm not a paedophile.'

D'Souza told me he understands 'that people have a way of justifying themselves if they commit a severe crime ... All I'm saying is that he said that to me'. Regardless of the evidentiary weight one places on this statement of innocence in the months before the trial, one can confidently assert that the impending trial and his legal situation were dominating Arkell's thinking at that stage. As D'Souza recalls it, Arkell was in 'a very high state of anxiety and distress'.[19] The approaching trial must have weighed heavily on him. His court date loomed and the pressure only increased.

---

17 Lisa Carty, 'Malicious Attacks on Arkell's House—Ex-Mayor Complains of Harassment', *Illawarra Mercury*, 25 November 1997: 5.
18 Hannan and Patty, 'Child Sex MP Slain'.
19 Interview with Michael D'Souza, 21 November 2022.

12. 'PEOPLE DON'T WAVE ANYMORE'

In early 1998 the Reverend Gordon Bradbery, a minister at the Wesley Uniting Church in Wollongong who would later become a long-serving Wollongong lord mayor—just like Arkell—was asked by a mutual friend to visit Frank. Bradbery found him in a near delusional state, disassociated from reality, and he spoke to the reverend of the visions of the Black Madonna, who had been appearing to him:

> I just sat with Frank and listened to his litany of delusional talk about the Black Madonna. It was quite disturbed and disorientated and, as I said, delusional. And this Madonna and the icon spoke to him and all sorts of things like this, so, yeah, his behaviour was quite bizarre, so it was very difficult to even talk to him rationally about things, and it was more or less a case of listening.[20]

The Madonna or Virgin Mary is the holiest of Catholic symbols, representing innocence, hope and faith, yet at various times the Catholic faithful claim to see or render images of the Madonna with darker skin. It is not apparent why Arkell was seeing visions of a Black Madonna. The city of Częstochowa in Upper Silesia in southern Poland was one of the spiritual homes of the Black Madonna, where Catholics revered a unique painting, *The Black Madonna of Częstochowa*, depicting the Madonna and baby Jesus. Did Arkell's visions have some deeper psychological or spiritual meaning or was it just a random image produced by an increasingly unstable mind? Perhaps in his diminished state he was becoming more and more influenced by his Polish-born housekeeper, Maria Subotic? Subotic was present in the house when Bradbery visited. Whatever the case, his demeanour was brittle and erratic. He was at various times angry and bitter towards the *Illawarra Mercury*, the Labor Party and others, then whimsically obsessed with his visions.

At this meeting between Bradbery and Arkell, there was no confession, no revelation of truth and no sense of a man reviewing and reflecting on his life. As Bradbery recalled, Arkell wanted to 'continually reassure me that he didn't do certain things. But he didn't go into the detail, and it wasn't my place to do so at the time.' Bradbery and Arkell shared a moment of prayer:

> I think I even had a prayer with him just to sort of try and relieve the agony … [I]t was cognitive agony basically, existential agony he was in at the time … Word was out that Frank Arkell had a past, and Frank's life was just imploding.[21]

---

20 Interview with Gordon Bradbery, 29 April 2023.
21 ibid.

Frank Arkell's committal hearing was at the Wollongong Magistrates Court in February 1998 before Magistrate Paul Johnson. Arkell attended each day of court, arriving on the first day in a neat dark-grey suit. He looked composed but he walked very slowly and hesitated before taking the stairs to the courthouse. One of the waiting media asked him, 'How are you feeling today sir?' 'Very well thank you,' replied Arkell, 'I'm in Wollongong.' Other than those few words, he offered no comment.

It is of great concern that the recording and transcript of Arkell's committal hearing are no longer available. Such an important case is now lost in the shadows of the very recent past. A court officer informed me that recordings of committal hearings are not kept beyond 10 years. Unless someone requests a transcript of the recording before that period elapses (which, apparently, they had not), the recording is destroyed and no record is available.

The only record we have of the committal hearing, then, are the reports from a handful of journalists who covered proceedings and the outcome.[22] The best accounts were written by Lisa Carty for the *Illawarra Mercury*, who provided a summary of each witness statement, the defence response to the statement and the prosecution's reply. For many years, Arkell and his legal representatives had denied all charges against him on the basis that the victims had mistaken Arkell for Tony Bevan or that Bevan had orchestrated a vendetta against Arkell. On the first point, it would seem very unlikely that victims could mistake the two men physically. Arkell was tall and broad-shouldered with a patrician bearing, standing more than 190 centimetres tall, while Bevan was a much smaller man, at 168 centimetres, with a nuggetty face and a missing front tooth. Bevan had a significantly receding hairline and, by the late 1970s, a horseshoe pattern of remaining thin black hair. Arkell, by contrast, kept a generous head of greying hair with a cowlick on his fringe throughout this period and into his sixties. On the existence of a conspiracy to frame Arkell, we have seen this has an element of truth to it, with the production and circulation of the Scorpion Tape, but how Bevan's conspiracy could have reached out beyond the grave after his death in 1991 was never explained. To that end, Magistrate Johnson 'rejected the defence's claim that one of the men [accusers] was still driven by a conspiracy orchestrated by Arkell's rival Tony Bevan'.[23]

---

22   See 'Arkell to Stand Trial', *Sunday Telegraph*, [Sydney], 13 February 1998: 17; Carty, 'Arkell Goes to Trial'; 'NSW: Arkell Fronts Committal Hearing into 29 Sex Charges', *AAP* [*Australian Associated Press*], 8 February 1998.
23   Carty, 'Arkell Goes to Trial'.

The relevant legislation guiding the proceedings for Arkell's committal hearing was the *Criminal Procedures Act 1986* (NSW). In 2018, major changes to this Act abolished committal hearings in the state. While still in force before 2018, however, the Act required a magistrate to determine whether a jury, if properly instructed, could find a defendant guilty. In some cases, a magistrate would find that a charge could not proceed because of evidentiary problems or a lack of substantiating evidence. As we saw in Chapter 8, this is a common issue in sexual assault cases, especially historical ones. The fact that the charges did not proceed to trial did not necessarily mean that they were false accusations. They may have been lacking evidence that would meet the threshold of 'beyond reasonable doubt'. In matters of law, the evidentiary threshold is high and the presumption of innocence sets a high bar to prove a case with a level of evidence that is well beyond what we would consider necessary in everyday life. Carty, our only guide to the details, suggests that several charges against Arkell were dismissed on 'legal technicalities'. The 29 charges involving five alleged victims were whittled down to five charges involving four victims. There was a further case that was yet to be indicted and would be heard later. The decision of the NSW Police to withhold the Arkell files means it is not possible to describe even in general terms the substance of the yet-to-be-indicted case.

Carty sat through all the evidence at the committal hearing. The claims of one man, whom we know as 'W26' from the royal commission, 'were rightly chucked out', she reported: 'But it was the other two men who convinced me—as I believe they would have convinced the jury in Parramatta District Court in September—that Arkell was not a hapless old homosexual.'[24]

Arkell's life was increasingly confined to his Reserve Street home and neighbourhood, punctuated only by his weekly check-in at Wollongong Police Station and the occasional outing to his favourite garden shop. For a man who had spent much of his adult life at meetings, events, festivals, parties, sporting presentations and celebrations in Wollongong, Sydney and elsewhere, it was a dramatic reduction in his sphere of activity. Arkell trudged up and down Reserve Street or walked into Gilmore Park, his demeanour distracted, his steps short and stilted. Arkell was now a lonely, isolated figure. Arkell told Michael D'Souza's father that one of the hardest things he found was that 'people don't wave anymore'.[25]

---

24 Carty, 'The Day Frank Turned from Kiss to Hiss'.
25 Interview with Michael D'Souza, 21 November 2022.

Just four months after the committal hearing, in June 1998, an east coast low-pressure system stalled over the state and flooded the Illawarra, Sydney and Newcastle regions with heavy rain. The entire month was wet and gale-force winds were recorded along the coast. On Wednesday 24 June 1998, there was rain across the Illawarra and cold, gusty winds that peaked that evening off Bellambi Point at almost 100 kilometres per hour. After the rain came a snap of even colder weather. Dorothy Johnson, a friend and neighbour of Arkell, told a journalist: 'He had a few disgusting things painted on his fence, windows broken, people yelling and screaming abuse as they drove by.'[26] At some point during that month's media coverage of Arkell and the allegations and charges of child sexual abuse, a deeply troubled young man called Mark Valera came across this information. Valera had already brutally murdered Albion Park man David O'Hearn on 12 June and his mind had turned to who would be his next victim. The seeds of a terrible idea were planted.

On windy nights, the curtains in the main house at 1 Reserve Street swung wildly in the wind. There were so many broken windows in the home that Arkell had not replaced them. Marcella's home—once maintained so assiduously—was in a state of disrepair as Frank flipped between the self-righteous angry man and the wandering lost soul with visions of the Black Madonna. It was only three months until his trial. The legal reckoning was almost on him. Tension was building in the Illawarra but no one expected anything so gruesome or shocking as what would happen in Reserve Street, West Wollongong, at the end of that month. No one anticipated the horror of what was to come.

---

26 Hannan and Patty, 'Child Sex MP Slain'.

13

'Our brother Frank was suddenly and violently taken from us': The death of Frank Arkell

Across the passage of time and the ebb and flow of change, families, loss, new homes and businesses, subdivisions and sales, elections, campaigns and years of political dominance of Wollongong City Council; through media moments, job losses and the turmoil of economic restructuring; through the endless formal events, speeches and tourism campaigns; and through the completion of impressive new high rise apartments along the beachfront—through all of this and more the years have rolled by and we arrive back in late June 1998 with Frank Arkell's best years behind him.

On Friday 26 June 1998, 19-year-old Mark Valera calls Frank from a phone box at Wollongong Railway Station. He secures an invitation to Frank's home for later that day on the pretext that he is a young gay man and he wants to talk. Frank heads out to his favourite garden shop on the Princes Highway at Fairy Meadow. He is driven there and back home by a chauffeur, but the name of that chauffeur is something the police never find out. At about 4 pm, neighbours see Frank in Gilmore Park next to his home. He had a habit of walking in the park, picking up rubbish and clearing away broken branches. That evening Frank opens his door. Given what we know about Frank's deteriorating health and his unsteady state of mind, it was highly unlikely he was in a fit state to judge personal risk or to intuit a potentially dangerous situation. Lonely and isolated, he may have welcomed the company.

Valera enters Frank's apartment at the rear of 1 Reserve Street and they speak for a few minutes. The trial judge rejected the argument from Valera's defence team, who claimed that Arkell and Valera had met in 1997 and previously had sex. As Justice Studdert wrote:

> I reject the prisoner's evidence that he was called upon by Mr Arkell to engage in sexual activity and that this prompted a loss of self control. I reject the prisoner's assertion that he lost control when he attacked this victim, and I accept Dr Milton's analysis that this was on the contrary a purposeful killing.

The judge determined that this was the men's first meeting and that Valera had gone to Arkell's with an intent to kill.

According to later trial evidence, Valera entered Frank's apartment and they spoke for a few minutes. Then Valera attacked. At the entrance to his bathroom, Frank raises his arms in defence. The coroner would later count 34 separate blows to his head. The attack is as unrelenting as it is brutal. Valera had already killed another man just two weeks earlier. Furniture is broken, a lampshade is wielded as a heavy weapon. Arkell crawls across the floor towards the bedroom, trying to fend off blows. Valera would later testify that Frank begged him to stop: 'I thought we were friends', he reportedly said. All to no avail. An electric cord, then a belt, is wound tight around Frank's throat. An ashtray is used to bludgeon his head. The property where Marcella and Frank had lived side by side for three decades is now the site of another Arkell tragedy. Clad in tracksuit pants and a white singlet, Frank lies prone on the floor next to his bed, blood pooling around him. It is a gruesome echo of the scene that confronted Frank's brother Richard in Sidney's bedroom so many years before. Personal items like tiepins and Rotary badges—emblems of a life of service—are deployed by Valera as ghastly finishing touches defiling the now-deceased body of Francis Neville Arkell (1929–1998).

Valera takes off his blood-stained clothes, discarding his running shoes and tracksuit pants. He finds something of Frank's to wear and leaves the premises later that night. Neighbours have heard nothing since some saw Frank in the park that afternoon. At 2.35 am on 27 June, a red Nissan station wagon is seen leaving Frank's driveway, though police are never able to identify that vehicle or its driver. Just another mystery in the Arkell tragedy. Maybe it was the wrong driveway? Maybe the witness was mistaken?

13. 'OUR BROTHER FRANK WAS SUDDENLY AND VIOLENTLY TAKEN FROM US'

Murder is the ultimate act of violence against a person. It is also an act of biographical intrusion. The murderer will always be a part of the subject's story, appearing in the closing act, bringing the inexorable end. Valera is now a permanent presence in Arkell's story. Mark Valera is the name most often attached to Frank Arkell. The best-known aspects of Frank's life will be the nature of his death, his association with paedophilia and the name of the man who killed him.

At 8 o'clock the morning after Valera's attack on Frank, a long-term family employee, Maria Subotic, arrives to clean the main house and the apartment and finds Frank's body. It is Maria who calls the police, and paramedics treat her for shock. Brett Martin was the first journalist at the Reserve Street scene early that Saturday morning. A neighbour who lived around the corner had tipped off Martin. This neighbour was on an early morning walk when he saw the police at Arkell's house. Martin jumped on his motorbike and arrived at about 8.30 am, and he watched as the police began setting up their cordon, roadblocks and the crime scene tape. There was not much to see except police vehicles. Martin knew both the crime scene detectives in attendance, but they would not give him any information at that stage. One of the detectives wondered how Martin could have arrived at the scene so quickly, but Martin did not divulge his source.[1] Lawyer and close friend Peter Daly arrived later that morning. Police began to examine the murder scene and remove evidence. Daly was reportedly in a 'distressed state', as you might expect after learning of the murder of his long-time friend and close business associate.[2]

The Sydney-based *Sun-Herald* wasted no time in declaring the now-dead Arkell guilty. 'Child Sex MP Slain' was its headline for the Sunday edition, summing up Arkell's life as they saw it in a headline before the weekend was over. The events of June 1998 left Wollongong people in shock. The following two months while the murder remained unsolved evinced a tangible sense of fear. It was the most high-profile murder case in recent memory. Everyone knew Frank Arkell, most people had come across him in one way or another and now he was dead. People to whom I spoke in researching this book still remembered the gruesome details of the murder. Though they were loath to repeat them, they were nonetheless etched into memory. What's more, a similarly gruesome murder had occurred only

---

1 Interview with Brett Martin, 23 November 2022.
2 Hannan and Patty, 'Child Sex MP Slain'.

two weeks earlier. There had been scandals, corruption and terrible crimes before, and have been since, but nothing that matched the brutality and intensity of the murders of David O'Hearn and Frank Arkell.

Plate 13.1 Front page of the *Illawarra Mercury*'s 'Special Arkell Murder edition', 29 June 1998

Photo: Author's copy.

13. 'OUR BROTHER FRANK WAS SUDDENLY AND VIOLENTLY TAKEN FROM US'

David O'Hearn, Valera's first victim in that fateful June, was a single man, one of a large family of three brothers and four sisters. He owned and managed a small shop on Kanahooka Road, kept a fastidiously neat home and led a quiet, private life. He was planning a move from his Albion Park home to be closer to his ailing mother, who was in a nursing home, but unfortunately, that move did not come soon enough. O'Hearn was a man caught in the wrong place at the wrong time as Valera's urge to kill became overwhelming. On 12 June 1998, Valera simply began knocking on doors in a street near his grandfather's house. Valera told police: 'I stayed at the door and asked if there was any, like accommodation around.' O'Hearn had replied, 'Come in and we'll talk about it.'[3]

Frank Arkell's funeral service, on 2 July, was a small, private affair at St Francis Xavier Church in Wollongong. It was attended by about 40 family members and close friends. The family and the funeral directors had kept the details secret but, even so, a large media contingent was present outside. Father John Stork, chaplain of Wollongong Hospital, led the service and refused to elaborate on its details to the waiting media. Security guards who accompanied family members told inquiring media with an air of menace, 'If you go anywhere near the family you'll get nothing.'[4] Officers from the Child Protection Enforcement Unit watched proceedings from a discreet distance.

Later, at the Wollongong Cemetery, a single bouquet of yellow flowers would be placed on the rosewood coffin as 10 relatives and close friends watched while Frank's coffin was lowered into a simple family plot.[5] Earlier, cemetery workers had told inquiring media representatives that they knew nothing about the Arkell service. A cross had been placed at Arkell's plot bearing another man's name to deceive the waiting media. Consulting their own records, the *Illawarra Mercury* found that this man had been buried the previous week. Moments before the Arkell party arrived, the decoy cross was removed. In death as in life, Arkell's family chose to keep their secrets.

---

3   *R v Valera* [2000] NSWSC 1220 [21 December 2000], www6.austlii.edu.au/cgi-bin/viewdoc/au/cases/nsw/NSWSC/2000/1220.html.
4   Louise Turk and Nalita Ferraz, 'Grave Scheme to Fool Waiting Media—The Arkell Murder', *Illawarra Mercury*, 3 July 1998: 3.
5   'NSW: Quiet Funeral for Frank Arkell', *AAP* [*Australian Associated Press*], 2 July 1998; Nalita Ferraz, 'Former Leader Given Secret Burial—The Arkell Murder', *Illawarra Mercury*, 3 July 1998: 2.

The following day there was a separate memorial mass at St Francis Xavier attended by almost 300 people. Security guards ensured that members of the public could not enter.[6] Reverend Father Paul Ryan led the congregation in prayer: 'Our brother Frank has been suddenly and violently taken from us.' But Father Ryan prayed that God would 'come swiftly to his aid, have mercy on him, and comfort his friends and family by the power and protection of the cross'. The congregation sang Psalm 31 ('I place my life in your hands, in your hands') and concluded the service with the Lord's Prayer: 'Forgive us our trespasses as we forgive those who trespass against us; and lead us not into temptation, but deliver us from evil.'[7]

The memorial mass was attended by senior political leaders, well-known Wollongong businessmen and senior Wollongong Council staff. Ordinary folk may wish for a memorial mass like this, but it was not the kind of service Frank Arkell would have wanted. Public standing and public respect were so important to him. His great uncle's funeral in 1906 may have been the template. Frank O'Donnell, a long-serving alderman and sometime mayor of the Central Illawarra Council, had been given a heartfelt send-off by his community amid the shock and genuine sadness at his sudden passing from his horseriding accident. By contrast, Frank Arkell's funeral had been a closely guarded secret watched by police officers from the CPEU and a large media contingent. The endless days and nights of civic work over decades must have warranted some final mark of respect, Arkell may have thought. The funeral should have been the moment when everyone farewelled 'Mr Wollongong', the city's favourite son. Even for a memorial mass, Arkell's ambitions would have extended further than 300 mourners. Only four weeks earlier, the whistleblower priest from Berkeley, Father Morrie Crocker, had 700 in attendance at his funeral. Father Crocker had led a remarkable life with ups and downs but led it with humility, honesty and Catholic piety. That he attracted a larger crowd to his funeral than the man who had dominated Wollongong public life for more than three decades was one small mercy coming out of his tragic suicide.

But the tide had turned against Arkell and the steady stream of revelations and stories had revealed a sordid network of well-connected powerful men who had transgressed. One Wollongong councillor, Terry Gallagher, refused to attend the funeral or stand for a minute's silence at a council meeting out of respect for what the *Illawarra Mercury* termed the 'alleged victims' of sexual

---

6   *Sydney Morning Herald*, 3 July 1998.
7   *Illawarra Mercury*, 3 July 1998.

abuse.[8] Arkell's murder, and the salacious and damning allegations against him, came on top of a steady decline in his popularity from the late 1980s as he became more and more associated with big development proposals and the big developers. To many, it appeared as though Mr Wollongong had already sold out.

In August, the Illawarra was once again drenched with huge amounts of rain. It was almost as though the weather was attempting to wash away the city's sins. Major flooding occurred throughout the region. At the back of the Hellenic Club, and only a few kilometres down the road from the old Arkell garage, Byarong Creek was in flood. Arkell's olive trees, now part of an established, peaceful hideaway from the travails of the city, got their feet wet as water rose over the embankment. Allans Creek, which runs past Arkell's childhood suburb of Cringila, flooded, as did American Creek, which flows through Figtree and feeds Allans Creek. Arkell's murder was bookended by flooding and wild rainstorms. And still, the murder remained unsolved. There was extensive coverage of Frank Arkell's murder in the Wollongong and Sydney print and TV media. The two brutal murders in close succession prompted speculation about the existence of a serial killer and several possible motives and links between the two victims were suggested. In July and August, everyone seemed on edge.

Contrary to media speculation at the time, David O'Hearn and Frank Arkell had no association at all. What lay behind some of the media speculation linking the two murders was the assumption that since both men were single, and were not apparently involved in any heterosexual relationship, their murders must somehow be linked to homosexuality or even paedophilia. The police investigation, needing to keep all lines of inquiry open, pursued the possibility that the two murders were hate crimes or revenge attacks by former victims of child sexual offences. Dr Richard Basham, a forensic anthropologist from the University of Sydney, took it one step further, writing an opinion piece for the *Sunday Telegraph*. With the murders unsolved and the police investigation ongoing, Basham speculated that the deaths of David O'Hearn, Frank Arkell and another man recently murdered in Sydney, Trevor John Parkin (who was facing charges of child sexual offences), were all related. Basham wrote: 'Since they

---

8   Geoff Failes, 'No Respect for Arkell—Councillor Refuses One-Minute Silence', *Illawarra Mercury*, 2 July 1998: 2.

bear the hallmark of revenge killings for paedophilia, the murderer must see himself as a victim of his victims. Most likely he feels his life was ruined by their sexual assaults on him as a youth.'[9]

Basham essentially presented David O'Hearn here as a paedophile. This and other similar coverage was deeply distressing for his family. O'Hearn had no engagement at all in child sexual abuse. He did not know Arkell, Tony Bevan or anyone else in the Wollongong paedophile network. Cruel fate alone brought him into contact with a man who was intent on killing someone, or anyone. And Valera was not responsible for Parkin's murder, so Basham was also incorrect on that count. As noted previously, some Wollongong perpetrators were men living what looked like typical heterosexual lives, married to a woman and with children. Others were single men who never had any long-term male partners, such as Arkell, while yet others, like Bevan, did have a long-term partner but were compulsive paedophiles. In a further twist, Bevan's partner was originally one of his teenage targets. The Wollongong case studies show there is no direct connection between male homosexuality and paedophilia. The parade of paedophiles was a mixed bunch of offenders, some living as heterosexual men, some gay who also abused boys and some who appeared solely focused on abusing boys and had little else in their private lives. David O'Hearn is still fondly remembered by his large family. As his sister Anne recalled, 'He was such a perfectionist. He was a really, really good person.'[10]

Valera surrendered himself to Wollongong Police Station on 30 September. During the investigation, he had been interviewed as a person of interest but had not been arrested or charged. On the evening he surrendered, he told police he targeted Arkell because of 'all the nasty things he has done to kids. Read about him. Heard about him in the papers and the media.' Psychologists working with the police found that Valera had an abusive childhood that included physical and sexual abuse, moments of dissociation and a macabre fascination with the occult and satanism.[11] The violent fatal attacks on both O'Hearn and Arkell and the mutilation of their bodies, especially in the case of O'Hearn, show Valera was a deeply damaged, unhinged individual. Justice Studdert summarised: 'The prisoner neither displayed in his demeanour nor did he express in his testimony during the trial any remorse for these killings.'

---

9   Richard Basham, 'Crimes Bear Hallmark of Vengeance', [*Sunday Style Magazine*], *Sunday Telegraph*, [Sydney], 30 June 1998: 2.
10 Notes from an interview with Anne Baron, 24 October 2022.
11 See *R v Valera* [2000] NSWSC 1220 [21 December 2000].

In police interviews that went on into the early hours of 1 October, Valera freely admitted his guilt for the murders of David O'Hearn and Frank Arkell. The following day, Valera was taken by Wollongong detectives to 1 Reserve Street. The trial judge noted that Valera seemed lucid and cooperative as he helped police reconstruct the terrible events of 26 June. The business-like manner in which Valera conducted himself hinted at deeper and darker things: Valera was completely devoid of any sense of the suffering of his victims. He walked through the home as though he was a visiting professional assessing it for sale or renovation. No wonder the Arkell family sold the property as soon as legal probate was approved.

The media returned to the story once Valera was charged in October 1998 and again when his case reached the courts in late 1999. In August 2000, Mark Valera was found guilty at a jury trial, and then sentenced in December of that year. Justice Studdert concluded: 'I am satisfied beyond reasonable doubt that the prisoner conducted the attack with intent to kill. The prisoner sought to explain, and indeed to justify, his attack upon an adverse judgment he had formed of his second victim.' The sentencing judge rejected Valera's trial evidence that he had met Arkell before and that they had already had sex. The defence made the case that both murders had been triggered by childhood abuse committed on Valera by his father. In the act of sex, the defence argued, he entered a dissociated state and was not fully in control of his violent aggression. Justice Studdert did not accept this argument, noting that 'the defence of substantial impairment was rejected by the jury in the case of each killing'. 'Once again,' declared Studdert, 'he demonstrated his utter contempt for his victim after inflicting the savage injuries which inevitably would have led to death … I find a complete absence of any facts such as might mitigate the seriousness of either crime.'[12] Valera is serving two concurrent life sentences for the murders of Arkell and O'Hearn. In April 2002, the NSW Supreme Court rejected an appeal against the severity of his sentence.[13] Legally, there is no prospect of parole. For Valera, a life sentence means his entire life spent in prison.

In history so much depends on when we choose to finish a story. A political biography focusing on Arkell's public life and his years of success might finish at his 1991 defeats in the state and council elections. In this version, Arkell can be remembered as Mr Wollongong—a successful politician,

---

12 See ibid.
13 *R v Valera* [2002] NSWCCA 50 [12 April 2002, revised 17 April], www8.austlii.edu.au/cgi-bin/viewdoc/au/cases/nsw/NSWCCA/2002/50.html.

an active figure in the community, a devoted son and a loyal servant to the Wollongong cause, whose popularity had waned and whose message had grown repetitive. But take the story up to his brutal death and the high-profile controversies that surrounded his secret life, including the police charges, and the tale ends very differently. In this story, Arkell is murdered and how he is remembered is shaped by that act of wanton cruelty and violence. Whatever has come before is wiped clean by the sheer brutality of his death.

There were some in Wollongong and elsewhere who saw the nature of Arkell's death as a kind of punishment for a life punctuated by depravity. Such ideas of a violent death as the ultimate retribution for a sinner or unethical subject have been present in biographical traditions since the Classical era. The villain meets an untimely and undignified end, as befits their misshapen character. In contrast, the hero dies a tragic death but with courage and for the right cause. The nature of a character's death is said to reveal much about their life and their fate. Throughout Arkell's life, there were stories of abuse, stories of suicide, stories of possible dishonesty that included his family, his political and business associates and, as we have seen, his own life in the most profound way. Frank's world was full of tragedy. Those around him suffered and perpetuated abuse, died by their own hand or simply died unexpectedly. Arkell's father shot himself in 1941. One of Arkell's older brothers, Richard, died an early death, aged 41, in 1963. In 1994 a Catholic clerical associate and friend, Brother Michael Evans, committed suicide. Close political ally Brian Tobin committed suicide only two years later. I do not hold with the argument that Arkell's violent death was justified in any way, but considering Arkell's whole life and the drama of those around him, somewhat surprisingly, his murder does not feel so much out of place.

14

'Wollongong is the "W" in NSW': Frank Arkell's political record

More than 25 years after the shocking murder of Frank Arkell, the scandals that preceded it and the high-profile media coverage that followed, it is now possible to offer a more sober assessment of Arkell's public contributions out from the shadow of his brutal death. Are the Arkell supporters right? Do Frank's public achievements outweigh his perversions?

The sheer energy that Arkell directed towards Wollongong's clubs and societies, and its civic life, was truly remarkable. It is among these groups—Rotary, Lions, the Illawarra Historical Society and the like—that he is best remembered. Among Wollongong's Italian, Greek, Polish and Philippine communities, he was also well known and respected. Sometimes with a shared faith in Catholicism, Arkell's respectful engagement and his conservative social values resonated well with these migrant groups and their second- and third-generation children. Arkell gave so much of his time and energy to these communities. He worked tirelessly on their issues and concerns. He was the sort of politician who turned up and participated. Especially in the earlier phase of his political career, he did not just make an appearance but took an active role. He loved the spotlight. He loved the engagement and the busy world of meetings and events. In this domain, he projected the image of an active and engaged leader who cared for his community.

POLITICS, PRIDE AND PERVERSION

John Martin was a Labor alderman on Wollongong City Council from 1977 to 1988. Martin, who in 1977 had only recently divorced, recalled that he and Arkell were the only two single men on the council at the time. While the other aldermen headed home to their families after meetings, he and Arkell would attend birthdays, weddings and other social events. Here Martin witnessed Arkell's incredible energy and his capacity to meet and greet everyone in the room. Despite his proximity, Martin never saw any evidence of illicit or illegal activities on Arkell's part.[1] Likewise, Bevan Fermor, another rival Labor alderman, this time from Arkell's own Ward 3, had a grudging respect for Frank. He called him a 'formidable' political opponent and praised his energy and commitment to Wollongong.[2] Both Martin and Fermor were aware of Arkell's limitations as a politician but both were also mindful of his political strengths. As Fermor recalled, the polling booths on election day were always well staffed with a wide variety of Arkell supporters: old family friends, business associates and members of Wollongong's multicultural community who all turned out in force, often decked out in Arkell T-shirts and other paraphernalia.

Arkell's embrace of multicultural Wollongong was one of the keys to his success and perhaps his most important achievement. He was a regular visitor to the Italian, Polish and Hellenic clubs and AGA Club Germania, among others, and his participation in national days and other key commemorative dates was widely reported in the ethnic press.[3] He helped those organisations with fundraising and attended their functions and events. As former *Illawarra Mercury* editor Nick Hartgerink remembers: 'For a lot of migrant communities that was a really big deal. It gave them an imprimatur that they mattered and it gave Frank a very loyal voter base.' The Illawarra had been through dramatic changes as large-scale migration from Central and Southern Europe transformed the population. Arkell regularly spoke of the multicultural makeup of the region and always in a positive manner. As he told Robyn Slater in a 1982 interview about the Friends of the University: 'It must be realised, Robyn, that in a Wollongong of 200,000 people we've got 80,000 people who came to us from 76 different countries.'

---

1   John Martin, Personal communication, 23 April 2023.
2   Interview with Bevan Fermor, 22 March 2023.
3   For example, 'Wollongong', *Le Courrier Australien*, [Sydney], 10 April 1983: 15; 'En Ce 14 Juillet [On This July 14]', *Le Courrier Australien*, [Sydney], 10 August 1983: 9.

The reference to '76 different countries' was an Arkell standard repeated many times. Also in 1982, as a guest of Rotary, he spoke of Wollongong's uniqueness:

> As you hove about [Wollongong] you get an understanding of that uniqueness … Immediately after the War people from all over the world came to our city as refugees. Today there is [sic] over 76 national groups in the City of Wollongong.[4]

And, of course, this favoured point would appear in his first speech to parliament in September 1984, when he spoke with real feeling about Wollongong as 'a city of warm friendly people, people from 76 different countries'. Arkell's empathy was channelled onto the city itself. It was more than just clever self-promotion when he told the *Illawarra Mercury* that 'I am married to Wollongong'.[5]

Political allies and rivals alike heard that stump speech about cultural variety many times, but its significance never waned in a region where migration had provoked ethnic tensions and resentment against the 'newcomers'. It gave Arkell a voter base among a group whom Labor had not yet fully developed. Arkell's unreserved celebration of multicultural diversity was also a vital part of the city's transition to a modern culturally diverse city. Unsurprisingly, Arkell was a strong supporter of the proposed Nan Tien Buddhist Temple. For Arkell, the temple would be both a major cultural tourism destination and a symbol that Wollongong was growing and changing with an affirmative embrace of religious differences and cultural tolerance.[6]

Arkell wanted Wollongong to be a modern clean and green city with a positive image. He worked tirelessly towards that end. He wanted the economy to diversify and flourish. He wanted education to thrive. He eschewed all negative publicity for Wollongong. In 1975 he railed against the ABC's *The Aunty Jack Show* for its tongue-in-cheek satire of local culture. The 1974 album spinoff from the show included the iconic song

---

4   'President's Report for the Year 1982', *Rotary News*, Rotary Club of West Wollongong, www.rotarynews.info/2/club/4445/3239 (site discontinued).
5   Frank Arkell, NSW, Parliamentary Debates, Legislative Assembly, 11 September 1984, 634–39; Geoff Failes, 'Married to Wollongong', *Illawarra Mercury*, 29 June 1998.
6   Gordon Waitt, 'A Place for Buddha in Wollongong, New South Wales? Territorial Rules in the Place-Making of Sacred Spaces', *Australian Geographer* 34, no. 2 (2003): 223–38, doi.org/10.1080/00049180301733.

'Wollongong the Brave'.[7] Arkell discussed a ban at the council, arguing that it was damaging to Wollongong's reputation.[8] Any perceived negativity was a target for Arkell. In the 1980s he became increasingly annoyed with the *Illawarra Mercury* for its reporting of high regional unemployment figures and overall adverse portrayal of the city, as he saw it. As *Sydney Morning Herald* journalist Gareth Powell wrote of Arkell in 1988:

> He is not a man who sees things in subtle shades. For him, there is black and white. You are for Wollongong and the Illawarra region or you are not.[9]

The cumulative effect of Arkell's relentless positivity from the mid-1970s and throughout the 1980s helped Wollongong become a city with a more self-assured and confident image nationally. When parliament was in session, Arkell would leave Sydney when the Legislative Assembly had finished its deliberations on Thursday and return to his electoral office in Wollongong on Friday. The transition from Thursday to Friday neatly summarised Arkell's sense of his dual mission. In 1988 he told the *Sydney Morning Herald*: 'On Thursday I sell Wollongong to the world. On Friday I sell Wollongong to Wollongong.'[10] In other words, his audience was both the outside world and Wollongong people themselves. And for those Wollongong people, from the mid-1970s, Arkell made it a little easier to be proud and appreciative of their place, often in the face of an undesirable national image that tended to be frozen on the utilitarian, hard-edged, polluted city of the 1950s and 1960s. Asked how many times he said 'wonderful' when describing Wollongong, Arkell delivered a classic riposte: 'It is a wonderful, wonderful city, so why shouldn't I say so? We have wonderful beaches, wonderful climate, wonderful shopping centres and wonderful people.'[11]

In terms of political achievements, Frank Arkell had a simple proposition that sought to pressure the major parties to take Wollongong seriously. 'Wollongong had been neglected for many years because it was a blue

---

7   'Raise your heads high / See a burnt sienna sky / Lands so free / Of trees / You may laugh, say we pong / But to me it's Wollongong / Wollongong the Brave'. Excerpt from 'Wollongong the Brave', *Aunty Jack*, [written and produced by Rory O'Donoghue, Grahame Bond and Maurice Murphy], 1974.
8   Grahame Bond, 'Interview Transcript from Illawarra Stories Wollongong City Libraries Oral History Project', Interviewer: Kirsten Bokor, 8 February 2009, Wollongong City Library, illawarrastories.com.au/grahame-bond-interview-transcript/.
9   Gareth Powell, 'This Man is the Secret Weapon of "Bustle City"—Wollongong and the Illawarra', [Supplement], *Sydney Morning Herald*, 20 April 1988: 3.
10 ibid.
11 Frank Arkell cited in ibid.

ribbon seat—a safe seat,' he wrote in 1985 in his first six-monthly report from his electoral office: 'Now Government takes notice of our needs and rights.' Against a viable rival in the figure of Arkell, the NSW Labor government began to make election promises designed to give their Wollongong candidate a fighting chance. The electrification of the rail line from Waterfall to Port Kembla began in earnest after the very close result in the 1981 state election when Eric Ramsay won by 51 votes. The line was electrified to Helensburgh by April 1984 and the service to Wollongong opened in February 1986. The total cost of the project when completed to Port Kembla was reportedly $230 million, with subsequent extensions to Dapto (1993) and Kiama (2001).[12]

It is not possible, of course, to ask Arkell himself what he thought his greatest political achievement was, but we can get close. Peter Daly, Arkell's long-term solicitor and close friend, asked him this question. As Daly told the Illawarra Historical Society in 2008:

> Frank Arkell told me of his greatest achievement for Wollongong, when I asked him. He said the Northern Distributor. It was agony before and disruptive. It ended the truck movements through the northern suburbs and they by-passed Wollongong. A visit to these areas today will show the steady renewal that has occurred.[13]

The Northern Distributor was part of the plan for the region's roads developed in the late 1940s. Land was progressively set aside or acquired in the corridor between the coast and the Princes Highway, which ran like a ribbon through the northern suburbs of Wollongong, from North Wollongong through Fairy Meadow, Towradgi, Corrimal, Russell Vale and Woonona. The aim was a freeway running all the way from North Wollongong to Bulli—a distance of almost 10 kilometres. The Northern Distributor would relieve the heavy traffic, including coal trucks, flowing in both directions along the Princes Highway, which also cut through a series of main street shopping centres in the townships along the way. There were many hands who helped secure this road, starting with the previous state member. Labor member for Corrimal Laurie Kelly led an adjournment debate on the 'Wollongong northern suburbs expressway' in 1974 and told

---

12 'Big Projects and New Faces in the SRA—The Essential Engineer', [Supplement], *Sydney Morning Herald*, 4 September 1987: 4.
13 Peter Francis Daly cited in *Bulletin*, [Illawarra Historical Society], September–October 2011: 60. See also Peter Francis Daly, 'The Law During the Last 50 Years: An Address Given to the Illawarra Historical Society', *Bulletin*, [Illawarra Historical Society], April–May 2011: 19–20; May–June 2011: 29–37; July–August 2011: 47–50; September–October 2011: 60–63.

the Legislative Assembly: 'Since entering Parliament [in 1968,] I have been promised that an early commencement would be made on the Wollongong northern suburbs expressway, an extremely important artery.'[14] In September 1975 the Department of Main Roads reported that the project was in 'the late stages of planning'.[15] Much to Kelly's dismay, the Northern Suburbs Distributor project (often just called 'the Northern Distributor' by locals) languished as road construction increasingly focused on the Wollongong bypass and extensions of the freeway to the south, and then on the F6 freeway between Bulli and Waterfall. I remember walking through Fairy Meadow, in the area where the Northern Distributor was planned to run, on the way to school sports at Dalton Park in 1979. It was a liminal space between the residential area of Fairy Meadow and the road behind the coastal dune. On the ocean side, the sporting fields of Dalton Park opened out to the north, and the wild expanse of Puckeys Estate behind Fairy Meadow Beach loomed to the south. It was an area of partly graded road and empty paddocks fed by creeks clogged with weeds and cut in half by the South Coast rail line. The Northern Distributor was completed between the North Wollongong Interchange and Towradgi Road by 1990 and subsequently extended north towards Russell Vale, Thirroul and Bulli.[16]

This new road took the coal trucks and heavy car traffic away from the Princes Highway and the main street shopping areas in Fairy Meadow and later Corrimal, but it still pointed to an unresolved issue for the region: the continued presence of coal trucks on the roads. By 1982, 4 million tonnes of coal was being transported by road to the Port Kembla coal loader. Between 1975 and 1982, 27 people died in truck-related road accidents in the region.[17] While Arkell lobbied for the various proposed rail links and coal conveyor systems that might have reduced coal truck movements, ultimately, he placed the jobs at the Port Kembla coal loader and in the trucking industry above the very many concerns that large-scale truck-based coal transport generated. Like many matters in Arkell's political life, his true legacy is debatable.

---

14   Laurie Kelly in NSW, *Parliamentary Debates*, Legislative Assembly, 24 September 1974, 'NSW Parliament Adjournment Debate—Wollongong Northern Suburbs Expressway', 1378–80.
15   *Main Roads* [NSW Department of Main Roads Journal] 41, no. 1 (September 1975), www.opengov.nsw.gov.au/publications/16335;jsessionid=B9372A9CEF496C4DF895DF386EE72371, 6.
16   Roads and Traffic Authority, *Environmental Impact Statement: Northern Suburbs Distributor*, prepared by Robert Purdon of Purdon & Associates Pty Ltd (Sydney: RTA, 2002).
17   Sophia Apolonia Everett, 'Port-Orientated Coal Transport Infrastructure: An Analysis of Locational Decision Making', MA (Hons) thesis (University of Wollongong, NSW, 1984), 121; Phillip Laird, 'The Maldon Port Kembla Railway and the Wentworth Deviation', Paper presented to the AusRAIL PLUS Conference, Adelaide, 17–19 November 2009.

Arkell's move to 'restart' the road project in 1989 combined his mayoral and parliamentary roles in a very specific way. This could be called either creative or problematic depending on your perspective, but by getting Wollongong Council to declare the Northern Distributor 'a standard arterial road', he effectively passed some responsibility to the council and reduced the state government's total funding burden. The Department of Main Roads (which became the Roads and Traffic Authority in 1989 and is now Roads and Maritime Services) adopted Wollongong Council's suggestion to define the road as a 'standard arterial road'. The regular progress report from Arkell's electoral office noted that this move 'substantially reduced both the future commitments of funds required and the extent of the lands required for the road'.[18] This meant that the Northern Distributor could be constructed on a smaller scale and the costs shared with the council. As Arkell's press release noted: 'I will be asking Minister for Transport, Bruce Baird, for a massive injection of funds to enable a two lane Arterial Road.'[19] Colin Markham, Labor member for Keira (a seat formed in 1988 based on the northern suburbs, replacing the seat of Corrimal), called the plan 'stupid' since it amounted to halving the capacity of the proposed road from four to two lanes.[20] Here was Arkell using his two elected positions in partnership but the ratepayers of Wollongong and the users of this crucial northern route may not have been too pleased with the compromise that was reached.

Coal transport and its necessary infrastructure are controversial issues in Wollongong, and it is not easy to extract a clear picture of the role that Arkell played. For a start, these proposals had a long history pre-dating his 1984 election win. To address Wollongong's perennial problems with the road transport of coal, the Maldon–Dombarton railway line was first proposed in the mid-1970s, but the state Labor government shelved the idea in October 1978. The proposal, with some variations over the years, was for a transport route that would take coal from the mines in the Burragorang Valley south-west of Sydney to the Port Kembla coal loader, joining the Illawarra Line near Unanderra.[21] The state Labor government returned to the project in October 1982 with an in-principle agreement.

---

18 'Progress Report from the Office of the Member for Wollongong, 1988–1989', Wollongong City Library.
19 Frank Arkell, 'Arkell Claims Northern Distributor Delays Unsatisfactory', Media release, 14 March 1989, Office of the Member for Wollongong, 1988–89, Wollongong City Library.
20 Colin Markham cited in 'Close Unsafe Roads: Owen', *Illawarra Mercury*, 13 March 1989.
21 See Dames & Moore, *Maldon–Dombarton–Port Kembla Rail Line: Environmental Impact Statement. Volume 2* (Sydney: State Rail Authority, 1983). The best analysis of the complex history and politics behind these coal transport infrastructure projects undertaken in the region is Everett, 'Port-Orientated Coal Transport Infrastructure'.

Ongoing concerns about the transport of millions of tonnes of coal by road, vigorous local lobbying, including from the South Coast Trades and Labour Council, as well as the prospect of losing the seat of Wollongong to an independent led to the project becoming a major part of Labor's platform for the 1984 election.

In the mid-1980s, driving south along the Princes Highway past Arkells' garage at Cobbler's Hill and towards Unanderra, you could see the impressive new railway bridge that spanned the highway and the new supports for electric cabling lining the track. NSW Labor cannily brought forward the work so that there were signs of construction activity before the 1984 election. Three months after the election, all went quiet when the government announced that the electrification of the South Coast Line would be prioritised. The completion date for Maldon–Dombarton would be delayed until 1990. Funding was subsequently provided in the 1984–1985 budget for the $150 million project.[22]

Significant progress was achieved but a few months after the election of the Greiner Coalition government in March 1988, the project was cancelled. During Premier Greiner's visit to Wollongong in June 1988, protestors, including sacked rail workers, surrounded the entrance to the Wollongong City Council building chanting 'Sack Greiner' and 'Tax the rich, not the poor'.[23] The premier, ushered through the crowd of hostile protestors by police, did his best to maintain a smile for the television cameras, surrounded, as he was, by 'representatives from almost every sub-group the new Government has managed to anger in its three months in office'.[24]

Inside the council building, Greiner met with Frank Arkell in the mayor's office on the tenth floor. Arkell put the case for Wollongong, with the chants of the protesters still audible. There was a broad political and ideological agenda at play in Greiner's decision. Despite an election promise to continue the project, after the election, Greiner emphasised the levels of unsustainable state debt, arguing that it would be 'criminally stupid' to continue the Maldon–Dombarton project since the State Rail Authority was 'bankrupt'. He also had the authority of a sweeping election victory behind him. More controversially, many alleged that the NSW Liberal Party was showing its bias towards the trucking companies, who were, it

---
22 Everett, 'Port-Orientated Coal Transport Infrastructure', 119–21.
23 'Greiner Jeered by Sacked Rail Workers', *Sydney Morning Herald*, 16 June 1988: 2.
24 Matthew Moore, 'Wollongong Waves Rock Greiner's Loveboat', *Sydney Morning Herald*, 18 June 1988: 32.

was claimed, major donors to their campaign. There is a popular belief in Wollongong that cancelling the Maldon–Dombarton project cost more in terms of paying out contracts than it would have to finish it. Over many years, the sturdy concrete bridge over the Princes Highway and the steel posts without cabling slowly lost their shine. Every trip down the highway towards Unanderra seemed to present the promise of modern rail-borne coal transport fading as the steel girders lost their silvery lustre. Further inland, an unfinished concrete rail bridge across the Nepean River near Maldon is now a popular and perplexing sightseeing destination. This unfinished infrastructure is a visible reminder of the cancelled project. It was also a testament to a new set of political calculations that arrived in 1988 with the first Coalition government in New South Wales since 1976.

Putting aside these statewide matters, including the Greiner government's approach to governing and its stated and allegedly hidden agendas, the election of the Coalition government was a serious blow to Arkell. The value of Wollongong being represented by an independent only made sense if the government of the day coveted the seat. The Liberals had not made a serious attempt to win the seat since they lost it to Labor in 1971. The eclectic mix of independents, of whom Arkell was the most high profile, had become the de facto opposition in Wollongong, effectively replacing the Liberals as a major alternative political force in the city. Therefore, the election of a Coalition government significantly reduced Arkell's leverage.

It is a strange irony that Arkell—for so long a thorn in the side of NSW Labor—was also reliant on Labor's desperate desire to win back the seat of Wollongong. The long list of state Labor ministers who visited Wollongong in the period 1984–1988 is a testament to that peculiar interdependence. Arkell invited Labor's Barrie Unsworth, then minister for health, to Wollongong and secured funding to improve psychiatric services in the city.[25] He invited Bob Carr, then minister for the environment, and managed to secure the restoration of resources that were to be removed from the local office of the State Pollution Control Commission. Arkell invited George Paciullo, the minister for police, and, in March 1986, secured the promise of a new police station and upgraded security for the police and court complex in Wollongong.[26]

---

25 'Psychiatric Plan Earns Support', *Illawarra Mercury*, 24 March 1986; Press release from the Office of the Member for Wollongong, 21 March 1986, Wollongong City Library.
26 Press release from the Office of the Member for Wollongong, 28 February 1986, Wollongong City Library; Clarke, 'Police Station Planning Begins'.

Most of these ministerial visits ended with a polite press release from Arkell. On the new police station, Arkell praised 'the responsiveness of this Minister to Wollongong's needs' and proclaimed 'that great things in Police Services are sure to come of it'.[27] When Carr reversed the decision to reduce Wollongong's pollution monitoring capacity, Arkell praised him 'for coming in person to see our problems' and hoped that 'Wollongong City Council and the State Government can continue to work as closely on environmental issues as we are at present'.[28] Arkell was playing a delicate game. He gave his opponents credit, but he also had to demonstrate that he was central to whatever was achieved.

There is a definite pattern of success for Arkell at the ministerial level in his first term as a member for Wollongong. These regular ministerial visits and the mostly good outcomes for Wollongong were a barometer of Arkell's political achievements and an indication of the electoral realities of a state Labor government that wanted to win back the seat. But the cancellation of the Maldon–Dombarton line in June 1988 was also a clear sign that the new Greiner Coalition government had other priorities including ideological ones that paid no heed to electoral realities in the seat of Wollongong. Labor's election loss in 1988 and the reduction in Arkell's political leverage might also explain his increasing levels of frustration and his sometimes ill-tempered interactions with staff. Arkell had become adept at glad-handing Labor ministers but he had no such political leverage with Greiner and his new ministry.

Wollongong was the first, second and third issue on Arkell's public agenda. He had a reputation for leaving Wollongong tourism brochures all around the NSW Parliament and liked to quip that 'Wollongong is the "W" in NSW'.[29] Arkell was nonetheless active on social issues, revealing his conservative stance and his natural synergy with other socially conservative members of parliament. This is where public, private and secret begin to collide in the most complex and disturbing of ways.

As we saw in Chapter 9, homosexual law reform legislation had been debated in parliament since at least 1978. The issue again came to the fore in 1984, this time in the shape of a private member's bill sponsored by

---

27 Press release from the Office of the Member for Wollongong, 28 February 1986; Clarke, 'Police Station Planning Begins'.
28 Frank Arkell, 'Arkell Applauds Carr Initiatives', Media release, 17 January 1986, Office of the Member for Wollongong; Peter Clarke, 'SPCC Forced to Back Down', *Illawarra Mercury*, 31 December 1985.
29 Interview with Nick Hartgerink, 24 November 2022.

Premier Neville Wran. Wran's bill to amend the *Crimes Act 1900* sought to decriminalise homosexual sex for all consenting males over the age of 18. Arkell voted against the bill and against an amendment put by the member for Illawarra George Petersen to make the age of consent for homosexual sex the same as the age of consent for heterosexual sex (16 years).[30]

Finding some common ground with the Reverend Fred Nile and his party as well as conservatives from the Catholic right wing of the Labor Party, Arkell also supported a series of petitions that were critical of the proposed legalisation of homosexual sex. These were made available in his electoral office for signing and he presented the signatures to parliament. All these petitions were organised and presented while the amendment to the *Crimes Act* was being debated in an effort to slow or stop the passage of the legislation. In one petition, the signatories supported 'your efforts to strengthen family life and protect children'. The petition continued:

> We totally oppose any moves in Parliament to legalize sodomy, or buggery, which God calls an abomination. Such moves would imply community approval and acceptance of these unnatural, unhealthy and immoral acts which would therefore also permit public soliciting and put teenagers at risk.[31]

It can be hard to fathom the personal motivations and occasional inconsistencies of our fellow humans, but this seems an especially dissonant and ultimately self-destructive position to have taken. It is well established by now that Arkell had sex with young men and boys, yet he opposed the legalisation of homosexual sex. If sodomy was an abomination in the eyes of God, how did Arkell reconcile this with his own behaviour over many decades? It is possible to suggest political reasons for this stance—in the maintenance of his support base, for example, which had coalesced around his conservative social values—or even social reasons as he may have feared the loss of friends or public standing if he took any other position. Yet, the personal activities and preferences of the man were so at odds with his public position we can only wonder how he reconciled the two.

Another disturbing confluence of public and private occurred when Arkell spoke out about services for young people in Wollongong. In early 1986 Frank had expressed concern about the levels of resourcing provided for the after-hours child abuse scheme. Youth and Community Service staff had

---

30 NSW, *Votes and Proceedings*, Legislative Assembly, 15 May 1984, 766, 769, 770, 772, 771.
31 ibid., 17 May 1984, 1054.

taken their concerns to the Industrial Court, claiming that the reduction in funding would 'leave between 15 to 20 child abuse cases unanswered each week'.[32] Arkell asked the minister responsible to intervene in the dispute, arguing that the 'provision of adequate child protection services was a "crucial responsibility"'.[33]

In May 1989 Arkell supported a phone-in for homeless youth organised by the Wollongong Youth Refuge in which 41 callers contacted the agency providing important insights into their situation. Before the phone-in, Arkell noted: 'I was deeply concerned that we do not fully understand the complex circumstances which force young people onto the streets.' Arkell wrote that 'family problems—including sexual and physical abuse—are the most common reasons for children becoming homeless' and 'most children do not wish to be homeless and wish for a happy family life'.[34]

Can we seriously imagine that the man who groomed Rene Mori for five years, had anonymous sex with Ray Leary, W13 and possibly others, as well as propositioned but was turned down by G17, had a purely policy-driven response to the question of sexual assault services for young homeless people? This press release from the man who had been having sex with boys as young as 13 since at least the early 1970s seems to be deliberately displaying the truth close to the public eye. Arkell knew at first-hand the existence of Tony Bevan's paedophile network and he had seen up close the edgy, troubled lives of boys in Kings Cross, yet his press release specifically mentions the threat of sexual abuse from within the family, ignoring the kind of threat represented by the paedophile networks.

Despite the lack of concern in the Coalition government about its electoral standing in Wollongong, leading up to the 1991 state election, Arkell had the leverage provided by the opposition Labor Party's keenness to return Wollongong to its column. Arkell's success disciplined the Labor Party in Illawarra to eventually preselect strong candidates and work harder to win back and retain the seat. Labor had spent two decades trying to impugn Arkell's character in and out of parliament. In 1991 the party took a novel approach when it preselected a viable alternative who was a strong campaigner: Gerry Sullivan. A commerce and accounting graduate from the University of Wollongong, Sullivan had enjoyed a long career as

---

32   Peter Clarke, 'Child Protection Crisis Goes to Court', *Illawarra Mercury*, 10 January 1986.
33   ibid.
34   Frank Arkell, 'Arkell Claims Phone-In Success', Media release, 8 June 1986, Office of the Member for Wollongong, Wollongong City Library.

a high school teacher before embarking on the 1991 campaign. He won in 1991 after a disciplined and effective campaign and won again in 1994, but internal party ructions led to a complicated deal that saw him lose preselection. Wollongong as a Labor stronghold was vulnerable again to a high-profile lord mayor and independent candidate in the shape of the Reverend Gordon Bradbery. Labor in the Illawarra was slow to learn the lessons of the Arkell era. Utilising the same energy and enthusiasm for community work as Arkell, Bradbery dominated the mayoral office from 2011 to 2024, defeating Labor candidates at every mayoral contest. In Bradbery's case, he was unsuccessful in his bid to win the state seat of Wollongong at the November 2016 state election, which highlights Arkell's achievement in wrestling the seat from Labor in 1984 and 1988.

Wollongong Council has been touched by corruption and maladministration time and time again. The conditions that allowed the problems experienced after Arkell departed the council in 1991 were shaped in the late 1970s and 1980s when Arkell was arguably the single dominant figure there. The tradition of long-serving staff, including Phil Bertold and Rod Oxley, who was general manager from 1988, continued from the Arkell era and proved problematic in later years. The relationship between entrepreneurial council staff and driven developers also triggered a series of behaviours that led to an ICAC inquiry, high-profile corruption issues and the sacking of the council in 2008.[35]

It is a testament to Arkell's energy and ambition that the list of his political achievements is long. We have sampled some of the major ones, particularly in his first term as a member for Wollongong, though we have seen with the Northern Distributor that his legacy is complex and vexed, and the

---

35   NSW ICAC established that internal checks and balances against corruption had been progressively removed by long-serving general manager Rod Oxley, thus 'increasing the likelihood of corrupt conduct occurring'. ICAC presented evidence that Oxley's dismantling of internal firewalls and lack of external or arm's-length scrutiny of the decision-making process allowed corruption to spread. ICAC found that Oxley had breached the council's code of conduct by having offsite face-to-face meetings with developers with no other council staff present and no formal record of the meetings taken. ICAC concluded that Oxley had engaged in corrupt conduct. These findings against Oxley, however, were never referred to the Director of Public Prosecutions and Oxley strenuously denied the imputation of corruption. He died in March 2022. See Independent Commission Against Corruption, *Report on An Investigation into Corruption Allegations Affecting Wollongong City Council. Part Three* (Sydney: ICAC, October 2008), www.parliament.nsw.gov.au/tp/files/7660/Investigation%20into%20corruption%20allegations%20 affecting%20Wollongong%20City%20Council%20-%20Operation%20Atlas%20-%20Part%203. pdf, 11, 69–81; Nick McLaren, 'Fallen Wollongong Leader Fights Back', *ABC News*, 4 December 2009, www.abc.net.au/news/2009-12-04/fallen-wollongong-leader-fights-back/1169476; 'Rod Oxley Funeral Notice', *Illawarra Mercury*, 26 March 2022.

outcomes debatable. But we can hardly separate his public achievements from his private life. There were simply too many connections between the two. The stark contrast between his public world of social conservatism and fierce opposition to homosexual law reform and his private world of indulgence and personal gratification in sex with boys and young men is especially heinous—the very definition of hypocrisy. His use of the perks and opportunities afforded by his office—his grand mayoral office and the resources and financial capacity of business success—to gain privileged access to boys and young men is also deeply troubling. Public standing gave him a high degree of protection. His public world shielded his private life, which is, of course, another link between his public life and private perversions. Despite the decades of rumours and innuendo, including that from my Year 7 classmate in 1979 and my university friend in 1991, and everything before and after, nothing was done, and no action was taken. The great and powerful of Wollongong, including Arkell, remained above the law, at least until the last few years of his life.

Perhaps the most compelling connection between Arkell's public achievements and his private illicit and illegal activities was how his important success in giving Wollongong a better reputation among outsiders and locals alike was undermined by the revelations about his sordid secret life, which had the potential to undermine all his good work. The counter-image that was presented was of a city with a pathological child abuse problem, a site of unspeakable abuse and possible corruption. For journalist Richard Guilliat, writing in the *Sydney Morning Herald*'s *Good Weekend* magazine, Wollongong was a 'city of secrets'. 'It now transpires,' Guilliat wrote in August 1998, 'that Wollongong was run for 20 years by two mayors who preyed sexually on their teenage constituents.' The secret activities of Arkell's private world became public in ways that completely undermined what had been his mission in public life for many decades: to present a positive picture of wonderful, wonderful Wollongong to the rest of Australia and indeed the world.

Arkell's life ended without resolution of these issues, with the legal proceedings against him cut short. In a visceral, physically sickening attack, Mark Valera swept aside all civility, law and words. He took away the impending reality of a legal reckoning, indulging in his own violent retribution, however inchoate and formless. Arkell had lived a life in the spotlight, an energetic life full of service and zeal, but perversion and deceit had shadowed him and, in the end, left him, and us, in darkness.

15
'I would rather him face the courts': The aftermath and the legacy

Wollongong people, including expatriates, still live with the legacy of Frank Arkell. Especially for those over 40 years of age, Arkell's history and his tragic murder are well known and have entered regional folklore. It is a topic that still divides people as they take sides on whether Arkell was a 'saint or a sinner' or attempt to navigate between the two. As Gordon Bradbery said, the revelations about Arkell's past and then his murder left Wollongong people with cognitive dissonance. How could they reconcile the hardworking, once very popular lord mayor with the alleged child abuser murdered 'for what he had done to kids'?

The question of Arkell's guilt or otherwise, as well as the proper legal processes that would have resolved the allegations and the charges one way or another, can never be determined. All these words and reflections were overtaken by events, and by the brutality of murder. The courts will never be able to pronounce on the charges. Arkell was murdered only three months before his September court date. As Rene Mori, who was abused by Arkell in the mayoral office in 1984, said to an ABC reporter:

> I don't believe he deserved to die the way he did. Regardless of what he did to me or anyone else ... I would rather him face the courts and face the consequences.[1]

---

1   Rene Mori quoted in 'Wonderful Wollongong', *Background Briefing*, [*ABC Radio*], 1 October 1998, C100, 1286175, National Archives of Australia, Canberra.

Arkell's murder has left a cultural ambiguity in Wollongong, a clear lack of certainty about which way to turn on the man who gave so much and yet was shrouded in a veil of controversies, allegations and rumours. The first person to take the Arkell story seriously and conduct in-depth research was journalist Brett Martin. Even before Arkell's death, he researched and wrote a long, detailed exposé of those involved in the Wollongong paedophile network, but publishers in the 1990s were not interested. One commissioning editor told Martin the manuscript was 'too dark'.

Before the Royal Commission into Institutional Responses to Child Sexual Abuse which ran from 2013 to 2017, there were hurdles to convincing gatekeepers in publishing houses and newspapers that this was a significant issue. Now we see headlines in Australia and around the world about child abuse being endemic and that in institutional settings and churches it was commonplace. A seven-year inquiry initiated by the UK Government, which reported in October 2022, found that 'child sexual abuse is not a problem consigned to the past' and the recent 'explosion in online-facilitated child sexual abuse underlines the extent to which the problem is endemic within England and Wales'.[2]

After the 2017 royal commission, the Arkell story seemed even more relevant. The commission provided a disturbing national snapshot of the extent of child sexual abuse. It led to a further reckoning within many communities throughout Australia, especially in the Catholic Church and in specific places where abuse was widespread—namely, the dioceses of Sale and Ballarat in Victoria, and in Wollongong. The material on Wollongong in the 2017 royal commission was a dreadful but not unexpected coda to the revelations about the city in the 1997 Wood Royal Commission. The ghosts of Tony Bevan, Brother Michael Evans and Father Peter L. Comensoli still haunted Wollongong and the royal commission found the rates of sexual offending against children among the clergy there among the highest in the country. Among the worst offenders were the Christian Brothers whose long tenure at Christian Brothers College (now Edmund Rice College) has bequeathed a bitter and often traumatic legacy for the children of Wollongong and their families. Arkell's alma mater was a deeply flawed institution. As well as being a site of child sexual abuse, it was staffed by and seemingly produced generations of abusers since its formation in 1926.

---

2 *The Report of the Independent Inquiry into Child Sexual Abuse* (London: UK Government, October 2022), www.iicsa.org.uk/reports-recommendations/publications/inquiry/final-report/executive-summary.

When I sought further information from Edmund Rice College to confirm the years of Frank's school attendance and ask for assistance to access any old yearbooks or annual reports, for example, it refused to cooperate, replying that 'at the present time it is not our practice to communicate such details to third parties in this way'.[3] Given the paucity of evidence, we can only speculate that Frank's school experiences, and the company it entailed, were possible reasons for the development of his preference for transitory asymmetrical relationships between himself as the older powerful male and boys and young men as less powerful dependants. In the absence of definitive evidence, this must remain only a possibility, but given the school and its history and the behaviour of many of his peers, there was a strong chance that Arkell was subjected to sexual abuse or had firsthand experience of a culture of abuse while a student at Christian Brothers College. There is only one tantalising piece of evidence that reflects on Arkell's time at the school. It comes from journalist Richard Guilliat in a quote from former Christian Brothers headmaster Brother Kevin O'Farrell. At a 1986 school silver jubilee function, O'Farrell reportedly said: 'Frank was one of the tender little boys at the school, and look what we've done to him.' Arkell, Bevan and Brian Tobin were reportedly all present.[4] No further evidence of Arkell's experience at the school has been found.

Aside from Brett Martin's early work on the paedophiles of Wollongong, several documentary filmmakers and podcast producers have more recently been considering the story again. It never lost its relevance even if it did fade from regional memory, reactivated on the tenth and twentieth anniversaries of Arkell's murder, in 2008 and 2018, respectively. The 2018 anniversary featured a story by ABC senior reporter Nick McLaren. It became McLaren's most shared story—a testament to the ongoing interest in the Arkell legacy and its brutal ending.

Then there were disturbing synergies between Frank Arkell's case and the high-profile trial of Cardinal George Pell, the investigative reporting done by ABC TV's *7.30* and *Four Corners* as well as Louise Milligan's biography of Pell and her follow-up book on the experiences of being a 'victim' in sexual abuse trials. That the now-deceased Pell was educated at a Christian Brothers high school was a further reminder of the role the Christian Brothers College played in Wollongong. This was reinforced when Stephen Jones, federal

---

3   Email from Edmund Rice College to Erik Eklund, 29 June 2023.
4   Guilliat, 'City of Secrets', 24.

Labor member for Whitlam (a seat that covers the city of Wollongong), said that the college, which he attended, 'felt like a dumping ground for paedophiles'.[5]

Understanding the social forces and prejudices that shaped Arkell's world, which made it so difficult to be his true self in his public and private lives, is not the same as excusing his subsequent behaviours. There is an important distinction between providing the context for a person's actions and providing an excuse. There is a fine balance to be struck between the social forces that shape us all and the real agency of our everyday choices and actions. The link between suffering abuse and becoming an abuser is not absolute and many can indeed break the chain of suffering. Many people have survived abusive actions and abusive conditions and have found the strength to live their best lives, even helping others to survive and heal.

The individual responsibility is clear, but context helps us understand motivation and action. Here, there seems little doubt that Arkell attended a high school that was a deeply flawed institution. Arkell was most likely subjected to, or aware of, predatory sexual practices committed by those in positions of power against young boys. The fact that some of his classmates and generations of the school's teachers would become some of Wollongong's most notorious abusers gives weight to this interpretation. In 1998 one of Arkell's political rivals, Paul Matters, secretary of the South Coast Trades and Labour Council, astutely observed: 'I think the men that were socialised in that environment learned early on that if you were powerful you could do it, provided it doesn't become public knowledge. I think they learned that from the church.'[6] Christian Brothers College was the beating heart of Wollongong's decades of sexual abuse and predation, and it seems a fair assessment to say that some of the abused became the next generation's perpetrators. It is also apparent that Arkell's long-time rival, Tony Bevan, orchestrated some of the allegations against Frank. Any allegation from one of 'Tony's Boys' must be assessed with the possibility that Bevan helped fabricate or exaggerate the claim.

---

5   Stephen Jones MP quoted in Angela Thompson, 'MP Stephen Jones Says Sexual Predators Moved Freely at Edmund Rice College in the 1980s', *Sydney Morning Herald*, 16 June 2016, www.smh.com.au/national/nsw/mp-stephen-jones-says-sexual-predators-moved-freely-at-edmund-rice-college-in-the-1980s-20160616-gpl1s6.html.
6   Guilliat, 'City of Secrets', 23–24.

15. 'I WOULD RATHER HIM FACE THE COURTS'

If the first question people ask about Arkell is whether he was a saint or a sinner, the second question is how did he get away with living a secret life for so long? The answer is not straightforward for it involves a myriad of personal, cultural and institutional factors. On the personal side, Arkell was a credible and convincing politician. He had excellent people skills when he wanted and needed to use them. His persona was so recognisable and so eccentric that it often diverted people from any concern about more serious matters. Like many successful well-to-do paedophiles, he utilised the skills and resources he had acquired through business and politics to aid and abet his activities. A ready supply of cash, regular travel, the successful family businesses, the real estate agency, the rounds of social gatherings and events, the trappings and the gravitas that came with the public office—all provided the tools with which he could pursue his desires. The paedophiles covered in this book were well-off, successful businessmen and politicians. All were driven, highly capable men with a dreadful secret. They leave many who had otherwise normal, personable interactions with these men floored because they were so good at hiding their private world of perversion. The public face of the committed, affable lord mayor or the high-profile volunteer pilot and former mayor becomes a shield to deflect suspicions. For Arkell as for Bevan and for many of the other men covered in this book, success, public standing and prestige were the perfect foils to cover their child sexual abuse.

There was strong community deference to those in high office. A lord mayor (and state MP) naturally commanded respect. Australians tend to confer respect on those in high office, especially in person, even if we might grumble about them when they are not in our presence. These patterns of deference have weakened in more recent decades, but in the 1960s, 1970s and 1980s, they were still strong. A visit from the lord mayor was a significant moment in the life of a community group or sporting club. Such visits were treated with formal proceedings, usually with an opportunity for a speech and often for one in reply by the host president or chair. This level of formality naturally gave Arkell an air of respectability and discouraged any robust debate or discussion. Arkell was seen in his official mayoral robes, lending further authority and gravitas to the person and the event. Challenging the mayor on something that only some knew as rumour or innuendo would have been unthinkable. Arkell, Bevan and all the paedophile Catholic priests and brothers also benefited from a culture of deference to those in power and high office. Many in the community quite reasonably expected those in such positions to be respectable decent men who were worthy of our trust.

That Arkell lived with his mother, was a lifelong bachelor and was never seen out in Wollongong with what contemporaries might have called a 'lady friend' meant that many in the city believed that he was gay. Being gay but not being 'out' functioned as a shield against prying eyes and invasive questions. To question his behaviour in this context would have appeared insensitive and disrespectful. The NSW Labor government had started to build a political conversation around decriminalising homosexuality. Experts in the field noted how violence against gay men including homicides increased as the public conversation around equality for people who were gay and lesbian took hold in the state and around Australia. There was no shortage of homophobic abuse and violence ('gay bashing') in Wollongong and few wanted to add to the general tone of gay hatred. In other words, Arkell slipped through the cracks as a closeted gay man who was able to quietly pursue his paedophile practices but benefit from a growing awareness that homophobia was unacceptable and sexuality was a topic best not spoken about.

If citizens were unwilling or unable to force the matter then police are exactly the right organisation to do the task. One of the many reasons we have a professional police force is to provide formalised procedures to investigate crimes and initiate criminal proceedings. We cannot expect vigilante engagement from citizens about the honesty and probity of community leaders since there are so many ways in which this form of scrutiny can go horribly wrong. NSW Police in Wollongong and Dapto were in receipt of information regarding Tony Bevan and his activities from as early as 1982. There were numerous reports, with one telling police intelligence report suggesting that Bevan's behaviour was well known. Using the somewhat insensitive language of the day, the report nonetheless accurately described Bevan was a 'well known homo and pederast'.

There is evidence from the transcripts of the Wood Royal Commission that the police information on Bevan included a reference to Frank Arkell. It has not been possible to confirm this by accessing the original police records as they are no longer available. But police witnesses and counsel assisting at the Wood Royal Commission referred to and even read from police evidence, meaning that the transcripts are the best record we have of these otherwise 'lost' original documents.

Bevan's network provided some of the boys against whom Arkell offended. Arkell had his own local boys whom he groomed and assaulted and those he picked up at gay beats. Police action against Bevan would have led to Arkell taking much greater care, perhaps even leading to the arrest of Arkell if police had uncovered the Bevan Tapes and followed up on the myriad Wollongong businessmen and politicians who were on those recordings.

A free and fearless local media is a vital protection against corruption and systemic sexual abuse. In Wollongong, many of the victims of child sexual abuse sought help from the *Illawarra Mercury* under the editorship of Peter Cullen only after they had not found a fair hearing from either the police or the Catholic hierarchy in the Wollongong diocese. In other regional cities, local newspaper journalists have also been able to uncover stories of child sexual abuse, often at great personal cost. In Newcastle and the Hunter Valley, it was the *Newcastle Herald* and especially journalist Joanne McCarthy who shone a light on these matters. The Ballarat *Courier* played a similar role in that regional Victorian city.

However, changes to the regional media landscape raise important concerns about whether the same thing could happen now or in the future. Numerous media outlets have closed since the early 1990s when the *Illawarra Mercury* championed the paedophile cases in the Illawarra. This process was only accelerated from 2020 with the effects of the Covid-19 pandemic on the media industry and regional newspapers especially. All media outlets in 2024 are working with fewer journalists while in many regional towns and cities, there is no longer a strong local newspaper, only free community papers that are mostly vehicles for advertising.[7]

So, if this same situation arose today, the *Illawarra Mercury* and many other regional papers would not have the resources or the staff to devote to such a big story. There may be opportunities now for citizen journalists and podcasters to fill the void but as far as I can tell that has not been the case in the child abuse scandals that have broken publicly in the past 20 years. The University of Wollongong, as we have seen, was compromised by its close relationship with Wollongong Council and by the way in which

---

7   See Nikolas Dawson, Sacha Molitorisz, Marian-Andrei Rizoiu and Peter Fray, 'Layoffs, Inequity and COVID-19: A Longitudinal Study of the Journalism Jobs Crisis in Australia from 2012 to 2020', *Journalism* 24 no. 3, 2023: 531–59, doi.org/10.1177/1464884921996286; Olav Muurlink and Elizabeth Voneiff, 'Out of Print: What the Pandemic-Era Newspaper Crisis in Australia Teaches Us about the Role of Rural and Regional Newspapers in Creating Sustainable Communities', *Sustainability* 15 no. 6, 2023: 5439, doi.org/10.3390/su15065439.

Wollongong paedophiles infiltrated the new institution. The university was another local organisation that could have turned a critical and independent eye to events that were occurring in the city, but it did not. The one ray of hope, however, is the growing importance of advocacy groups such as Broken Rites, who have done much to research and publicise ongoing issues of systemic child abuse.

There are also legal and judicial reforms that have the capacity to protect children and unmask child abuse perpetrators such as independent corruption commissions and legal protections for whistleblowers. Some of these reforms came out of the recommendations of the Wood Royal Commission, including the formation of a special police unit to deal with child sexual abuse cases. If Wollongong City Council, for example, had stronger corruption protections in the 1970s and 1980s, then Arkell may not have been able to continue to secure the financial benefits that flowed to his family's companies by securing council contracts. His success here emboldened him to pursue other, more risky activities including using his mayoral office as a venue for grooming and abuse. Criminologists have found that timely action on corruption can rein in more extreme behaviours with early intervention being one of the best ways to ensure against widespread abuse.

Finally, extensive silence on this matter did not serve Wollongong well. To try to ensure this does not happen again we would be well served by a public culture in Australia and globally that allows robust discussion and debate, in which all issues can be raised and nothing is off the table. Asking questions should not immediately be assumed offensive even if the topic is complex and emotionally and politically difficult. A situation in which silences are allowed to grow, in which they are allowed to sit undisturbed beneath a patina of assumed civility or progressive sensibility, is a situation in which accomplished and skilled perpetrators like Arkell and many others thrive.

Arkell also tried to use defamation law to silence the *Illawarra Mercury*. He made public statements threatening legal action. In November 1996, he told ABC TV that he would sue all those who had defamed him: 'If they embarrass me, I'm going to embarrass them. I hope they've got a lot of money because legal fees are going to be pretty high. I am going to come out right on top.'[8]

---

8   *ABC TV News*, 4 November 1996, T315653, ABC Archives, Sydney.

15. 'I WOULD RATHER HIM FACE THE COURTS'

In March 1998 he began legal proceedings against the *Illawarra Mercury* and one of its senior journalists, Lisa Carty. Free speech is often the enemy of the perpetrator while threats or cases of defamation often come to the aid of those in power and those with extensive resources.

A robust public culture of debate and accountability backed up by anticorruption bodies and legal protections for whistleblowers were all factors that together would have helped to at least minimise the extent and harmful impact of Arkell's offending. But most importantly, if NSW Police had acted on early reports of Bevan's activities and vigorously followed up intelligence and, later, complaints of child abuse, many boys who became victims of Arkell and the other paedophiles in the Wollongong network would have been spared that trauma.

***

The city of my youth carries the burden of being the site of a network of abusers, which included Bevan, Tobin, Arkell, Evans, Comensoli, Roberts and many others. It is a heavy weight carried by a place that provided a warm embrace for my youth and is now a good home for many, sandwiched between the blue-green escarpment and the expanse of the Tasman Sea. On my last trip to Wollongong, I visited my sister and her family and consulted the final records while finishing this book. Once again, I was able to enjoy this coastal vista up close, though it is nonetheless etched in memory from the seemingly endless summers of my childhood. During these times there were a few constants in life: the dominance of the steelworks and the coalmines, the casual, everyday insult of being called 'gay' or a 'homo' at an all-boys high school, long days at the beach and, of course, Frank Arkell's ascendancy on Wollongong Council.

On my most recent visit to Wollongong, the swell moved smoothly along the breakwaters at Wollongong harbour, the air was alive with seaspray and salt and the continental baths where my late mother swam for many years were a reassuring presence clinging to the rocky coast between the harbour and North Beach. The city has grown and changed much since I left. Time seems not so much at a standstill but racing forward. So much of what was once seen as normal has been swept away. The old weatherboard and solid brick homes along Cliff Road have been replaced with high-rise modernity wrapped in coloured glass. The iconic Art Deco 'South Beach' Surf Club (as we knew it) was demolished in 2003 and replaced with a 'viewing platform', subsequently renamed the Ted Tobin Observation Deck.[9] Wollongong now resembles the kind of city that Arkell imagined somewhat prophetically back in the early 1980s. While it was not necessarily his vision, he made it his own with his lively and ceaseless engagement. The steelworks and the coalmines employ a fraction of the workforce compared with the 1980s. The University of Wollongong and the area health service are now the two biggest employers. Wollongong is cosmopolitan and appealing, its public image polished and slick like the new Sea Cliff Bridge that traverses the steep coastline from Clifton to Coalcliff and Stanwell Park in the north of the region. The bridge brings the tourists south from Sydney to wonderful, wonderful Wollongong.

Frank Arkell would have been proud, but the grimy underside of his secret life, his sordid dealings and networks has not been fully exorcised. The city still lives with its share of corruption and poverty. The council is still a magnet for controversy and salacious behaviour. Cringila, the location of the old Arkell family home, where Frank's father killed himself more than 80 years ago, is one of the most disadvantaged suburbs in New South Wales. If Arkell's ghost, heavy with unredeemed sin, walks the streets near Wollongong's new office blocks and beachside cafes and nods with approval at the tourism campaigns, then he also turns up in its mean streets and alleyways, at its illicit liaisons and private parties and is occasionally there to witness its desperate times and desperate people. For in Frank Arkell's life we see the modern city revealed in all its contradictions. We see Wollongong's prosperity and splendour, its success and progress, but we also see its private grief and greed, its illicit desire and human fallibility—all shadowed by the inevitability of decline and death. So much energy, so much optimism, so much civic service—all tainted by a warped and illicit desire and ended by a shocking act of violence. Even the biggest swell on the stormiest day cannot wash away wonderful Wollongong's past or sweep clean its sordid history. It is time to embrace this modern city and see all the dysfunction and darkness that underpinned its making.

One opens a door to many things in life—a chance encounter, a quirk of fate bringing a new person into our lives or a fleeting exchange with a new neighbour. Frank Arkell opened his door to his murderer. The energy,

---

9 The official name of the club was the Wollongong City Surf Lifesaving Club, but locals knew the beach and the club as 'South Beach'. Regular maintenance had not been kept up on the building and it was demolished apparently because it had structural defects. See John Madry, *The Blue Mile: Wollongong Foreshore Master Plan*, 2010, www.coastalconference.com/2010/papers2010/John%20Madry%20full%20paper.pdf.

the meetings, the plans, the hopes and dreams—suddenly gone. In a life unresolved, Arkell had been down but not entirely out, charged but not convicted, the denouement to his secret life of illicit dealings and pornographic liaisons not yet fully delivered. A rich but tragically flawed life ended.

Who knows what Mr Wollongong would have done on receipt of a conviction? But no chance for a fair trial now, nor redemption much less salvation. No opportunity to make amends or apologise. Many Arkell supporters still earnestly believe that the trial would have delivered a verdict of not guilty. We will never know. Regardless, there was no chance for last rites as Frank Arkell lay dying on the floor of his apartment in West Wollongong.

Our brother Frank has been suddenly and violently taken from us. His fate, dear Lord, is in your hands. Had he attended confession and gained religious absolution before that fateful day? Was he able to pray directly to Jesus asking for forgiveness? The speed and brutality of Valera's attack may have taken even that chance from him. We have no way of knowing. But if not, in Arkell's own religious worldview and Catholic practice, he passes into purgatory as a soul with unforgiven sins, while his band of survivors—where they have survived—find the strength to carry on in this world. The city that was Arkell's first love is now transformed into a modern, twenty-first-century place—all light and dark, industry and nature, good and evil, mountains and sea, public and private—shadowed by a secret that overwhelmed us all.

Afterword

In July 2023, when I was in the middle of editing and finalising the chapters for this book, an email arrived from NSW Police. It was an email I had been eagerly awaiting. I had applied to the NSW Police to access any material on Frank Arkell held by the Dapto or Wollongong police commands and the former NSW Child Protection Enforcement Unit. Furthermore, since the recording and the transcript of Frank Arkell's committal hearing in February 1998 had been either destroyed or never made, I also applied to secure a copy of the original 29 charges of child sexual abuse that were the basis of Arkell's arrest and pending court case. In short, I wanted to know whether Frank Arkell had a police file and whether it dated from as early as 1956 or whether it was essentially based on the material provided by the Wood Royal Commission and those who offered testimony to it. Was it the case that, as with Bevan, the police knew of Arkell's activities and had not acted? Was it the high-profile publicity surrounding the royal commission that finally forced NSW Police to take Arkell's case seriously?

In April 2023 I had applied for access to this material under the *Government Information (Public Access) Act 2009* (NSW). Over the next two months, there would be multiple requests from NSW Police for a deadline extension, with correspondence confirming that 'searches are currently being undertaken to obtain the information you seek. There has, however, been a delay in the return of the information from the Command that holds the documents.'[1]

In mid-July 2023 the NSW Police extended the deadline further. This time they did not require my agreement. 'In order to decide whether or not access should be granted to information held,' the email explained, 'it is necessary for the NSW Police Force to consult with a third party.'[2]

---

1   Email from NSW Police Information Review Officer to Erik Eklund, 5 June 2023.
2   Email from NSW Police Information Review Officer to Erik Eklund, 13 July 2023.

It was a Tuesday when the final extension of time was due to expire. Nothing arrived in the morning. But then, at 3.11 pm, the email on which I was so desperately waiting arrived. I was to be profoundly disappointed. My request to gain access to Frank Arkell's police files was rejected, thus providing a further barrier to uncovering the nature and true extent of his offending.

Despite the rejection, the correspondence confirmed that two main file groups had been located. The first file was titled 'Police Intelligence Reports Referring to Frank Arkell' (no date range provided), which came from the NSW Police COPS database. The second file was the 'Brief of Evidence' against Arkell that came from the Sex Crimes Squad.

The final determination by the NSW Police stated that 'there is an overriding public interest against disclosure of the information'. The Act attempts to protect individual privacy and does not authorise the release of an individual's personal information until 30 years after their death. Furthermore, as NSW Police told me, 'no conviction was recorded against this individual and these matters were not proven in court'. And it is here we can see how much it matters that Frank Arkell was never convicted. Arkell's murder was not simply a heinous crime, it was also the means by which justice was denied. Now legally, despite the weight of evidence against Arkell, 'these matters were not proven in court'.[3]

Since the brief of evidence had been passed on to the Director of Public Prosecutions (DPP), that agency was consulted. The Act defines any inquiry, investigation or complaint as 'excluded information'. The DPP did not consent to the release of documents relating to the investigation of Arkell or his pending court case.

The rejection of my request does confirm several things. It confirms there was a file or files on Frank Arkell's past engagement with NSW Police. It had been searched for, found and then a 'third party' had been consulted about its contents. Two further grounds for rejecting my request were that the 'disclosure could reasonably be expected to prejudice the effective exercise by the agency of the agency's functions' and that 'disclosure could reasonably be expected to prejudice the prevention, detection or investigation of a contravention or possible contravention of the law or prejudice the enforcement of the law'. These two grounds for rejection hint

---

3   Email from NSW Police Information Review Officer to Erik Eklund, 25 July 2023.

AFTERWORD

at another story, hidden deeper still, that relates to the role of the police in the Wollongong area, but at this point I can only speculate what that might be.

Even 25 years after the death of the former lord mayor, Frank is too controversial for the official record. We are left with fragments of evidence reflected in the mirror of a royal commission, in newspaper and court reports of the committal hearing and in the memories of those who experienced this tumultuous time. Even after all these years, there are still secrets to be kept in the Arkell case.

One cannot shake the feeling that there is more to be told. But while documents remain outside the public domain, while royal commission evidence lies frozen in storage for 100 years, while NSW Police remain concerned that their actions with regard to a man who was murdered more than 25 years ago can still 'prejudice the effective exercise of an agency', and while local actors like Edmund Rice College still refuse access for legitimate research in the public interest, we are left piecing together the truth, reflecting on its meaning and our place in it. Some secrets have been brought into the light, some truths made manifest, but others await their day. Torn in two by its public swagger and its depravity, Frank Arkell's life is over, but his story is not.

Arkell family tree

Michael O'Donnell Sr   &   Sarah Meade   (m. 1840)
(1815?–1861)   (1820–1887)

Michael O'Donnell Jr   &   Ada Isobel Smith   (m. 10 April 1894)
(17 June 1854 –   (1868–1937)
18 March 1945)

                          &   Alma Annabella?   (m. 1939)
                                (1939–1945)

Sidney Arkell   &   Marcella Veronica   (m. 10 June 1921)
(21 October 1881 –   O'Donnell
23 March 1941)   (1898 – 3 April 1979)

Richard Sidney Bruce Arkell
(8 August 1921 – 6 March 1963)

James Edward (Bill)
(1923–2009)

Harold Francis Norman (Harry)
(1924–2013)

Francis Neville Arkell (Frank)
(13 September 1929 – 26 June 1998)

Frank Arkell: Timeline

21 October 1881: Frank's father, Sidney Arkell, is born in Bibury in the United Kingdom. Sidney migrates to Australia in 1911.

1898: Frank's mother, Marcella Veronica O'Donnell, is born on the Five Islands Estate at Port Kembla, NSW, the third child of Michael O'Donnell and Ada Isobel O'Donnell (nee Smith).

10 June 1921: Sidney and Marcella marry at St Paul's Catholic Church in Albion Park.

13 September 1929: Francis Neville (Frank) Arkell is born, the fourth son of Marcella and Sidney Arkell.

23 March 1941: Frank's father, Sidney Arkell, commits suicide using his eldest son's rifle.

May 1941: Marcella purchases land and at least two properties in Reserve Street, West Wollongong. The entire family moves to 11 Reserve Street in 1945, while Marcella and Frank would live at 1 Reserve Street from about 1960.

18 March 1945: Michael O'Donnell Jr, Marcella's father, dies in a private hospital in Sydney.

December 1946: Frank secures his Leaving certificate from Christian Brothers College in Wollongong.

December 1965: After several years working in Sydney, Frank returns to Wollongong and is elected as an alderman on Wollongong City Council representing Ward 5.

1969: Frank serves a one-year term as deputy mayor on Wollongong Council.

13 February 1971: Frank stands as an independent candidate for the state seat of Illawarra, losing to Labor's George Petersen.

27 September 1974: A narrow majority of Wollongong City aldermen vote for Arkell to become Lord Mayor of Wollongong—a position he will hold for the next 17 years.

3 April 1979: Marcella Arkell, who shared the West Wollongong home with Frank, dies after several years of failing health and possible dementia.

19 September 1981: Frank Arkell stands for the state seat of Wollongong, losing by only 51 votes to Labor's Eric Ramsay.

24 March 1984: Arkell wins the seat of Wollongong, defeating the Labor candidate, Rex Connor Jr.

19 March 1988: Arkell wins a second term as the member for Wollongong, defeating Labor's Laurie Kelly.

3 May 1991: Labor candidate Gerry Sullivan defeats Frank in a convincing victory, with Arkell's two-party preferred vote declining to 45 per cent.

14 September 1991: After 17 years as the Lord Mayor of Wollongong, Frank narrowly loses the mayoral vote to Labor's David Campbell.

1 December 1994: Labor member Deirdre Grusovin reads a statutory declaration from Colin Fisk into Hansard in the NSW Upper House, which includes a claim that police failed to follow up on a number of high-profile paedophiles, including Frank Arkell.

9 March 1995: The *Illawarra Mercury* publishes a front-page story identifying former mayor Tony Bevan as a key organiser of a Wollongong-based paedophile network. The story includes an allegation that Arkell is involved in the network.

May 1996: The Wood Royal Commission hears detailed evidence on the operation of Tony Bevan's paedophile network, including evidence from four witnesses who identify 'W1' as a person of interest.

August 1996 – onward: Arkell withdraws from public life.

30 October 1996: NSW Labor parliamentarian Franca Arena identifies Frank Arkell as 'W1' in NSW Parliament.

5 November 1996: Both the *Illawarra Mercury* and the *Sydney Morning Herald* publish major stories airing evidence given under oath to the Wood Royal Commission identifying Arkell as a man involved in Tony Bevan's Wollongong paedophile network. Arkell issues a statement denying all these allegations.

1 March 1997: Frank Arkell is arrested and charged with 29 counts of child sexual abuse. He is detained at Wollongong Police Station and released that evening on bail.

February 1998: At Arkell's committal hearing in Wollongong, the 29 charges involving four 'victims' are reduced to five charges involving four victims. The trial is set to be heard in the Parramatta Local Court in September 1998.

12 June 1998: Mark Valera brutally murders Albion Park man David O'Hearn. O'Hearn had no prior association with Valera.

26 June 1998: Valera contacts Arkell and arranges to visit him at his West Wollongong home. Shortly after his arrival, Valera brutally murders Arkell and slips away early the next morning.

29 June 1998: The *Illawarra Mercury* publishes a special 'Arkell Murder Edition'. The eight-page spread includes several allegations from men claiming they were assaulted by Arkell when they were boys or young men.

3–4 July 1998: A small, private funeral is held for Arkell followed by a larger commemorative service the next day.

30 September 1998: Valera gives himself up at Wollongong Police Station, offering a full confession to the murders of David O'Hearn and Frank Arkell.

21 December 2000: Mark Valera is sentenced to life in prison for the murders of David O'Hearn and Frank Arkell (Valera's appeal in 2002 against the severity of the sentence is unsuccessful).

Bibliography

Primary sources

Australian Bureau of Statistics. 1966. 'Part 1: New South Wales.' In *2106.0 Census of Population and Housing, 1966. Volume 4: Population and Dwellings in Local Government Areas*. Canberra: Commonwealth of Australia. www.ausstats.abs.gov.au/ausstats/free.nsf/0/D311C20059D36DDFCA257880008306D7/$File/1966%20Census%20-%20Volume%204%20Population%20and%20Dwellings%20in%20LGA%20-%20Part%201%20NSW.pdf.

Birth Certificate for Richard Sidney Bruce Arkell, 38762/1921, State Records NSW, Sydney.

'City of Wollongong Council Elections, Independent How to Vote Leaflet, Ward 1.' 20 September 1980, C1/19/01, University of Wollongong Archives.

'City of Wollongong, How to Vote Independent for Ward 5, 23 September 1977.' Collection C1/10/16, University of Wollongong Archives.

Dames & Moore. 1983. *Maldon–Dombarton–Port Kembla Rail Line: Environmental Impact Statement. Volume 2*. Sydney: State Rail Authority.

Deed of Sale, No. 6, Book 549, 17 July 1894, Land Titles Office. State Records NSW, Sydney.

Deed of Transfer, No. 276, Book 2483, 29 April 1959, Land Titles Office. State Records NSW, Sydney.

Department of Main Roads. 1970–80. *Main Roads*. [NSW Department of Main Roads Journal]. Sydney: NSW Government.

Department of Main Roads. 1972. *Annual Report 1971–72*. Sydney: Roads and Traffic Authority of New South Wales. www.opengov.nsw.gov.au/publications/16108;jsessionid=D58927032234A24C62E82E8CEB1C8505.

Department of Main Roads. 1975. *Main Roads* [NSW Department of Main Roads Journal] 41, no. 1 (September). www.opengov.nsw.gov.au/publications/16335;jsessionid=B9372A9CEF496C4DF895DF386EE72371.

Department of Main Roads. 1978. *Annual Report 1977–78*. Sydney: Roads and Traffic Authority of New South Wales. www.opengov.nsw.gov.au/publications/16102;jsessionid=B8724FC7B4F5AFFD5BD34015FC17697D.

Electoral Roll for Wollongong, 1977. National Library of Australia, Canberra.

Harry Francis Norman Arkell, Service Number 73391, 1942–1948, A9301, 73391. National Archives of Australia, Canberra.

Illawarra Historical Society 1960–2010. *Bulletin*. Archives Online, University of Wollongong. archivesonline.uow.edu.au/nodes/view/13327/.

'Inquest Held at the Court House, Bulli on the 15 September 1960 on the Cause of Death of Arthur Frank Bevan.' AF00288285. State Records NSW, Sydney.

'Inquiry into a Plane Crash Near Wollongong', 12 April 1958. State Records NSW, Sydney.

James Edgar Osbourne Beale, Service Number NX125047. National Archives of Australia, Canberra.

John Sands. 1912. *Sands Sydney, Suburban and Country Commercial Directory*. Sydney: John Sands Limited. [City of Sydney Archives.]

John Sands. 1915. *Sands Sydney, Suburban and Country Commercial Directory*. Sydney: John Sands Limited. [City of Sydney Archives.]

John Sands. 1917. *Sands Sydney, Suburban and Country Commercial Directory*. Sydney: John Sands Limited. [City of Sydney Archives.]

John Sands. 1920. *Sands Sydney, Suburban and Country Commercial Directory*. Sydney: John Sands Limited. [City of Sydney Archives.]

NSW Marriage Certificate, Sydney [sic] Arkell & Marcella O'Donnell, 10 June 1921, St Paul's Catholic Church, Albion Park, 9041/1921. State Records NSW, Sydney.

NSW Police File on Edgar Beale, CNI Number 3013464.

Office of the Member for Wollongong, Research Centre, Progress Reports and Press Releases, 1984 to 1991. Wollongong City Library.

Probate of Michael O'Donnell, NRS-13660-26-6700-Series 4_304286. State Records NSW, Sydney.

Probate of the Late Richard Sydney Bruce Arkell, NSW Supreme Court, No. 642257, 11 December 1965. State Records NSW, Sydney.

R v Valera [2000] NSWSC 1220 [21 December 2000]. www8.austlii.edu.au/cgi-bin/viewdoc/au/cases/nsw/NSWSC/2000/1220.html.

R v Valera [2002] NSWCCA 50 [12 April 2002, revised 17 April]. www8.austlii.edu.au/cgi-bin/viewdoc/au/cases/nsw/NSWCCA/2002/50.html.

Smiles, Peter H. 1983. *Report of an Inspection of Wollongong City Council under Section 212 of the Local Government Act (1919)*. Sydney: NSW Government Printer.

Transcripts of Conversations between Tony Bevan and Various Business and Personal Associates, [Bevan Tapes], nos 1–49. Originally transcribed by the *Illawarra Mercury*. Personal collection of Brett Martin.

'The UK 1911 Census.' 2024. *UK Census Online*. Jersey: Genealogy Supplies Limited. ukcensusonline.com/census/1911/.

University of Wollongong Campus News. 1975–1998. Archives Online, University of Wollongong. archivesonline.uow.edu.au/nodes/view/9165?.

US National Archives and Records Administration. 1910. 'Household Returns for Carey, Idaho.' In *Thirteenth Census of the United States, 1910*. Microfilm Publication T624, Record Group 29. www.archives.gov/research/census/online-resources.

Wollongong Outlook: The University Alumni Magazine. Autumn–Winter 1995. Archives Online, University of Wollongong. archivesonline.uow.edu.au/nodes/view/18082.

Wood, J.R.T. 1997. *Royal Commission into the NSW Police Service. Final Report. Volume 1: Corruption*. Sydney: NSW Government. www.australianpolice.com.au/wp-content/uploads/2017/05/RCPS-Report-Volume-1.pdf.

Wood, J.R.T. 1997. *Royal Commission into the NSW Police Service. Final Report. Volume 4: The Paedophile Inquiry*. Sydney: NSW Government. www.opengov.nsw.gov.au/publications/17129;jsessionid=152611E7FD89AE98D77ADD531D7484DE.

Wood, J.R.T. 2011[?]. *Royal Commission into the New South Wales Police Service: Public Hearing Transcripts*. Sydney: Police Integrity Commission. [State Library of New South Wales.]

State Records NSW, Sydney

Royal Commission into the New South Wales Police Service
Evidence of Patrick Cassidy, PR238, PR240.
Evidence of J. Dooley, PR238.
Evidence of Bill King, PR248, PR257, PR307.
Evidence of Ken Watson, PR309.
Evidence of W13, PR248.
Evidence of W26, PR251, PR307, PR309.

Interviews by the author

Anthony, Andrew, 24 October 2022.
Bahlmann, Peter, 8 July 2023.
Baron, Anne, 24 October 2022.
Bradbery, Gordon, 29 April 2023.
Cullen, Janine, 20 October and 23 November 2022.
D'Souza, Michael, 21 November 2022.
Fermor, Bevan, 22 March 2023.
Hanson, Harold, 3 April 2023.
Hartgerink, Nick, 24 November 2022.
Leary, Ray, 19 October 2022.
Martin, Brett, 23 May 2022.
Martin, John, 23 April 2023.
McInerney, Paul, 21 November 2022.
Richmond, Mark, 13 October 2022.
Tziolas, Antonios, 13 November 2022.

Interviews by other researchers

Bongiorno, Paul. 1974. 'Interview with Lord Mayor Frank Arkell.' *WIN4 TV*, 29 September, WIN4 Collection, D75/srs/1974/09/29/pt3. Archives Online, University of Wollongong. archivesonline.uow.edu.au/nodes/view/4338.

Mitchell, Winifred, and Geoffrey Sherington. 1982. 'Interview with Frank Arkell as part of research for the book "Growing up in the Illawarra".' July, D153/1/1. Archives Online, University of Wollongong. archivesonline.uow.edu.au/nodes/view/8780.

O'Ferrell, Steve, and Terry Moore. 1973. 'Interview with Mayor John Parker—Mayor 1972 and 1973.' *WIN4 TV*, 5 August 1973. Archives Online, University of Wollongong. archivesonline.uow.edu.au/nodes/view/3736.

Slater, Robyn. 1982. 'Interview with Professor Ken McKinnon and Mr Frank Arkell.' Friends Session on the FM Test Broadcast, 24 March, U59/03/03a. Archives Online, University of Wollongong. archivesonline.uow.edu.au/nodes/view/3259.

Stewart, Peter. 2011. 'Interview with Giles Pickford—Academic Manager and Epicure.' July, The Australian National University, Canberra. openresearch-repository.anu.edu.au/bitstream/1885/12924/2/giles_pickford.html.

New South Wales election results

Parliament of New South Wales

State Election Results for the Seat of Bulli, 1965. www.parliament.nsw.gov.au/electionresults18562007/1965/Bulli.htm.

State Election Results for the Seat of Corrimal, 1968. www.parliament.nsw.gov.au/electionresults18562007/1968/Corrimal.htm.

State Election Results for the Seat of Illawarra, 1971. www.parliament.nsw.gov.au/electionresults18562007/1971/Illawarra.htm.

State Election Results for the Seat of Illawarra, 1981. www.parliament.nsw.gov.au/electionresults18562007/1981/Illawarra.htm.

State Election Results for the Seat of Wollongong, 1968. www.parliament.nsw.gov.au/electionresults18562007/1968/Wollongong.htm.

State Election Results for the Seat of Wollongong, 1976. www.parliament.nsw.gov.au/electionresults18562007/1976/Wollongong.htm.

State Election Results for the Seat of Wollongong, 1981. www.parliament.nsw.gov.au/electionresults18562007/1981/Wollongong.htm.

State Election Results for the Seat of Wollongong, 1984. www.parliament.nsw.gov.au/electionresults18562007/1984/Wollongong.htm.

State Election Results for the Seat of Wollongong, 1988. www.parliament.nsw.gov.au/electionresults18562007/1988/Wollongong.htm.

State Election Results for the Seat of Wollongong, 1991. www.parliament.nsw.gov.au/electionresults18562007/1991/Wollongong.htm.

Secondary sources

ABC News. 1998. 'Raw Footage from Wollongong Court House.' *ABC News*, 9 February. ID: T352758. ABC Archives, Sydney.

ABC Radio. 1998. 'Wonderful Wollongong.' *Background Briefing*, [*ABC Radio*], 1 October. C100, 1286175. National Archives of Australia, Canberra.

ABC TV. 1996. *ABC News*, [*ABC TV*], 4 November. T315653. ABC Archives, Sydney.

Anon. n.d. 'O'Donnell Family History.' [Online]. www.wagsoft.com/FamilyHistory/ODonnell.pdf.

Arena, Franca. 2012. 'We Must Deliver on Important Promises.' *Daily Telegraph*, [Sydney], 14 November. www.news.com.au/national/nsw-act/we-must-deliver-on-important-promises/news-story/baff1c87f18db93961804ead6885912e.

Arkell, Frank. 1986. 'Arkell Applauds Carr Initiatives.' Media release, 17 January, Office of the Member for Wollongong. Wollongong City Library.

Arkell, Frank. 1986. 'Arkell Claims Phone-In Success.' Media release, 8 June, Office of the Member for Wollongong. Wollongong City Library.

Arkell, Frank. 1989. 'Arkell Claims Northern Distributor Delays Unsatisfactory.' Media release, 14 March, Office of the Member for Wollongong, 1988–1989. Wollongong City Library.

Arkell, Frank. 1989. 'Inbound Tourism Increase.' Media release, 29 May, Office of the Member for Wollongong. Wollongong City Library.

Arkell, Frank. 1989. 'Arkell Demands New Realistic Train Timetables.' Media release, 20 June, Office of the Member for Wollongong. Wollongong City Library.

Arklay, Tracey, John Nethercote, and John Wanna, (Eds). 2006. *Australian Political Lives: Chronicling Political Careers and Administrative Histories*. Canberra: ANU E Press. doi.org/10.22459/APL.10.2006.

Armstrong, David. 1983. 'A Steel City Sings the Blues.' *Bulletin*, [Sydney], 19 April: 27–29.

Aubin, Tracey. 1988. 'Mr Speaker Is Called Out of Order.' *Sydney Morning Herald*, 14 January: 3.

Australian Associated Press (AAP). 1996. 'NSW: Arkell Denies in Commission He Is a Paedophile.' *AAP*, 7 November. [Access global NewsBank, National Library of Australia, Canberra.]

Australian Associated Press (AAP). 1998. 'NSW: Arkell Fronts Committal Hearing into 29 Sex Charges.' *AAP*, 8 February.

Australian Associated Press (AAP). 1998. 'NSW: Quiet Funeral for Frank Arkell.' *AAP*, 2 July.

Australian Press Council. 1997. 'Adjudication No. 901.' *Australian Press Council News*, February. www5.austlii.edu.au/au/journals/AUPressClNews/1997/8.pdf.

Bailey, Paul, and Danielle Cook. 1991. 'Candidates Agree on the Monorail: It Has to Go—Local Government Elections.' *Sydney Morning Herald*, 14 September: 6.

Baker, Jacquelyn. 2021. 'Q&A with Jenny Hocking, Author of "The Palace Letters".' *Australian Policy and History*, 11 February. aph.org.au/2021/02/qa-with-jenny-hocking-author-of-the-palace-letters/.

Barwick, Kathleen H. 1978. *History of Berkeley, New South Wales*. Wollongong: Illawarra Historical Society. ro.uow.edu.au/ihspubs/21.

Basham, Richard. 1998. 'Crimes Bear Hallmark of Vengeance.' [*Sunday Style Magazine*], *Sunday Telegraph*, [Sydney], 30 June: 2.

Beale, Edgar. 1977. *Illawarra Sketchbook*. Illustrations by Gillian Trigg. Adelaide: Rigby.

Beale, Edgar. 1979. *Sturt, the Chipped Idol: A Study of Charles Sturt, Explorer*. Sydney: Sydney University Press.

Bearup, Greg. 1996. 'I'm No Pederast, Says Former Mayor.' *Sydney Morning Herald*, 5 November: 2.

Bearup, Greg. 2001. 'Death Surrounds Her.' *Sydney Morning Herald*, 19 May. www.smh.com.au/national/death-surrounds-her-20130524-2k6km.html.

Bindel, Julie. 2001. 'Gay Men Need to Talk Straight about Paedophilia.' *Guardian*, 4 March.

Birkin, Andrew. 2003. *J.M. Barrie and the Lost Boys: The Real Story behind Peter Pan*. New Haven: Yale University Press.

Bita, Natasha. 1990. 'Club Gong?—Forget It, Unions Tell Japanese.' *Sydney Morning Herald*, 2 August: 1.

Bond, Grahame. 2009. 'Interview Transcript from Illawarra Stories Wollongong City Libraries Oral History Project.' Interviewer: Kirsten Bokor, 8 February. Wollongong: Wollongong City Library. illawarrastories.com.au/grahame-bond-interview-transcript/.

Brickell, Chris. 2009. 'Sexuality and the Dimensions of Power.' *Sexuality & Culture* 13: 57–74. doi.org/10.1007/s12119-008-9042-x.

Brown, Malcolm. n.d. 'James Seymour (Jim) Hagan (1929–2009).' *Obituaries Australia*. Canberra: National Centre of Biography, The Australian National University. labouraustralia.anu.edu.au/biography/hagan-james-seymour-jim-16951.

Brown, Malcolm. 1996. 'Pedophile Claims "Confused": Arkell.' *Sydney Morning Herald*, 9 November: 11.

Brown, Nicholas. 2006. 'Public Lives, Private Lives: The Fundamental Dilemma in Political Biography.' In *Australian Political Lives: Chronicling Political Careers and Administrative Histories*, edited by Tracey Arklay, John Nethercote, and John Wanna, 35–42. Canberra: ANU E Press. doi.org/10.22459/APL.10.2006.05.

Cahill, Desmond, and Peter Wilkinson. 2017. *Child Sexual Abuse in the Catholic Church: An Interpretive Review of the Literature and Public Inquiry Reports*. Melbourne: Centre for Global Research, School of Global, Urban and Social Studies, RMIT University. religionsforpeaceaustralia.org.au/download/child-sex-abuse-and-the-catholic-church.pdf.

Carty, Lisa. 1997. 'Victims Wanted Their Day in Court.' *Illawarra Mercury*, 29 June: 2.

Carty, Lisa. 1997. 'Arkell Sex Case Held Next Year—Preliminary Hearing.' *Illawarra Mercury*, 10 September.

Carty, Lisa. 1997. 'Malicious Attacks on Arkell's House—Ex-Mayor Complains of Harassment.' *Illawarra Mercury*, 25 November: 5.

Carty, Lisa. 1998. 'Arkell Goes to Trial—Wollongong Magistrate Decides: Former MP Faces 11 Sex Charges.' *Illawarra Mercury*, 13 February: 1.

Carty, Lisa. 1998. 'Old Wounds Still Raw.' *Illawarra Mercury*, 28 June: 2.

Carty, Lisa. 1998. 'The Day Frank's World Came Crashing down—The Arkell Murder.' *Illawarra Mercury*, 29 June: 2.

Carty, Lisa. 1998. 'New Arkell Victim Speaks Out.' *Illawarra Mercury*, 30 June: 1.

Carty, Lisa. 1998. 'The Day Frank Turned from Kiss to Hiss—'96 Cup One to Remember: My View.' *Illawarra Mercury*, 1 July: 8.

Carty, Lisa. 2002. 'He's Gone: Harrison Quits as Mayor.' *Illawarra Mercury*, 26 July: 1, 4.

Castle, Josie. 1991. *University of Wollongong: An Illustrated History.* Wollongong: University of Wollongong.

Catholic Diocese of Wollongong. 2019. 'Statement by Bishop Brian Mascord on the Death of Mr Peter Lewis Comensoli.' Press release, 20 March, Catholic Diocese of Wollongong. www.dow.org.au/resource/statement-from-bishop-brian-mascord-on-the-death-of-mr-peter-lewis-comensoli/.

Christian, Kerrie Anne. 2009. 'Alderman Rube Hargrave—Ward 1, Wollongong City Council.' *Linga Longa: Stories of Women and Thirroul,* 27 March. lingalongathirroul.wordpress.com/2009/03/27/alderman-rube-hargrave-ward-1-wollongong-city-council/.

Clark, Pilita. 1998. 'The Media and the Murder.' *Sydney Morning Herald,* 4 July: 33–34.

Clarke, Peter. 1985. 'SPCC Forced to Back Down.' *Illawarra Mercury,* 31 December.

Clarke, Peter. 1986. 'Child Protection Crisis Goes to Court.' *Illawarra Mercury,* 10 January.

Clarke, Peter. 1986. 'Police Station Planning Begins.' *Illawarra Mercury,* 1 March: 7.

Clifford, Jessica. 2018. 'Known Paedophile Pleads Guilty to Fresh Charges.' *ABC Illawarra,* 7 August. www.abc.net.au/news/2018-08-07/known-nsw-paedophile-pleads-guilty-to-fresh-charges/10083596.

Colvin, Mark. 'Independents' Day.' *Four Corners,* [*ABC TV*], 7 March. T87476. ABC Archives, Sydney.

Cook, Danielle. 1991. 'Gong Upset Stunned the Winner—The Cliffhanger.' [*Spectrum*], *Sydney Morning Herald,* 27 May: 7.

Cook, Danielle. 1991. 'Labor Ends Arkell's Reign—Local Council Election.' *Sydney Morning Herald,* 16 September: 6.

Cordell, Michael, Geraldine O'Brien, and John O'Neil. 1988. 'Labor's Lost Heartland.' [*Spectrum*], *Sydney Morning Herald,* 29 March: 61.

Coultan, Mark. 1988. 'Pecuniary Disclosures of MP Queried.' *Sydney Morning Herald,* 4 February: 5.

Coultan, Mark. 1994. 'Outrage over Paedophile Accusation.' *Sydney Morning Herald,* 2 December: 3.

Cousins, Arthur. 1994 [1948]. *The Garden of New South Wales: A History of the Illawarra and Shoalhaven.* [First published NSW: Producers' Co-operative Distributing Society Limited]. Wollongong: Illawarra Historical Society.

Cox, Brett. 2009. 'The Hawks Fan Who Lived to Help Others.' *Illawarra Mercury*, 26 October, [Updated 5 November 2012]. www.illawarramercury.com.au/story/623533/the-hawks-fan-who-lived-to-help-others/.

Crime and Corruption Commission. 2019. 'The Fitzgerald Inquiry.' *Our History*. [Online]. Brisbane: Crime and Corruption Commission Queensland. www.ccc.qld.gov.au/about-us/our-history/fitzgerald-inquiry.

Cushing, Nancy, Katrina Quinn, and Caroline McMillen. 2015. 'University of Newcastle: Recasting the City of Newcastle as a "Univer-City"—The Journey from "Olde" Newcastle-Upon-Tyne to the New Silk Road.' In *Univer-Cities: Strategic View of the Future. From Berkeley and Cambridge to Singapore and Rising Asia. Volume II*, edited by Anthony S.C. Teo, 93–118. Singapore: World Scientific Publishing. doi.org/10.1142/9789814644457_0006.

Daly, Peter Francis. 2011. 'The Law During the Last 50 Years: An Address Given to the Illawarra Historical Society.' *Bulletin*, [Illawarra Historical Society], April–May 2011: 19–20; May–June 2011: 29–37; July–August 2011: 47–50; September–October 2011: 60–63.

Davies, Dan. 2015. *In Plain Sight: The Life and Times of Jimmy Savile*. London: Quercus.

Davis, Joseph. 1998. 'Obituary: Frank Arkell, the Public Face.' *Bulletin*, [Illawarra Historical Society], September: 72.

Dawson Nikolas, Molitorisz Sacha, Rizoiu Marian-Andrei, Fray Peter. 2023. 'Layoffs, Inequity and COVID-19: A Longitudinal Study of the Journalism Jobs Crisis in Australia from 2012 to 2020', *Journalism* 24 no. 3: 531–559. doi.org/10.1177/1464884921996286.

Dempster, Quentin. 1997. *Stateline*, [*ABC TV*], 18 April. ID: T336611. ABC Archives, Sydney.

Dinneen, Martin. 2008. 'Tributes Paid to George Keegan.' *Newcastle Herald*, 26 November, [Updated 1 November 2012]. www.newcastleherald.com.au/story/490466/tributes-paid-to-george-keegan/.

Dwyer, Neil. 2022. 'Diocese Celebrates 70th Anniversary of its Foundation Decree! (Pt 2).' [Online]. 24 February. Catholic Diocese of Wollongong. www.dow.org.au/diocese-celebrates-70th-anniversary-of-its-foundation-2/.

Edmund Rice College. n.d. 'Our History.' [Online]. Wollongong: Edmund Rice College. www.edmundricecollege.nsw.edu.au/our-college/our-history/.

Eklund, Erik. 1995. '"Putting into Port": Society, Identity and Politics at Port Kembla, 1900 to 1940.' PhD diss., University of Sydney.

Eklund, Erik. 2002. *Steel Town: The Making and Breaking of Port Kembla*. Melbourne: Melbourne University Press.

Evans, Rachel. 2010. 'David Campbell "Scandal" Reveals Gay Bigotry.' *Green Left Weekly*, [Sydney], 29 May, no. 839. www.greenleft.org.au/content/david-campbell-scandal-reveals-gay-bigotry.

Everett, Sophia Apolonia. 1984. 'Port-Orientated Coal Transport Infrastructure: An Analysis of Locational Decision Making.' MA (Hons) thesis, University of Wollongong, NSW.

Failes, Geoff. 1988. 'Ex-Diggers Object to Japanese Resort Plan.' *Sun-Herald*, [Sydney], 18 September: 41.

Failes, Geoff. 1998. 'Married to Wollongong.' *Illawarra Mercury*, 29 June: 7.

Failes, Geoff. 1998. 'The Arkell Murder: Death Shocks and Saddens Colleagues.' *Illawarra Mercury*, 29 June: 7.

Failes, Geoff. 1998. 'No Respect for Arkell—Councillor Refuses One-Minute Silence.' *Illawarra Mercury*, 2 July: 2.

Failes, Geoff. 1998. 'Friends Praise Arkell: "We Hope the Good … Will Be Remembered".' *Illawarra Mercury*, 7 July: 5.

Fanning, Ellen. 1996. 'Interview with Julie Posetti.' *AM*, [*ABC Radio*], 6 November. R67432. ABC Archives, Sydney.

Fernandez, Tim. 2023. 'Police Criticised for Bungled Investigation into Possible Gay Hate Death in Wollongong.' *ABC Illawarra*, 18 May. www.abc.net.au/news/2023-05-18/lgbtiq-inuiry-hears-evidence-of-bill-rooney-death/102361452.

Ferraz, Nalita. 1998. 'Former Leader Given Secret Burial—The Arkell Murder.' *Illawarra Mercury*, 3 July: 2.

Frame, Tom. 2005. *The Life and Death of Harold Holt*. Sydney: Allen & Unwin.

Fynes-Clinton, Matthew, and Michael Ware. 1998. 'Shadowland: A Special Courier-Mail Investigation.' *Courier-Mail*, [Brisbane], 16 May.

Ginnane, Paddy. 1985. 'Frank Arkell.' [*Weekend Magazine*], *Illawarra Mercury*, 17 August.

Glassock, Andrew. 2018. *70 Years of Inflation in Australia*. [Online.] Canberra: Australian Bureau of Statistics. www.abs.gov.au/statistics/research/70-years-inflation-australia.

Green, Antony. 1996. *NSW Legislative Council Elections, 1995*. Background Paper, 1996/2. Sydney: NSW Parliamentary Library Research Service.

Green, Antony. 1998. *Changing Boundaries, Changing Fortunes: An Analysis of the NSW Elections of 1988 and 1991*. Occasional Paper No. 7, October. Sydney: NSW Parliamentary Library Research Service. www.parliament.nsw.gov.au/researchpapers/Documents/changing-boundaries-changing-fortunes-an-analysi/op07-98.pdf.

Guilliat, Richard. 1995. 'Brotherly Love.' [*Spectrum*], *Sydney Morning Herald*, 22 July: 1A–4A.

Guilliat, Richard. 1998. 'City of Secrets.' [*Good Weekend*], *Sydney Morning Herald*, 22 August: 22–27.

Hagan, Jim, and Andrew Wells, (Eds). 1997. *A History of Wollongong*. Wollongong: University of Wollongong Press.

Hannan, Liz, and Anna Patty. 1998. 'Child Sex MP Slain.' *Sun-Herald*, [Sydney], 28 June: 7.

Harris, Lachlan. 1986. 'Mr Wollongong Plans a Long Run as Mayor.' *Wollongong Advertiser*, 29 January.

Harris, Lachlan. 1986. 'The Great Jobs Boom.' *Illawarra Mercury*, 29 January: 1.

Haupt, Robert. 1988. 'With Rex, There's a Fight in the Heir.' *Sydney Morning Herald*, 2 March: 1.

Hayton, Ethel. 1984. *Wollongong 150 Years: The City of Greater Wollongong, 1834–1984*. Port Kembla: South Coast Printers.

Hemsley, Paul. 2012. 'No More Government Dual Roles.' *Government News*, [Sydney], 5 April. www.governmentnews.com.au/no-more-government-dual-roles/.

Herben, Carol. 2012. 'Timeless Wollongong: Little Shopping Lane Once an Attractive Park.' *Illawarra Museum*, [Online], 20 August. illawarramuseum.wordpress.com/category/wollongong-rest-park/.

Hocking, Jenny. 2009. *Gough Whitlam: A Moment in History. Volume 1*. Melbourne: Melbourne University Press.

Hocking, Jenny. 2011. 'It's a Ripping Good Yarn: Political Biography and the Creative Imagination.' *Adelaide Law Review* 32, no. 1: 69–82.

Hoctor, Michelle. 2007. 'Arkell Turned City's Blues to Green, Says Historian.' *Illawarra Mercury*, 22 June.

Hoctor, Michelle. 2010. 'Ted Tobin: A True Gentleman of the Illawarra.' *Illawarra Mercury*, 9 February, [Updated 5 November 2012]. www.illawarramercury.com.au/story/626361/ted-tobin-a-true-gentleman-of-the-illawarra/.

Illawarra Historical Society. 1979. 'BEALE, Edgar (1916–1989).' *Bulletin*, [Illawarra Historical Society], June. www.illawarramuseum.com/page/beale-edgar-1916-1989.

Illawarra Museum. 2012. 'Timeless Wollongong: Kembla Grange Marks 100 Years of Racing.' *Illawarra Museum*, 8 September. illawarramuseum.wordpress.com/category/kembla-grange-racecourse/.

Independent Commission Against Corruption. 2008. *Report on An Investigation into Corruption Allegations Affecting Wollongong City Council. Part Three*. October. Sydney: ICAC. www.parliament.nsw.gov.au/tp/files/7660/Investigation%20into%20corruption%20allegations%20affecting%20Wollongong%20City%20Council%20-%20Operation%20Atlas%20-%20Part%203.pdf.

Independent Inquiry into Child Sexual Abuse. 2022. *The Report of the Independent Inquiry into Child Sexual Abuse*. October. London: UK Government. www.iicsa.org.uk/reports-recommendations/publications/inquiry/final-report.html.

Jain, Purnendra. 1991. 'Japan's Urban Governments, Their International Activities and Australia–Japan Relations: An Exploratory Essay.' *Policy, Organisation and Society* (Summer), [Special Japan Issue]: 33–44. doi.org/10.1080/10349952.1991.11876767.

Jespersen AF, Lalumière ML, Seto MC. 2009. 'Sexual Abuse History among Adult Sex Offenders and Non–Sex Offenders: A Meta-Analysis'. *Child Abuse & Neglect* 33, no.3: 179–92. doi.org/10.1016/j.chiabu.2008.07.004.

Jordan, Matthew. 2004. *A Spirit of True Learning: A Jubilee History of the University of New England*. Sydney: UNSW Press.

Laird, Phillip. 2009. 'The Maldon Port Kembla Railway and the Wentworth Deviation.' Paper presented to the AusRAIL PLUS Conference, Adelaide, 17–19 November.

Laneyrie, Frances. 2010. 'Between Class and Gender: Female Activists in the Illawarra 1975–1980.' PhD diss., Auckland Institute of Technology. openrepository.aut.ac.nz/items/da3c59fa-da19-4c82-b8e1-0371d7bc550c.

Lawson, Michael. 1997. 'Former Mayor Faces Sex Charges.' *Sydney Morning Herald*, 28 May: 6.

Lawson, Michael. 1997. 'Doctors Treat Sick Arkell—Bail Too Tough on Frank, Claims Lawyer … but Magistrate Stands Firm.' *Sydney Morning Herald*, 9 July: 1.

Leary, Ray, with Kate Shayler. 2016. *A Beautiful Boy: Ray's Story*. Hazelbrook: Moshpit Publishing. www.scribd.com/read/307228103/A-Beautiful-Boy-Rays-Story.

Linton, John Suter. 2004. *Bound by Blood: The True Story behind the Wollongong Murders*. Sydney: Allen & Unwin.

Madry, John. 2010. *The Blue Mile—Wollongong Foreshore Master Plan*. www.coastalconference.com/2010/papers2010/John%20Madry%20full%20paper.pdf.

Martin, Brett. 1995. 'Bevan's Double Life Shocks Former Lover.' *Illawarra Mercury*, 9 March: 7.

Martin, Brett. 1995. 'Former Mayor Ran Child Sex Ring.' *Illawarra Mercury*, 9 March.

Martin, Brett. 1995. 'Tapes Shame Former Mayor.' *Illawarra Mercury*, 9 March: 1–9.

Mathews Ben, Bromfield Leah, Walsh Kerryann, Cheng Qinglu, Norman Rossana E. 2017. 'Reports of Child Sexual Abuse of Boys and Girls: Longitudinal Trends over a 20-Year Period in Victoria, Australia', *Child Abuse & Neglect* 66: 9–22, doi.org/10.1016/j.chiabu.2017.01.025.

Mathews Ben, Lee Xing Ju, Norman Rosanna E. 2022. 'Impact of a New Mandatory Reporting Law on Reporting and Identification of Child Sexual Abuse: A Seven Year Time Trend Analysis', *Child Abuse & Neglect* 56: 62–79, doi.org/10.1016/j.chiabu.2016.04.009.

McClymont, Kate. 1997. 'Former MP Frank Arkell Faces 29 Child Sex Charges.' *Sydney Morning Herald*, 2 May: 1.

McClymont, Kate. 1998. 'The Demise of the Double Life.' *Sydney Morning Herald*, 29 June: 15–16.

McLaren, Nick. 2009. 'Fallen Wollongong Leader Fights Back.' *ABC News*, 4 December. www.abc.net.au/news/2009-12-04/fallen-wollongong-leader-fights-back/1169476.

McLaren, Nick. 2016. 'Wollongong MP Speaks of Sadness as Edmund Rice College Apologises over Historical Abuse of Student.' *ABC Illawarra*, 16 June. www.abc.net.au/news/2016-06-16/mp-opens-up-on-child-sex-abuse/7515624.

McLaren, Nick. 2018. 'Frank Arkell: How a Vicious Murder Unmasked a City's Darkest Secrets.' *ABC Illawarra*, 26 June, [Updated 27 June]. www.abc.net.au/news/2018-06-26/how-vicious-murder-unmasked-wollongong-paedophiles/9904280.

Meek, Vincent Lyn. 1984. *Brown Coal or Plato? A Study of the Gippsland Institute of Advanced Education.* ACER Research Series No. 105. Melbourne: Australian Council for Educational Research.

Milligan, Louise. 2019. *Cardinal: The Rise and Fall of George Pell.* Melbourne: Melbourne University Press. doi.org/10.2307/jj.1744966.

Milligan, Louise. 2020. *Witness: An Investigation into the Brutal Cost of Seeking Justice.* Sydney: Hachette.

Moore, Daniel. 1987. 'Jackson Guilty of Bribes Plot.' *Sydney Morning Herald*, 29 August: 1.

Moore, Matthew. 1988. 'Wollongong Waves Rock Greiner's Loveboat.' *Sydney Morning Herald*, 18 June: 32.

Moore, Terry. 1968. 'Tony Bevan to Run for Parliament.' *WIN4 News*, 31 January. Archives Online, University of Wollongong. archivesonline.uow.edu.au/nodes/view/14768.

Moore, Terry. 1973. 'Interview with Alderman Harold Hanson.' *WIN4 News*, 5 August. Archives Online, University of Wollongong. archivesonline.uow.edu.au/nodes/view/3558.

Mullins, Patrick. 1992. 'Cities for Pleasure: The Emergence of Tourism Urbanization in Australia.' *Built Environment* 18, no. 3 (1992): 187–98.

Muurlink Olav, Voneiff Elizabeth. 2023. 'Out of Print: What the Pandemic-Era Newspaper Crisis in Australia Teaches Us about the Role of Rural and Regional Newspapers in Creating Sustainable Communities', *Sustainability* 15 no. 6: 5439. doi.org/10.3390/su15065439.

Neales, Sue, and Sheryle Bagwell. 1989. 'The Nine Lives of Alan Bond.' *Australian Financial Review*, 15 September: 12.

New Zealand Herald. 1998. 'Fighting Priest Loses Last Round: Fr. Morrie Crocker, Australian Whistle-Blower, Apparently Commits Suicide.' *New Zealand Herald*, 7 June. www.bishop-accountability.org/news/1998_06_07_NewZealandHerald_FightingPriest.htm.

Newell, Peter. 2012. 'Long Struggle to Expose Evil Abuse of Children in the Illawarra.' *Illawarra Mercury*, 17 November, [Updated 20 February 2017]. www.illawarramercury.com.au/story/1126599/long-struggle-to-expose-evil-abuse-of-children-in-the-illawarra/.

Norton, Andrew. 2010. 'The Minister, the Gay Sauna and the Seven Reporter.' *Crikey*, 21 May. www.crikey.com.au/2010/05/21/the-minister-the-gay-sauna-and-the-seven-reporter/.

NSW Parliament. n.d. 'Mr Ernest George KEEGAN (1928–2008).' *Members*. [Online]. Sydney: Parliament of New South Wales. www.parliament.nsw.gov.au/members/Pages/member-details.aspx?pk=1876.

NSW Parliament. n.d. 'Mr (Frank) Francis Neville ARKELL (1935–1998).' *Members*. [Online]. Sydney: Parliament of New South Wales. www.parliament.nsw.gov.au/members/Pages/member-details.aspx?pk=1930.

O'Neil, John. 1987. 'Epidemic's Source Still Not Certain.' *Sydney Morning Herald*, 19 May: 4.

Organ, Michael. 1992. 'The "Discovery" of the Wreck of the Queen of Nations.' *Bulletin*, [Illawarra Historical Society], March: 14.

Overington, Caroline. 1998. 'Public Lives and Private Perversions: They Called Him Mr Wollongong, but the City's Favourite Son was Leading a Double Life.' *Sunday Age*, [Melbourne], 5 July: 4.

Parliamentary Joint Committee on the National Crime Authority. 1995. *Organised Criminal Paedophile Activity. A Report by the Parliamentary Joint Committee on the National Crime Authority*. Canberra: Commonwealth of Australia. www.aph.gov.au/Parliamentary_Business/Committees/Joint/Former_Committees/acc/completed_inquiries/pre1996/ncapedo/report/index.

Patty, Anna, and Linton Besser. 2010. 'Tough Tactics Forged in the City of Steel.' *Sydney Morning Herald*, 21 May. www.smh.com.au/national/nsw/tough-tactics-forged-in-the-city-of-steel-20100520-vpd8.html.

Piggin, Stuart. 1983[?]. 'Interviews with Kathleen Skipp and daughter, and Frank Arkell: Saint Michael's, Wollongong (Anglican).' D158/04/13a. Archives Online, University of Wollongong. archivesonline.uow.edu.au/nodes/view/3050.

Piggin, Stuart. 1984. *Faith of Steel: A History of the Christian Churches in the Illawarra, Australia*. Wollongong: University of Wollongong.

Powell, Gareth. 1988. 'This Man is the Secret Weapon of "Bustle City"—Wollongong and the Illawarra.' [Supplement], *Sydney Morning Herald*, 20 April: 3.

Powerhouse Museum. 1990. 'Diazo Print Normandie Hotel Wollongong.' *Architectural Plans and Drawings by Cyril Ruwald and Others*, Object no. 90/317-350, 1955. Sydney: Powerhouse Museum Collection. collection.powerhouse.com.au/object/104303.

Price, Lisa. 1995. 'MP Vows to Fight Pedophile Claims.' *Sun-Herald*, [Sydney], 5 February: 23.

Reserve Bank of Australia. n.d. *Pre-Decimal Inflation Calculator*. [Online]. Sydney: Reserve Bank of Australia. www.rba.gov.au/calculator/annualPreDecimal.html.

Ring, Beverly Anne. 1989. 'Legionnaires' Disease: The Wollongong Experience.' *Australian Journal of Physiotherapy* 35, no. 3: 167–76. doi.org/10.1016/S0004-9514(14)60506-7.

Roads and Traffic Authority. 2002. *Environmental Impact Statement: Northern Suburbs Distributor*. Prepared by Robert Purdon of Purdon & Associates Pty Ltd. Sydney: RTA.

Rodrigues, Mark, and Scott Benton. 2010. *The Age of Independence? Independents in Australian Parliaments*. Parliamentary Library Research Paper, 21 September, no. 4, 2010–11. Canberra: Parliament of Australia. parlinfo.aph.gov.au/parlInfo/download/library/prspub/228202/upload_binary/228202.pdf;fileType=application/pdf.

Rose, S.C. 1939. 'Mrs Alice B.C. O'Donnell—An Appreciation.' *Illawarra Mercury*, 14 July: 1.

Rotary Club of West Wollongong. 1975. 'President's News, 1975 to 1983.' [Notes from meeting dated 13 August 1975.] *Rotary News*. www.rotarynews.info/2/club/4445/3239 (site discontinued).

Royal Commission into Institutional Response to Child Sexual Abuse. 2017. *Royal Commission into Institutional Responses to Child Sexual Abuse. Final Report*. 17 vols. Sydney: Commonwealth of Australia. www.childabuseroyalcommission.gov.au/.

Sheldon, Peter. 1997. 'Local Government since 1947.' In *A History of Wollongong*, edited by Jim Hagan and Andrew Wells, 115–28. Wollongong: University of Wollongong Press.

Simpson, Lindsay. 1990. 'Verdict a Blow to Father.' *Sydney Morning Herald*, 4 April: 2.

Singh, Jimmy. 2017. 'Is Homosexuality an Offence?' *Criminal Defence Lawyers Australia Blog*, 5 September. www.criminaldefencelawyers.com.au/blog/is-homosexuality-an-offence/.

Steward, John. 1996. *ABC TV News*, 4 November. T315653. ABC Archives, Sydney.

Thompson, Angela. 2016. 'MP Stephen Jones Says Sexual Predators Moved Freely at Edmund Rice College in the 1980s.' *Sydney Morning Herald*, 16 June. www.smh.com.au/national/nsw/mp-stephen-jones-says-sexual-predators-moved-freely-at-edmund-rice-college-in-the-1980s-20160616-gpl1s6.html.

Tiffen, Rodney. 2021. 'Was Neville Wran Corrupt?' *Inside Story*, [Melbourne], 31 August. insidestory.org.au/was-neville-wran-corrupt/.

Tonkin, Shannon. 2016. 'Former Edmund Rice Brother John Vincent Roberts Jailed for a Decade for Child Abuse.' *Sydney Morning Herald*, 30 September. www.smh.com.au/national/nsw/former-edmund-rice-brother-john-vincent-roberts-jailed-for-a-decade-for-child-abuse-20160930-grspxz.html.

'Transport (Division of Functions) Act, 1932–1952—Main Roads Act, 1924–1954—Proclamation.' *Government Gazette of the State of New South Wales*, 1901–2001. Sydney: NSW Parliamentary Counsel's Office.

Turk, Louise, and Nalita Ferraz. 1998. 'Grave Scheme to Fool Waiting Media—The Arkell Murder.' *Illawarra Mercury*, 3 July: 3.

Tydd, Michelle. 2011. 'Murray Schipp's Sex Assault Appeal Fails.' *Illawarra Mercury*, 21 April, [Updated 6 November 2012]. www.illawarramercury.com.au/story/635019/murray-schipps-sex-assault-appeal-fails/.

University of Wollongong. n.d. 'History of Gleniffer Brae.' [Online]. University of Wollongong. documents.uow.edu.au/content/groups/public/@webdev/@webserv/documents/doc/uow129339.pdf.

University of Wollongong. 2019. 'Ethel Hayton: Avid Arts Advocate or Social-Climbing Busybody?' Media release, 9 April, University of Wollongong. www.uow.edu.au/media/2019/ethel-hayton-avid-arts-advocate-or-social-climbing-busybody.php.

Waitt, Gordon. 2003. 'A Place for Buddha in Wollongong, New South Wales? Territorial Rules in the Place-Making of Sacred Spaces.' *Australian Geographer* 34, no. 2: 223–38. doi.org/10.1080/00049180301733.

Wilkinson, John. 2011. *The Illawarra: An Economic Profile*. e-brief 18/2011, December. Sydney: NSW Parliamentary Library Research Service. www.parliament.nsw.gov.au/researchpapers/Documents/the-illawarra-an-economic-profile/Illawarra%20Region%20An%20Economic%20Profile%20GG2.pdf.

WIN Television. 1988. 'Prince Charles and Princess Diana in the Illawarra, 1988.' *WIN Television*. NFSA ID 590255. National Film and Sound Archive, Canberra. www.nfsa.gov.au/collection/curated/prince-charles-and-princess-diana-illawarra-1988.

Winters, Georgia M., Leah E. Kaylor, and Elizabeth L. Jeglic. 2022. 'Toward a Universal Definition of Child Sexual Grooming.' *Deviant Behaviour* 43, no. 8: 926–38. doi.org/10.1080/01639625.2021.1941427.

Wollongong City Libraries. n.d. 'Cringila.' *Your Suburb*. [Online]. Wollongong: Wollongong City Libraries. wollongong.nsw.gov.au/library/explore-our-past/your-suburb/suburbs/cringila.

Wollongong City Libraries. n.d. 'Kembla Grange.' *Your Suburb*. [Online]. Wollongong: Wollongong City Libraries. wollongong.nsw.gov.au/library/explore-our-past/your-suburb/suburbs/kembla-grange.

Yates, Alan. 1982. 'Thank Goodness It Couldn't Happen Here.' *Canberra Times*, 20 November: 13.

www.ingramcontent.com/pod-product-compliance
Lightning Source LLC
Chambersburg PA
CBHW071737150426
43191CB00010B/1606